Climate-Conscious Investing

Climate-Conscious Investing

Portfolios Aligned With the Paris Accords

Chenjiazi Zhong, PhD

BEP

BUSINESS EXPERT PRESS

Leader in applied, concise business books

First published in 2024 by
Business Expert Press, LLC
222 East 46th Street, New York, NY 10017
www.businessexpertpress.com

ISBN-13: 978-1-63742-700-2 (paperback)
ISBN-13: 978-1-63742-701-9 (e-book)

Business Expert Press Environmental and Social Sustainability
for Business Advantage Collection

First edition: 2024

10 9 8 7 6 5 4 3 2 1

This book is lovingly dedicated to the two pillars of my life, who have provided unwavering support and joy throughout this journey.

To my dear husband, Yu Zhuang, whose understanding, and strength have been my constant. Your ability to balance the demands of our life with grace and love, especially in taking care of our son Aiden, has been nothing short of remarkable. Your support has been a beacon of light, guiding me through the challenges and triumphs of writing this book. Your sacrifices and unspoken acts of love have not gone unnoticed, and for that, I am eternally grateful.

And to our son, Aiden Zhong Zhuang, the sweetest and most delightful soul I have had the privilege of calling my own. Aiden, your innocence, laughter, and pure joy have been a source of inspiration and motivation. In the midst of the busiest days, your presence has been a gentle reminder of what truly matters in life. You are the embodiment of hope and the future that this book aims to protect and nurture.

To Yu and Aiden: thank you for being my sanctuary and for filling my life with love and purpose. This book is not just a product of my dedication but a testament to the love and support you both have so generously given me.

Description

In the face of the urgent global issue of climate change, this book, *Climate-Conscious Investing: Portfolios Aligned With the Paris Accords,* takes a deep dive into the intricacies and complexities of climate investing.

It explores climate investment themes, approaches, and processes, and provides insights into constructing climate-conscious portfolios. The book also reviews successful climate-conscious investment cases, evolving policy developments, and regulatory changes and offers a glimpse into the future of climate-conscious investing.

This book stands out in financial literature for its innovative approach in integrating climate science with investment strategies. Unlike other books, it relies on meta-studies, ensuring that each conclusion drawn is up-to-date and deeply rooted in scientific consensus. This unique approach enhances the credibility of the investment advice and underscores the critical role of informed, science-based decision making in addressing climate change through financial practices.

Climate-Conscious Investing is a must-read for investors, policy makers, asset managers, investees, regulators, civil society and academia, and anyone who recognizes the financial ecosystem's critical role in addressing climate change.

Keywords

finance; investment; climate change; Paris agreement; climate-conscious investing; thematic investing; investment process; engagement; investment vehicles; portfolio construction; portfolio management; strategic asset allocation; investment selection; climate policies; technological innovations

Contents

Preface

Climate change, a change of climate, directly or indirectly attributed to human activity, that alters the composition of the global atmosphere and that is, in addition to natural climate variability, observed over comparable time periods, is one of the most pressing issues confronting the world today. Climate change presents different types of risks, such as physical risks (e.g., damage from extreme weather events), transition risks (e.g., the introduction of carbon pricing or regulations limiting greenhouse gas [GHG] emissions), and regulatory and legal risks that render certain business models or products obsolete. If left unaddressed, climate change can cause significant socioeconomic impacts on natural capital, physical assets, infrastructure services, food systems, liveability, and workability.

The financial ecosystem, including asset owners, policy makers, asset managers, investees, financial intermediaries, and regulatory bodies could play a crucial part in resolving climate change, as their decisions can significantly influence the shift to a low-carbon economy. In the wake of the *Paris Agreement* adopted in 2015, a landmark international treaty that aims to limit global warming to well below 2°C above preindustrial levels, and to pursue efforts to limit the temperature increase to 1.5°C, there has emerged a profound shift in the landscape of investing.

Climate-conscious investing is an investment philosophy integrating climate-change considerations into investment decision making. It acknowledges that climate change presents both significant risks and opportunities for investees and, consequently, for investors. Investing in companies that prioritize sustainability can contribute to positive climate change while seeking to improve financial returns. Investing in companies that are proactive about environmental issues may also reduce exposure to regulatory and reputational risks, as policy makers and regulatory bodies around the world are implementing climate policies to reduce GHG emissions, which can benefit companies in the sustainable sector.

However, the relatively new and evolving nature of climate-conscious investing means that historical performance data may be limited, making it challenging to balance ethical considerations with investment objectives. Investing in climate-conscious investment vehicles may involve higher fees and costs, potentially reducing returns. Changes in environmental regulations and climate policies can also impact investment success. Moreover, limited climate-conscious assets may meet strict "green" investment criteria in different markets. Additionally, since no universal standard exists for "green" investment, issuers may falsely claim assets to be environmentally friendly, leading to confusion and potential *greenwashing*.

Beyond these, integrating climate-conscious investments into an existing portfolio requires significant adjustments and a clear understanding of how these investments align with different investors' preferences and goals. In addition to choosing the right investments, climate-conscious investing is also about influencing corporate behavior. As shareholders, investors have certain rights that they can use to influence the companies they invest in and encourage them to act on climate change, depending on the jurisdiction and the type of shares.

This book is a timely exploration of the paradigm shift in the investment landscape, offering insights, strategies, and techniques for investors who seek to align their portfolios with the goals of the Paris Agreement. Throughout these pages, this book aims to explore the intricacies of climate investing and the complexities of this emerging field, from measuring the impact of climate change and assessing investment opportunities to managing risks and navigating the evolving regulatory environment. This book will explore various climate investment themes, approaches and processes, and investment vehicles to construct climate-conscious portfolios. This book will review successful climate-conscious investment cases, explore evolving policy developments and regulatory changes, and explore the future of climate-conscious investing.

This book stands out in the realm of financial literature due to its rigorous and innovative approach to integrating climate science with investment strategies. What sets this book apart is its reliance on meta-studies, which are comprehensive analyses of the most recent peer-reviewed research papers. This method ensures that each conclusion drawn in the book is up-to-date and deeply rooted in scientific consensus. By synthesizing a wide array of current research, the book offers a unique blend of environmental science and investment wisdom, providing readers with evidence-based strategies. This approach enhances the credibility of the investment advice and underscores the critical role of informed, science-based decision making in addressing climate change through financial practices.

This book is more than a guide; it is a call to action. This book is intended for investors, policy makers, asset managers, investees, regulators, civil society and academia, and anyone who recognizes the critical role the financial ecosystem must play in addressing climate change. By embracing the principles outlined in this book, readers can contribute to the vital task of building a sustainable future for all. As we stand at this critical juncture in history, the choices we make in the realm of investing have the power to shape the future of our planet. This book aims to equip readers with the information, knowledge, and tools they need to make those choices wisely and with a clear conscience.

CHAPTER 1

Introduction

The Paris Agreement

The Paris Agreement, a historic international treaty adopted in December 2015, has been a game-changer in the global fight against climate change. The primary goal of the Agreement is to limit global warming to well below 2°C above preindustrial levels, preferably to 1.5°C, compared to preindustrial levels. The Intergovernmental Panel on Climate Change (IPCC) 2018 Special Report clarified that net zero around or before 2050 is necessary to limit average temperature increases to 1.5°C, and around 2070 to 2°C. The IPCC report provided strong arguments that temperatures above 1.5°C should be viewed as dangerous, and to meet the 1.5°C target, all investments from now on, replacements and new, should be consistent with net zero by 2050. To achieve these temperature goals, the Paris Agreement aims to significantly reduce global greenhouse gas (GHG) emissions.

The Paris Agreement entered into force on November 4, 2016, after a sufficient number of countries had ratified it. As of April 2023, 193 out of 197 Parties to the *United Nations Framework Convention on Climate Change (UNFCCC)* have ratified the Agreement. This number represents the vast majority of the world's countries, demonstrating a global commitment to addressing climate change. Accounting for uncertainties regarding the damage curve, climate sensitivity, socioeconomic future, and mitigation costs, Glanemann et al. (2020) showed that the Agreement also represents the economically favorable pathway, if carried out properly.

The Paris Agreement emphasizes *Nationally Determined Contributions (NDCs)*, where each country determines, plans, and regularly reports on the contribution it undertakes to mitigate global warming. NDCs are intended to be ambitious, representing a progression over time. Every five years, there is a global stocktake to assess the collective progress toward achieving the purpose of the Agreement and to inform further individual actions by parties; as such, the NDCs are updated every five years. NDCs can also yield substantial health cobenefits in the process (Hamilton et al. 2021).

Using a 10-region model of the world economy to analyze the economic and environmental outcomes that are likely to result from the Paris Agreement, Liu et al. (2020) found that if all regions achieve their NDCs, the Agreement significantly reduces CO_2 emissions relative to baseline; however, the resulting paths were quite different across regions, indicating significant differences in marginal abatement costs. Focusing on evaluations of its institutional structure and its ability to induce member countries to implement policies, Dimitrov et al. (2019) found evidence that the key challenge for the Paris Agreement will likely be to facilitate sufficiently fast ratcheting-up of NDCs while keeping compliance rates high.

Liu et al. (2020) constructed additional scenarios to explore how the outcomes of the Paris Agreement would change if particular countries (the United States, China, and Australia) were to unilaterally withdraw from it without undertaking alternative climate policies. The results indicate that leaving the Agreement not only raises gross domestic product (GDP) for the country that leaves but also sharply reduces the domestic cobenefits the country receives as a side effect of controlling CO_2. Liu et al. also found that the net effect of withdrawing is negative, or the loss of cobenefits exceeds the gain in GDP. Based on the results, Liu et al. argued that it is in each country's self-interest to remain in the Agreement when cobenefits are considered.

In addition to NDCs, the Paris Agreement emphasizes international cooperation and financial support to achieve its goals. Developed countries are to provide financial resources to assist developing countries in both mitigation and adaptation practices in line with their own national objectives. Other countries are encouraged to provide or continue to provide financial support voluntarily. The Agreement is significant because it is the first truly global commitment to fight climate change, with participation from both developed and developing nations.

The Paris Agreement also emphasizes transparency and accountability, and technology development and transfer. The Agreement establishes an enhanced transparency framework for action and support to build mutual trust and confidence and to promote effective implementation. The Agreement aims to foster innovation and the development of climate-friendly technologies and to enhance the technology development and transfer framework. Recognizing the importance of adaptation in responding to climate change, the Agreement calls for greater levels and support for adaptation efforts.

Financial Implications

The United Nations (UN)'s *Sustainable Development Goals (SDGs)*, agreed to by all UN members in 2015 in replacement of the UN Millennial Goals, are the UN's blueprint to address key global challenges, including those related to poverty, inequality, climate change, environmental degradation, peace, and justice. The 17 goals are interconnected and particularly aimed at governments. The Paris Agreement, though negotiated in parallel to the SDGs, became one of its goals. The findings of Zhan and Santos-Paulino (2021) concluded that international private investment would be essential to alleviate public sector resource shortfalls for SDG-relevant investment and to spearhead the global campaign to build back better. With only 10 years left to complete the sustainable development agenda, the recent stagnation in private flows to developing countries—further affected by the COVID-19 pandemic—poses a daunting mission. Policy makers, asset owners, asset managers, investees, and financial intermediaries all face tremendous challenges and regulatory dilemmas in mobilizing and channeling investment for sustainable development.

The transition to a low-carbon and sustainable economy, as outlined by the Paris Agreement, brings with it a myriad of financial implications. Beyond its environmental implications, the Agreement has profound effects on risk assessments and investment opportunities. Understanding these implications is crucial for asset owners, asset managers, investees, and financial intermediaries to manage risks and capitalize on new opportunities.

Transition Risks

As the world shifts toward a low-carbon economy, sectors reliant on fossil fuels may face devaluation or become stranded assets. As a result, there is a risk that assets in these sectors, such as coal mines or oil fields, may lose their value or become obsolete before the end of their economic life. *Transition risks* may include policy and legal risks, technology risks, market risks, and reputation risks.

1. Policy and Legal Risks: As governments implement new regulations, taxes, or phase out certain industries to meet their climate goals, companies may face risks from changing regulations, carbon pricing, and potential litigation, which impact profitability. Some industries, particularly those heavily reliant on fossil fuels, may face a phase-out in favor of cleaner, renewable energy sources. This transition can have significant impacts on companies in sectors such as coal, oil, and gas.

2. Technology Risks: Changing technological advancements can lead to reduced demand for nonsustainable products and services. Rapid advancements in green technologies might render existing products or services obsolete.

3. Market Risks: Changing consumer preferences toward more sustainable products can affect demand. Additionally, there is the risk of stranded assets, where fossil fuel-based assets lose value. Transitioning to greener supply chains may also lead to short-term disruptions and increased costs.

4. Reputation Risks: Companies that are not proactive in addressing climate change might face backlash from consumers, investors, and the public.

Physical Risks

Physical risks are the risks arising from the physical impacts of climate change, which include acute risks and chronic risks. Acute risks are climate-change-related event-driven risks such as floods, hurricanes, wildfires, and other extreme weather events. They can cause direct damage to assets and infrastructure and disrupt trade, supply chains, and transportation. Chronic risks are long-term shifts in climate patterns, such as rising sea levels, changing precipitation patterns, and increasing temperatures.

These can affect crop yields and agricultural outputs, lead to water scarcity and volatility in food prices and supply, and impact human health. Modeling the energy, food and agriculture, and transport sectors, and mortality related to risk factors of air pollution, diet, and physical activity, Hamilton et al. (2021) found that greater consideration of health in the NDCs and climate change mitigation policies had the potential to yield considerable health benefits as well as achieve the "well below 2°C" commitment across a range of regional and economic contexts.

Liability Risks

Liability risks arise when parties who have suffered loss or damage from the effects of climate change seek compensation from those that are held responsible. Liability risks can lead to significant financial costs for companies, either from legal fees, compensation payouts, or both. This can affect a company's profitability and, consequently, its stock price. Being involved in high-profile climate-related litigation can also harm a company's reputation, potentially leading to a loss of consumer trust and decreased sales.

Regulatory and Legal Risks

The implementation of policies to meet NDCs under the Paris Agreement can have wide-ranging effects on businesses, as policy makers and regulatory bodies may introduce new environmental regulations and standards that businesses must comply with, such as emissions limits, energy efficiency requirements, and mandates for the use of renewable energy sources. To encourage environmentally friendly practices, policy makers and regulatory bodies might also impose taxes on carbon emissions or provide incentives for reducing GHG emissions. These climate policies and financial mechanisms are designed to steer businesses toward more sustainable practices. Companies that fail to adhere to environmental regulations or commitments may face legal repercussions. This can include fines, penalties, and in some cases, litigation—the cost of noncompliance can be substantial.

Reputational Risks

There is a growing public and consumer awareness of environmental issues—consumers are increasingly prioritizing sustainability, and asset owners, asset managers, and financial intermediaries are considering environmental factors in their decision making. This demand is driving companies to integrate sustainable practices into their business models, not just as a compliance measure, but as a core part of their strategy. Companies that align with sustainability goals can significantly enhance their brand value, as consumers are more likely to support brands that demonstrate a commitment to environmental stewardship. This alignment can lead to increased customer loyalty, market value, and potentially higher sales.

Conversely, companies not aligning with sustainability goals, are not taking steps to reduce their carbon footprint, or are perceived as environmentally unfriendly, may face reputational risks. Meanwhile, as aligning with sustainability goals is increasingly seen as essential for the long-term viability of a business, companies that ignore environmental issues may find themselves at a competitive disadvantage as the global economy continues to move toward more sustainable practices.

Opportunities

On the flip side, the transition to a low-carbon economy presents an opportunity for the development and innovation of new technologies, which can lead to both environmental and financial benefits. Companies that can adapt to sustainable business models, products, and services have the potential to gain new markets, growth opportunities, and open up new revenue streams. For asset owners and asset managers, this shift toward sustainability presents vast investment opportunities in climate themes. Eventually, companies that perform well on *environmental, social, and governance (ESG)* dimensions may attract more investment and potentially at more favorable terms.

The Rise of ESG Investing

ESG investing has emerged as a transformative force in the financial world, which represents a significant shift in the investment landscape, reflecting a growing awareness of sustainability issues among the financial ecosystem and the broad public. *ESG investing* is an approach to managing assets where asset owners and asset managers explicitly incorporate ESG factors in their investment decisions with the long-term return of an investment portfolio in mind. ESG investing aims to correctly identify, evaluate, and price social, environmental, and economic risks and opportunities. No longer a niche or secondary consideration, ESG factors are now central to many investment strategies, reflecting a broader societal shift toward sustainability and ethical business practices.

- *Environmental factors* refer to the factors pertaining to the natural world. They focus on a company's impact on the environment. Examples of environmental issues include carbon emissions, product carbon footprint, natural-resource conservation, energy efficiency, waste management, water usage, sustainable resource use, environmental policies and compliance, climate change mitigation and adaptation, biodiversity, and land use.
- *Social factors* refer to the factors that affect the lives of humans. They examine how a company manages relationships with employees, suppliers, customers, and communities. Examples of social issues include human rights, labor management/practices, diversity, equity, and inclusion (DEI), modern slavery, employee health and safety, stakeholder engagement, and community relations.
- *Governance factors* refer to the factors that involve issues tied to countries and/or jurisdictions or are common practice in an industry, as well as the interests of broader stakeholder groups. Examples of governance issues are accounting, business ethics, bribery and corruption, executive pay, board diversity, board independence, organizational structure, pay, and proxy access.[1]

Historically, ethical investing focused on excluding certain sectors (e.g., tobacco, weapons). ESG investing, on the other hand, is more comprehensive, evaluating companies based on their overall ESG performance. It is essential to note that there is currently no universal standard for assigning "E," "S," and "G" issues, and they may overlap with one another. The assignment of these issues depends on the specific properties of the financial ecosystem. Large asset owners, such as pension funds and endowments, have played a pivotal role in mainstreaming ESG considerations.

The rise of ESG investing is a result of growing awareness of climate change, social justice issues, and corporate–governance scandals. It is a fundamental shift in how asset owners and investee companies think about long-term value creation, risk management, and their broader impact on society and the environment. ESG investment strategies have experienced a massive inflow of capital over the past decade, and this capital inflow also happened without asset owners possessing the information, tools, and methods needed to evaluate and communicate their specific ESG values, objectives, and preferences (Horan et al. 2022). Monasterolo and de Angelis (2020) indicated the weight of the low-carbon indexes within an optimal portfolio tended to increase after the Paris Agreement, suggesting that stock market investors started to consider low-carbon assets as an appealing investment opportunity after the Agreement but have not penalized yet carbon-intensive assets. Using the Agreement as a shock to expected climate risk regulations, Seltzer et al. (2022) provided evidence that the composition of institutional ownership changes after the Agreement.

Efficiency and Productivity

Sustainable business practices build efficiencies by conserving resources, reducing costs, and enhancing productivity. Significant cost reductions can result from improving operational efficiency through better management of natural resources, such as water and energy, as well as from minimizing waste. A study analyzing data from the global climate database provided by the *Carbon Disclosure Project (CDP)* estimated that companies experience an average internal rate of return (IRR) of 27 to 80 percent on their low-carbon investments.

Employees, especially from younger generations, are increasingly demanding sustainable and ethical business practices, and seeking to work for companies that share their values, including environmental responsibility. A strong ESG proposition can help companies attract and retain talent and enhance employee motivation and productivity overall. Employee satisfaction is a key driver of long-term value and is positively correlated with shareholder returns.

Risk Management

Integrating ESG factors into business practices can reduce the risk of fines and state intervention. Regulatory pressure is a significant factor driving the adoption of sustainable practices and the growth of ESG investing. State and federal government agencies are enacting regulations to protect the environment and promote sustainability, in the form of environmental regulations, social responsibility laws, and corporate governance standards. Integrating sustainability into a business will position it to anticipate changing regulations in a timely manner, while failure to comply with regulations can lead to reputational damage, affecting customer loyalty and investor confidence. The anticipation of stricter environmental regulations is also prompting asset owners to prioritize companies that are better prepared to adapt to these changes.

In addition to regulatory considerations, ESG integration is becoming integral in identifying and managing the risks that could have a significant impact on an investee's performance and resilience. High-profile corporate governance failures have underscored the risks of poor governance practices, leading asset owners and asset managers to seek companies with strong governance structures.

Moreover, the market perceives companies with high carbon footprints as more likely to default, ceteris paribus, and exposure to climate risks affects the creditworthiness of their debt. Capasso et al. (2020) investigated the relationship between exposure to climate change and corporate credit risk. They showed that the distance-to-default, a widely used market-based measure of corporate default risk, is negatively associated with the amount of a company's carbon emissions and carbon intensity. Similarly, Seltzer et al. (2022) found that companies with poor environmental profiles or high carbon footprints tend to have lower credit ratings and higher yield spreads, particularly when their facilities are located in states with stricter regulatory enforcement.

Carbon risk exposure is also correlated with exposures to other common risk factors (D'Orazio, 2021; Görgen et al. 2021). D'Orazio (2021) suggested that failure to account for climate change could amplify the build-up of additional climate-related financial risks and existing vulnerabilities in the financial system, leading to increased overall exposure to climate risks and thus undermining the low-carbon transition in *G20 countries*. D'Orazio pointed out that tackling climate-related financial risks, scaling up green finance for a more sustainable recovery, and preserving the resilience of the global financial system are three interrelated objectives. On currencies, Cheema-Fox et al. (2022) showed that vulnerability is correlated with higher losses from natural disasters. The results of the study also suggest that non-*G10* currencies are more vulnerable to physical risk.

Financial Performance

There is a growing body of evidence suggesting that ESG-focused investments can perform comparable or better than non-ESG investments over the long term (Joshi and Dash 2023; Mueller et al. 2023). The increasing evidence is rooted in the consensus that sustainable practices often correlate with prudent management, innovation, and long-term strategic planning. As such, asset owners and asset managers are increasingly favoring companies with strong social responsibility records.

Corporate social responsibility (CSR) is a broad business concept that describes a company's commitment to conducting its business in an ethical way, which directly impacts a company's financial performance, and this impact becomes more significant as the company's ESG scores improve. Coelho et al. (2023) and Joshi and Dash (2023) found evidence to support that companies that are committed to mitigating climate change or with strong ESG practices tend to have strong financial performance, with higher returns on investment and lower volatility compared to companies that are not focused on climate change, especially in the long run. Cakici and Zaremba (2022) investigated whether socially responsible investing (SRI) pays off in 49 developed and emerging markets. The results indicate that stocks with the highest ESG scores underperform their low-rated counterparts by 4.68 percent per year; however, this is driven by the small-firm effect. Once isolated, the financial performance of ESG companies no longer differs significantly from their peers.

Summary

The introductory chapter sets the stage by delving into the Paris Agreement, its profound financial implications, and the rise of ESG investing. The first section introduces the landmark Paris Agreement, a pivotal moment in global climate policy. Signed in 2015, the Agreement unites nations in combating climate change by aiming to limit global warming to well below 2°C above preindustrial levels, with efforts to restrict it to 1.5°C. This section discusses the Agreement's significance, goals, and the challenges in achieving these ambitious targets. It highlights the collaborative effort required from countries, industries, and the financial ecosystem to make substantial changes in reducing GHG emissions.

The second section begins by outlining the implications of the Paris Agreement for asset owners and asset managers. It emphasizes that climate change presents both risks and opportunities in the investment landscape. On the risks side, this section discusses transition risks, physical risks, liability risks, regulatory and legal risks, and reputational risks; on opportunities, it highlights those in emerging technologies, sustainable business models, and environmentally friendly industries that are poised to grow in a low-carbon economy. Understanding these risks and opportunities is crucial for long-term investment success in a world increasingly shaped by climate concerns.

This chapter then transitions to presenting the rise of ESG investing, which has gained significant traction in the wake of the Paris Agreement. ESG investing represents a profound shift in how asset owners approach the financial markets, emphasizing the interconnectedness of financial returns with societal well-being. This section highlights how increased awareness of "E," "S," and "G" issues has led to a surge in ESG investing and emphasizes the impact of ESG investing, such as improved efficiency and productivity and enhanced risk management. This section also explores the relationship between ESG integration and financial performance, suggesting that ESG strategies can lead to comparable or even superior returns compared to traditional investments.

This comprehensive overview underscores a fundamental shift in how asset owners and asset managers evaluate and manage investments in the context of broader societal and environmental challenges. This chapter sets the stage for understanding the complex interplay between climate change, financial markets, and policy making offering insights into how these domains are increasingly intertwined in shaping a sustainable future.

CHAPTER 2

Navigating the Carbon Footprint Maze

Understanding and managing carbon footprint in investments is a crucial aspect for asset owners and asset managers who are conscious of their impact on the environment. This chapter delves into the intricate process of measuring carbon footprints, an essential first step in our collective journey toward environmental sustainability. This chapter explores the methodologies and tools used to quantify the carbon emissions associated with various activities, aiming to offer readers a clear and comprehensive understanding of how these environmental impacts are calculated. With a solid grasp of carbon-footprint measurement, the chapter transitions into a critical discussion on three pivotal approaches for carbon reduction: divestment, low-carbon investing, and carbon offsetting.

Carbon Footprint Measurement

Carbon footprint in investments refers to the total amount of GHG emissions, specifically carbon dioxide (CO_2), and it measures the total GHG emissions caused directly and indirectly by a particular business activity, product, or investment. Carbon footprint is usually expressed in terms of equivalent tons of carbon dioxide (CO_2e). This concept has gained significant attention in recent years.

Carbon footprint in investments involves evaluating how investment activities contribute to carbon emissions, which are a leading cause of climate change. It can encompass emissions from a company's operations (direct emissions) and emissions from the entire value chain, including suppliers and product use (indirect emissions). Carbon footprint is increasingly seen as a factor in managing financial risk, as regulatory pressures and shifting public preferences can impact the performance of high-carbon industries.

Measuring carbon footprint in investments involves quantifying the GHG emissions associated with an asset or investment portfolio and calculating the total amount of GHG emitted directly or indirectly due to the associated activities. This process is multifaceted, encompassing different methodologies and data sources.

Step 1: Define the Scope

Scope 1 Emissions (Direct Emissions)

- *Scope 1 emissions* are direct emissions from sources that are owned or controlled by the company;
- If a company owns or controls the source of the emission, it falls under Scope 1 emissions;
- Examples include emissions from combustion in boilers, furnaces, vehicles, and emissions from chemical production in owned or controlled process equipment.

Scope 2 Emissions (Energy Indirect Emissions)

- *Scope 2 emissions* are indirect emissions from the generation of purchased electricity, steam, heating, and cooling consumed by the company;
- While the company does not produce these emissions directly, they result from the energy the company purchases and uses;
- For instance, if a company buys electricity from a power plant that burns coal, the emissions from burning that coal are Scope 2 emissions for the company.

Scope 3 Emissions (Other Indirect Emissions)

- *Scope 3 emissions* are all other indirect emissions that occur in a company's value chain but are not owned or controlled by the company;
- This can include emissions from the extraction and production of purchased materials, transportation of purchased fuels, and use of products and services;

- For example, if a company sells a product that emits GHGs when used by consumers, those emissions are Scope 3 emissions for the company.

The earliest concept of carbon footprint was used to measure the level of CO_2 emissions in the direct and indirect GHG emissions of a product or service during its life cycle. Focusing on the carbon footprint in the agriculture sector, one of the main sources of CO_2 emissions, and using Strengths, Weaknesses, Opportunities, and Threats (SWOT) analysis, Zhang et al. (2023) reviewed different definitions of carbon footprint at macroscopic and microscopic levels and two main accounting methods, Life Cycle Assessment, and Input-Output Analysis, and found that there was no agreement with the definition of carbon footprint that only considers carbon emissions.

However, the academia reached a consensus on key elements, such as CO_2 emission in the whole life cycle or the whole process of production activities. Accordingly, Zhang et al. (2023) suggested carbon footprint cover the GHG emissions of the entire life cycle of a product or the whole process of an activity, including all sources and other pollutants, water, and energy footprints.

Step 2: Data Collection

A company-level analysis looks at the direct and indirect emissions of each investee company within an investment portfolio, which includes Scope 1, Scope 2, and Scope 3 emissions.

- Gather data on activities that result in emissions;
- Emission factors are coefficients that specify the amount of GHG emitted per unit of activity;
- For example, how much CO_2 is emitted per gallon of gasoline burned or per kilowatt-hour of electricity consumed.

Many companies disclose their carbon emissions in annual reports or sustainability reports, often following standards such as the *Global Reporting Initiative (GRI)* or the *CDP*. However, since not all companies report their emissions, the reported data vary in quality and completeness. Accurate and comprehensive data on carbon emissions can be hard to come by, especially for smaller companies and certain asset classes. Asset owners and asset managers are increasingly using advanced models and algorithms to estimate the emissions of the companies that do not report them.

Step 3: Calculation

- Multiply the activity data by the appropriate emission factors to calculate the emissions for each source;
- For instance: Emissions = Activity data x emission factor.

The two major emissions intensity metrics are absolute emissions and emission intensity. *Absolute emissions* refer to the total emissions in metric CO_2e. This is a straightforward measure but does not account for company size or economic output. *Emissions intensity* are emissions relative to a financial metric, such as revenue or market capitalization. Emissions intensity allows for comparison across companies of different sizes.

Step 4: Portfolio-Level Assessment

A portfolio-level assessment evaluates the overall carbon footprint of an investment portfolio, considering the emissions of all constituent assets. Aggregation and normalization are typically performed during this step.

1. Sum up the emissions from all sources to get the total carbon footprint:
   - If measuring the carbon footprint of a product or service, consider the entire life cycle, from raw material extraction to end-of-life disposal;
   - The carbon footprint of an investment portfolio is calculated by aggregating the emissions of each holding, weighted by the size of the investment in each holding.
2. The footprint is often normalized to a per-dollar-invested basis, allowing for comparison with other portfolios or benchmarks.

Different sectors and asset classes have varying levels of emissions. For instance, the energy sector typically has a higher carbon footprint than the technology sector. Asset owners and asset managers can utilize carbon accounting methodologies and tools that provide insights into the emissions associated with different investments.

Focusing on an approach consisting of measuring the sensitivity of stock prices with respect to a carbon risk factor, Roncalli et al. (2021) suggested that carbon betas are market-based measures that are complementary to carbon intensities or fundamental-based measures when managing investment portfolios. Roncalli et al. argued that carbon betas should be an extension or forward-looking measure of carbon footprint, which could be used to build minimum variance strategies for portfolio construction.

Measuring carbon footprint is a detailed process that requires careful consideration of various emission scopes, data sources, and analytical methods. While challenges exist, particularly in data quality and standardization, advancements in technology and reporting standards are continually improving the accuracy and usability of these measurements. There are also third-party data providers and specialized platforms that aggregate and analyze emissions data, providing more comprehensive insights, especially for asset owners with diverse portfolios.

Carbon Mitigation Strategies

Divestment, low-carbon investing, and carbon offsetting represent three major strategies that asset owners and asset managers can employ to reduce the carbon footprint of their portfolios and contribute to the broader goal of mitigating climate change.

Divestment

Divestment from high-carbon industries, particularly fossil fuels, has become a notable strategy among investors who are concerned about climate change and its associated risks. This strategy aims to reduce financial support for industries that are harmful to the environment, potentially leading to a shift in corporate behaviors and policies. This approach involves the deliberate withdrawal of investments from sectors and companies that are major contributors to carbon emissions.

In implementing a divestment, asset owners and asset managers first identify the assets in their portfolio that are linked to high-carbon industries. These can include direct investments in fossil fuel companies or indirect exposure through fund vehicles or financial instruments. Some asset owners and asset managers choose to divest gradually, reducing their exposure over time, while others opt for immediate divestment. The approach depends on the specific strategy, financial goals, and the size of their holdings in these industries. Divestment is often accompanied by a reallocation of funds into lower-carbon or green investments that align with their investment objectives and ethical standards.

Low-Carbon Investing

As awareness of climate change grows, investing in low-carbon industries and assets is one way to align financial goals with environmental values. Low-carbon investments prioritize environmental sustainability by focusing on industries, companies, or assets that emit fewer GHGs compared to others in the market or their sector. By directing capital toward environmentally friendly industries, companies, or assets, asset owners and asset managers can encourage and support sustainable business practices.

Carbon Offsetting

Carbon offsetting through investment is a strategy used by asset owners and asset managers to counterbalance the carbon emissions from their investment portfolios. This approach involves directing funds into projects or assets that are designed to reduce or absorb an equivalent amount of GHG from the atmosphere to compensate for the emissions associated with their investments. Carbon offsetting contributes to a net reduction in global carbon emissions. Ji et al. (2021) argued that developing a carbon-neutral economy is more important for emerging economies that have constrained financial markets.

The five major types of carbon-offset projects are reforestation and afforestation, renewable energy, energy efficiency, methane capture, and *carbon capture and storage* (CCS). Asset owners can directly fund specific carbon-offset projects or companies specializing in these initiatives.

1. Reforestation and Afforestation: Investing in projects that plant trees or restore forests. Trees naturally absorb CO_2 from the atmosphere, making these projects effective in sequestering carbon.
2. Renewable Energy: Funding the development of renewable energy sources such as wind, solar, hydro, and geothermal power. These projects reduce reliance on fossil fuels, thereby preventing carbon emissions.
3. Energy Efficiency: Investing in projects that improve energy efficiency in buildings, manufacturing, and transportation. Enhanced efficiency leads to reduced energy consumption and, consequently, lower emissions.
4. Methane Capture: Supporting projects that capture methane emissions from landfills, agricultural operations, or waste management facilities. Methane is a potent GHG, and its capture significantly reduces its impact on the environment.
5. CCS: CCS involves capturing CO_2 emissions produced from the use of fossil fuels in electricity generation and industrial processes, and then transporting and storing it underground to prevent it from entering the atmosphere.

Purchasing carbon credits is another common method of participating in carbon offsetting—one carbon credit typically represents the removal or avoidance of one metric ton of CO_2 emissions. Asset owners can also invest in climate-conscious investment vehicles that prioritize carbon-offsetting projects, which will be detailed in Chapter 4.

In addition to the types of carbon-offset projects, it is important to consider the aspects of verification and certification, *additionality*, long-term impact, and alignment with investment goals.

1. Verification and Certification: Ensuring that the carbon-offset projects are legitimate and effective. This often involves looking for projects that are verified or certified by reputable standards such as the *Verified Carbon Standard* or the *Gold Standard*.

2. Additionality: Refers to ensuring that the carbon reduction would not have occurred without the carbon-offset project, thus making a real difference in emissions levels.

3. Long-Term Impact: Evaluating the long-term sustainability and impact of the carbon-offset projects. For instance, reforestation projects should ensure the long-term survival and maintenance of the forests.

4. Alignment With Investment Goals: Balancing carbon-offsetting goals with other investment objectives, such as financial returns, risk management, and portfolio diversification.

Each of these carbon mitigation strategies has its unique benefits, implications, and limitations. While divestment can send a strong message and align investments with environmental values, its direct impact on reducing emissions can be debated. Low-carbon investing often uses ESG criteria to evaluate investments, and it often involves investing in green technologies, sustainable products, and services. In the context of carbon offsetting, it is important to ensure the credibility and effectiveness of the offset projects. This strategy is often used in conjunction with other methods, as it does not reduce the emissions of the investments themselves.

Divestment, low-carbon investing, and carbon offsetting strategies also play a role in risk management, as they can protect asset owners and asset managers from the financial risks associated with climate change and regulatory shifts toward a low-carbon economy. Many asset owners and asset managers find that a combination of these strategies can be more effective. For instance, divesting from high-carbon industries, investing in low-carbon alternatives, and offsetting any remaining emissions. There are also various tools and resources available, such as climate-conscious investment vehicles, ESG ratings, and carbon footprint calculators for investment portfolios.

Summary

This chapter delves into the critical role of carbon footprint analysis in modern investment strategies. This section emphasizes the importance of recognizing the environmental impact of investments, particularly in terms of carbon emissions. It explains how every investment contributes to carbon footprint, either directly or indirectly. The section outlines methods for assessing the carbon footprint, highlighting tools and metrics used to quantify and compare the carbon emissions associated with different companies, sectors, and investment portfolios.

This chapter then explores multifaceted approaches toward reducing carbon footprints, focusing on divestment, low-carbon investing, and carbon offsetting. Divestment is highlighted as a powerful tool for influencing corporate behavior and steering investments away from fossil-fuel-dependent industries. Low-carbon investing is presented as a proactive strategy, emphasizing investments in companies, projects, or products with minimal carbon emissions, aligning financial goals with environmental responsibility. Lastly, carbon offsetting is explored as a compensatory approach, allowing asset owners to invest in environmental projects to balance out their own carbon emissions.

CHAPTER 3

Climate-Conscious Approaches and Processes

Responsible investment (RI) is an umbrella term for the various ways in which asset owners and asset managers consider climate-conscious, sustainability, or ESG factors within investment selection and portfolio construction and in active ownership. Climate-conscious investing or green investing, impact investing, socially responsible investing (SRI), thematic investing, and so on are all types of RI—there is no standard classification in the industry (Thompson, 2023; Yasuda, 2023), and RI evolves over time. These approaches have some overlap but they differ in their objectives, focus, and investment process. This chapter particularly focuses on climate-conscious investing and thematic investing.

Climate-Conscious Investing

Climate-conscious investing or green investing refers to allocating capital to assets that mitigate climate change, biodiversity loss, resource inefficiency, and other environmental challenges. It focuses specifically on companies or projects that are proactive in minimizing their environmental footprint, developing innovative solutions to environmental problems, and support environmental sustainability.

Climate-conscious investments can include low-carbon power generation and vehicles, smart grids, energy efficiency, pollution control, recycling, waste management and waste of energy, and other technologies and processes that contribute to solving particular environmental problems. For example, investing in a solar panel manufacturing company, a green bond funding a clean water project, or an exchange-traded fund (ETF) focused on low-carbon technologies. Climate-conscious investing often excludes industries such as fossil fuels, mining, and others perceived as harmful to the environment.

Climate-conscious investments benefit the industrial structure (Chen et al. 2023), and increasing these investments up to top-level design for green industrial development is essential. Sharif et al. (2023) investigated the impact of climate-conscious investments on green technology innovation in selected six Association of Southeast Asian Nations (ASEAN-6) countries from 1995 to 2018, and found that the impacts of climate-conscious investment on green technology innovation are positive yet stronger in the long run.

In risk management, climate-conscious investments are more effective than gold for hedging oil market risk without ignoring the hedging ability of technology stock investment. Dutta et al. (2023) investigated the effect of climate risk on the return and volatility of climate-conscious investments. The results indicate that an upward demand for climate-conscious assets statistically increased the crude oil prices and decreased their volatility level. In other words, when climate risk increases, the correlation between crude oil and climate-conscious investment returns decreases.

Climate-conscious investment approaches reflect a growing recognition of the interconnectedness of financial performance, societal well-being, environmental stewardship, and ethical conduct. The growth of climate-conscious investing also reflects a shift in the investment landscape, where nonfinancial factors are increasingly seen as material to long-term success. SDGs, investment approaches, and financial knowledge all play a substantial role in investment success (Yang and Liu, 2022).

Thematic Investing

Asset owners and asset managers can generate investment ideas by exploring the themes associated with specific megatrends. *Thematic investing* refers to investing in themes or assets specifically related to sustainability or ESG factors. Building climate-conscious portfolios focuses on *climate investment themes*, which refer to the broad categories or focus areas within the field of climate-related investments. Climate investment themes encompass a diverse and interconnected landscape of investment opportunities that align with the global effort to mitigate climate change, adapt to its impacts, and transition to a more sustainable and resilient economy. These themes reflect various sectors, technologies, and strategies that contribute to global climate agenda. Asset owners and asset managers can pursue strategies that align with their investment objectives, risk tolerance, and values. The most common types of climate investments are in renewable energy, energy efficiency, water and waste management, sustainable agriculture, green transportation, green buildings and infrastructure, and climate resilience and adaptation (Joshi and Dash, 2023).

Renewable Energy

Energy is the "prime mover" of the economy, and reducing the emissions associated with energy production has knock-on effects across all sectors. Renewable energy investments are directed toward the development, expansion, and integration of energy sources that are sustainable, environmentally friendly, and inexhaustible. The production of low-carbon electricity has been at the forefront of these developments, from sources such as solar photovoltaics, onshore and offshore wind, hydroelectricity, geothermal energy, and more. Renewable energy investments offer a range of opportunities for asset owners seeking to support clean energy generation and capitalize on the transition to a sustainable energy future. These investments play a crucial role in the global transition from fossil fuels to cleaner energy, helping to reduce GHG emissions, enhance energy security, and foster economic growth.

Solar Energy

Solar energy is one of the fastest-growing renewable energy sectors. Investments in solar energy focus on harnessing the sun's energy through photovoltaic (PV) panels and solar thermal systems. Investing in solar PV projects, such as utility-scale solar farms, rooftop solar installations, and solar thermal systems presents opportunities for long-term returns.

Solar farms are large-scale solar power plants that generate electricity for the grid. Rooftop solar refers to smaller solar installations on residential and commercial buildings. Solar thermal systems use sunlight to heat water or generate steam. Solar investment funds, solar developers, and solar equipment manufacturers are avenues for investing in this sector.

Van de Ven et al. (2022) incorporated investment portfolio analysis into three different energy-economy models to examine the climate employment cobenefits of green recovery packages in six major emitting regions. The resulted three models all indicate that a dominance of funding toward solar power can lead to reductions in both CO_2 emissions and unemployment, most notably in the European Union (EU) and China.

Wind Energy

Wind energy is a mature and widely deployed renewable energy source. Investments in wind energy target the capture of wind power through wind turbines. Investments in onshore and offshore wind farms provide opportunities to support large-scale clean energy generation. The wind turbines located on land are onshore wind farms and those located in coastal waters are offshore wind farms, which often generate more energy due to stronger winds. Wind energy investment can involve partnerships with wind project developers, manufacturers of wind turbines, or renewable energy funds focused on wind power.

Investments in renewable energy, especially solar and wind power, have been proven to perform well with low risk (Joshi and Dash, 2023). The findings of Joshi and Dash (2023) indicate that solar and wind energy has led the change with highest potential in Asian region. East Asia and Pacific have highest potential in terms of attracting likely investments in ecofriendly instruments.

Hydropower

Hydroelectric power is a well-established renewable energy source with significant investment potential. Investments in hydropower focus on generating electricity from flowing or falling water. Opportunities exist in large-scale hydropower projects as well as smaller run-of-river or mini hydro installations. Large-scale hydropower refers to dams and reservoirs that generate significant electricity, while small-scale hydropower is smaller installations that have less environmental impact. Investing in hydroelectric power can involve partnerships with project developers, equipment manufacturers, or funds specializing in hydropower.

Geothermal Energy

Geothermal energy harnesses the heat from the Earth's subsurface for electricity generation and heating purposes. Investments in geothermal energy target the extraction of heat from the Earth's core, and focus on geothermal power plants and geothermal heating systems. Investing in geothermal projects can provide stable, baseload renewable energy. Geothermal project developers, equipment manufacturers, or specialized geothermal investment funds can be avenues for investment.

Biomass and Bioenergy

Biomass and bioenergy technologies utilize organic matter, such as agricultural residues, wood waste, or dedicated energy crops, to generate heat, electricity, or biofuels. Investments in biomass and bioenergy focus on generating energy from organic materials. The facilities that burn organic matter to generate electricity are biomass power plants. The fuels derived from organic materials used in transportation are biofuels. Investments in biomass power plants, biogas facilities, or bioenergy technology companies offer opportunities to support renewable energy generation from organic sources.

Energy Storage

As renewable energy penetration increases, investments in energy storage technologies are crucial for grid integration and ensuring a stable and reliable power supply. Investments in energy storage are essential for managing the intermittent nature of some renewable sources. Energy storage refers to the technologies that store renewable energy for later use. Batteries, pumped hydro storage, and other advanced storage technologies offer investment opportunities, and investing in energy storage manufacturers, project developers, or funds focused on energy storage can also capture the growing demand for grid-scale energy storage solutions.

Grid Integration

Investments in grid integration are essential for managing the intermittent nature of some renewable sources. Off-grid renewable energy solutions and distributed generation systems offer investment potential, particularly in areas with limited access to reliable electricity grids. Investing in off-grid solar, wind, or hybrid systems can provide energy access solutions for remote communities and commercial establishments.

Renewable energy investments are a multifaceted and rapidly growing field that offers opportunities to address climate change, reduce pollution, and create sustainable energy systems. They encompass various energy sources, each with unique characteristics, potentials, investment vehicles, and instruments. In a world committed to achieving the UN's SDGs and the targets of the Paris Agreement, renewable energy investments represent a promising and essential pathway toward a cleaner, more resilient, and sustainable energy future.

Energy Efficiency

Energy efficiency investments present numerous opportunities for asset owners seeking to promote sustainability, reduce energy consumption, and generate financial returns. Energy efficiency investments focus on reducing energy consumption through the implementation of technologies, practices, and systems that optimize energy use. These investments are essential for lowering GHG emissions, reducing energy costs, enhancing energy security, and contributing to sustainability.

Energy Management Systems

Investing in energy management systems (EMS) and software platforms that enable real-time monitoring, analysis, and optimization of energy usage is an emerging opportunity. These systems help businesses and organizations track energy consumption, identify inefficiencies, and make data-driven decisions to optimize energy use. EMS platforms often integrate with smart devices and sensors to provide comprehensive energy management solutions.

Industrial Energy Efficiency

Investing in energy efficiency measures in industrial sectors offers substantial potential. Investments in industrial energy efficiency aim to optimize energy use in manufacturing and production processes. Technologies and practices such as energy-efficient equipment, process optimization, waste heat recovery, and cogeneration can significantly reduce energy consumption and operational costs. Industrial energy service companies provide expertise in identifying and implementing energy-saving opportunities in manufacturing plants.

Transportation Energy Efficiency

Investments in transportation energy efficiency focus on reducing energy consumption in the transportation sector. Fuel-efficient vehicles support the development and adoption of fuel-efficient cars, trucks, and buses. Investing in energy-efficient public transportation systems and smart transportation technologies that optimize traffic flow and reduce fuel consumption also contribute to reducing fuel consumption, lowering costs, and minimizing environmental impacts.

Utility and Grid Efficiency

Investments in utility and grid efficiency aim to enhance the efficiency of energy distribution and consumption. Investments in smart grid technologies contribute to the modernization of energy infrastructure. Smart meters, demand response systems, grid monitoring, and control technologies enable efficient energy distribution, load management, and integration of renewable energy sources. Investing in businesses or projects involved in smart grid equipment, software, and infrastructure can drive energy efficiency gains and enhance grid resilience.

Investments in renewable energy microgrids support decentralized and resilient energy systems. These microgrids integrate renewable energy sources, energy storage, and smart grid technologies to provide reliable and sustainable power, particularly in areas prone to power outages or grid disruptions. Investing in renewable energy microgrid projects or collaborating with energy technology providers can contribute to climate resilience in the energy sector.

Energy-Efficient Appliances and Equipment

Investing in energy-efficient appliances, lighting, and equipment is a straightforward opportunity in the consumer and commercial sectors.

Energy Star-certified products and technologies that meet high energy efficiency standards offer attractive investment prospects. Companies involved in the development, manufacturing, and distribution of energy-efficient products can benefit from increasing demand and regulatory incentives.

Energy efficiency investments are a vital tool in the global effort to reduce energy consumption and mitigate climate change, which represent a practical and promising pathway toward a more sustainable and resilient energy future. They offer a wide range of opportunities across various sectors, including industry, transportation, and utilities. Energy efficiency investments align with global efforts to achieve the UN SDGs, particularly those related to affordable and clean energy (SDG 7) and climate action (SDG 13).

Water and Waste

Water and waste management investments are essential components of sustainable development. They address critical challenges related to water scarcity, sanitation, waste reduction, and recycling. Water and waste management investments offer opportunities to address pressing environmental challenges, ensure sustainable resource management, and generate financial returns.

Water Management

Water-management investments focus on the sustainable use, conservation, and distribution of water resources. Investing in water management can enhance water efficiency, treatment, and conservation, and contribute to environmental protection, public health, and economic growth.

1. Water Treatment and Purification: Investments in water treatment technologies and infrastructure address the need for clean and safe water supplies. Opportunities exist in water treatment plants, desalination facilities, filtration systems, and advanced water purification technologies. Investing in companies that develop innovative water treatment solutions can contribute to water security and quality.

2. Water Infrastructure Development: Investments in water infrastructure development, such as dams, reservoirs, pipelines, and water distribution systems, contribute to water resource management and supply reliability. Infrastructure projects that improve water storage, distribution, and efficiency offer investment opportunities. Collaborating with public entities and infrastructure development companies can unlock potential investment avenues in this sector.

3. Stormwater Management: Stormwater management investments focus on mitigating the impacts of urban runoff, reducing flooding, and improving water quality. Green infrastructure solutions, such as bioswales, permeable pavements, and rainwater harvesting systems, offer opportunities for sustainable stormwater management. Investing in companies specializing in stormwater management technologies or collaborating with municipalities for stormwater management projects can drive environmental and financial benefits.

4. Water Efficiency Technologies: Investments in water efficiency technologies help conserve water and optimize water use in various sectors. Opportunities exist in precision irrigation systems, leak detection technologies, water monitoring and management platforms, and smart water meters. Investing in companies that develop and deploy water-efficient technologies supports sustainable water management practices.

Waste Treatment and Recycling

Waste-management investments focus on the collection, treatment, disposal, and recycling of waste, aiming to minimize environmental impact. These investments also support technologies that promote waste reduction, recycling, and the conversion of waste into energy.

1. Wastewater Treatment and Reuse: Wastewater treatment and reuse projects help conserve water resources and reduce pollution. Investments in wastewater treatment plants, decentralized treatment systems, and water reuse technologies offer potential returns. Supporting companies that provide wastewater treatment and recycling services, or developing innovative solutions for wastewater management, can create sustainable water management practices.

2. Waste-to-Energy Conversion: Waste-to-energy projects focus on converting waste materials into renewable energy sources. Investments in waste-to-energy facilities, such as anaerobic digestion, landfill gas recovery, and waste incineration with energy recovery, present opportunities for sustainable waste management and renewable energy generation. Collaborating with waste management companies or investing in waste-to-energy technology providers can drive returns in this sector.

3. Recycling and Circular Economy: Investments in recycling and circular economy initiatives help reduce waste generation and promote resource conservation. Opportunities exist in recycling facilities, waste sorting and processing technologies, and companies involved in recycled material utilization. Investing in companies that develop innovative recycling technologies or support circular economy practices can contribute to sustainable waste management.

4. Waste Management Infrastructure: Investments in waste management infrastructure, including waste collection systems, recycling centers, and waste treatment facilities, play a vital role in responsible waste management. Collaborating with waste management companies or investing in infrastructure projects can support efficient waste collection, recycling, and disposal practices.

5. Land Remediation and Brownfield Development: Investments in land remediation and brownfield development involve revitalizing contaminated sites for productive use. Opportunities exist in cleaning up polluted land and transforming it into renewable energy installations, urban parks, or sustainable developments. Collaborating with environmental consulting firms or investing in brownfield redevelopment projects can contribute to land restoration and sustainable land-use practices.

6. Waste Reduction Technologies and Practices: Investments in waste reduction technologies and practices aim to minimize waste generation and promote sustainable consumption patterns. Opportunities exist in companies that develop waste reduction solutions, waste minimization consulting services, or innovative packaging alternatives. Supporting initiatives that promote waste reduction education and behavior change can also be an impactful investment practice.

Water- and waste-management investments can address both immediate needs and long-term resilience. They encompass a wide range of activities, from ensuring clean water access to promoting recycling and waste reduction. Water- and waste-management investments not only offer environmental and social benefits but also provide economic opportunities, as the demand for innovative water- and waste-management solutions continues to grow. The financial ecosystem can contribute to these efforts through various financial instruments and collaborative approaches. Water- and waste-management investments align with global efforts to achieve the UN SDGs, particularly those related to clean water and sanitation (SDG 6) and responsible consumption and production (SDG 12).

Sustainable Agriculture

The agriculture sector is one of the backbones of many countries' economies. Its processes have been changing to enable technology adoption to increase productivity, quality, and sustainable development. Sustainable agriculture and food investments aim to support farming practices and food systems that are environmentally responsible, economically viable, and socially just. Sustainable food investments focus on the broader food system, including production, processing, distribution, and consumption.

Sustainable agriculture investments are crucial for addressing global challenges such as food security, climate change, and natural resource depletion. Investment opportunities in sustainable agriculture and food offer avenues for asset owners to support environmentally friendly and socially responsible practices in the food system. Joshi and Dash (2023) found that sustainable agriculture investments yielded strong financial returns with low risk.

The key investment opportunities and practices in sustainable agriculture and food investments include:

1. Organic Farming: Investing in organic farming practices involves supporting agricultural methods that minimize the use of synthetic inputs such as pesticides and synthetic fertilizers. Opportunities exist in organic crop production, livestock farming, and organic food

processing. Investing in organic farming can involve partnerships with individual farmers, organic food companies, or organic-focused investment funds.

2. Precision Agriculture: Precision agriculture utilizes technology, data analytics, and remote sensing to optimize farm management practices. Investments in precision agriculture technologies, such as sensors, drones, and satellite imaging, can enhance resource efficiency, reduce environmental impact, and improve crop yields. Start-ups developing precision agriculture solutions and equipment manufacturers offer potential investment avenues.

3. Vertical Farming and Controlled Environment Agriculture (CEA): Vertical farming involves growing crops in vertically stacked layers, often in urban areas, using controlled environments and artificial lighting. CEA encompasses various technologies such as hydroponics, aeroponics, and aquaponics. Investments in vertical farming companies, CEA infrastructure providers, or urban farming start-ups can support sustainable food production in resource-constrained areas.

4. Sustainable Aquaculture: Sustainable aquaculture practices promote responsible fish farming that minimizes environmental impact and preserves aquatic ecosystems. Investments in sustainable aquaculture projects, such as land-based fish farms or recirculating aquaculture systems (RAS), offer opportunities for supporting environmentally sound fish production. Engaging with sustainable seafood producers or aquaculture technology providers can provide investment avenues in this sector.

5. Alternative Protein Sources: Investments in alternative protein sources, such as plant-based proteins or cultivated meat (cellular agriculture), address the environmental and ethical challenges associated with traditional animal agriculture. Start-ups focused on developing plant-based meat substitutes, insect protein, or lab-grown meat offer opportunities for investors interested in sustainable protein solutions.

6. Food Waste Reduction: Investing in technologies and initiatives that reduce food waste throughout the supply chain presents opportunities to address both environmental and economic challenges. Start-ups focused on food waste prevention, recovery, and upcycling

can offer investment potential. Additionally, investing in companies that facilitate food redistribution, composting, or anaerobic digestion can support sustainable waste management practices.

7. Sustainable Supply Chains: Investments in sustainable supply chains involve supporting initiatives that promote transparency, traceability, and ethical sourcing practices. Companies working on sustainable sourcing, fair trade, regenerative agriculture, and certification systems offer investment opportunities. Sustainable sourcing platforms and technologies that enable supply chain transparency are also areas for potential investment.

8. Agricultural Technology (AgTech) and Farm Management Systems: AgTech innovations, such as farm management software, remote sensing, and Internet-of-Things (IoT) applications, enhance productivity and sustainability in agriculture. Investing in AgTech start-ups that develop solutions for farm management, irrigation optimization, pest management, or soil health monitoring can support sustainable agriculture practices.

9. Soil Health and Regenerative Agriculture: Regenerative agriculture focuses on building healthy soil ecosystems, optimizing nutrient cycling, and sequestering carbon in agricultural soils. Investments in regenerative agriculture practices, including cover cropping, crop rotation, and agroforestry, can promote soil health and contribute to climate-change mitigation. Supporting organizations that provide education, training, or resources for farmers transitioning to regenerative practices is another investment avenue.

10. Sustainable Food Retail and Distribution: Investments in sustainable food retail and distribution channels support the availability and accessibility of environmentally friendly and ethically produced food products. Investing in organic food retailers, farmers' markets, sustainable food delivery services, or companies focused on reducing food miles can align with sustainable food system goals.

Sustainable agriculture and food investments are vital for building a food system that nourishes people without depleting the planet's resources. They encompass a wide range of strategies, from promoting environmentally friendly farming practices to supporting local food economies and reducing food waste. Sustainable agriculture and food investments represent a promising pathway toward a more resilient, equitable, and sustainable food system that can meet the needs of a growing global population while preserving the environment for future generations.

Green Transportation

Green transportation investments are critical to the global effort to reduce GHG emissions and mitigate climate change. These investments focus on developing and promoting transportation modes and technologies with a reduced carbon footprint. Asset owners may find ample opportunities in the green transportation sector, aligning financial goals with positive environmental impact through investments in electric vehicles (EVs) and public transportation, for example, which have been found to have a moderate financial risk (Joshi and Dash, 2023).

Electric Vehicles

The electrification of industrial processes—from clean sources—is an essential lever for the decarbonization of industry. Investing in EV and the necessary charging infrastructure, which is at the forefront of low-carbon transportation opportunities, is a key strategy to reduce emissions from the transportation sector. The expansion of charging infrastructure is essential for the widespread adoption of EVs. Investments in charging network operators, fast-charging technologies, and smart charging solutions can help address range anxiety and enhance the accessibility and convenience of EV charging. Collaborating with charging infrastructure companies or investing in charging networks are also potential avenues for investment. Other investment opportunities include investing in EV manufacturers and EV supply chain components. As the demand for EVs continues to rise, investing in this sector can support the development and adoption of clean and efficient transportation.

Public Transportation

Enhancing public transportation systems can significantly reduce individual car usage and associated emissions, and promote sustainable mobility options. Investment opportunities exist in electric buses, light rail systems, and other forms of low-emission public transportation. Investing in public transportation infrastructure projects or working with public transportation authorities can contribute to sustainable urban mobility.

Shared mobility services, such as car-sharing, ride-sharing, and bike-sharing, offer sustainable alternatives to individual vehicle ownership. Investments in shared mobility platforms, technology providers, and fleet operators can support the growth of these services and reduce the overall number of vehicles on the road. Collaborating with shared-mobility providers or investing in innovative shared mobility models can align with low-carbon transportation goals.

Investments in sustainable aviation solutions offer opportunities to reduce the environmental impact of air travel. These solutions can include electric aircraft, biofuels, and hydrogen-powered aviation technologies. Investing in aviation-technology companies or partnering with airlines and aviation authorities can drive advancements in low-carbon aviation. Wang et al. (2020) found that the aviation sector presents challenges in terms of carbon emissions.

Investments in low-carbon logistics and freight solutions also aim to reduce emissions in the transportation of goods. Opportunities exist in electric or hybrid delivery vehicles, sustainable logistics management platforms, and last-mile delivery innovations. Collaborating with logistics companies or investing in sustainable freight transportation solutions can support efficient and low-emission goods movement.

Active Transportation

Promoting walking and cycling as viable transportation options can reduce reliance on motorized transport. Investments in active transportation infrastructure, such as bicycle lanes, pedestrian walkways, and multimodal transportation hubs, promote sustainable and low-carbon modes of transportation. Investing in infrastructure projects that support walking, cycling, and other forms of active transportation can contribute to healthier and greener cities.

Alternative Fuels

Investing in alternative fuels such as hydrogen and biofuels can reduce emissions from existing internal combustion engines. Investments in alternative fuels, such as biofuels, hydrogen, and renewable natural gas, can contribute to decarbonizing transportation. Opportunities exist in biofuel-production facilities, hydrogen infrastructure, and renewable natural-gas projects. Collaborating with alternative fuel manufacturers or investing in research and development (R&D) of advanced fuel technologies can support the transition to low-carbon transportation.

Smart Transportation Technologies

Implementing smart technologies can optimize transportation systems and reduce emissions. Intelligent transportation systems (ITS) leverage technology and data to optimize traffic management, reduce congestion, and improve transportation efficiency. Investments in ITS solutions, including traffic management systems, smart traffic lights, and real-time transportation information platforms, can enhance the sustainability and performance of transportation networks.

Autonomous and connected vehicle technologies have the potential to improve transportation efficiency, reduce congestion, and enhance safety. Investments in autonomous vehicle technology companies, connected vehicle platforms, and associated infrastructure can drive the development and deployment of low-carbon transportation and ITS.

Focusing on the climate-adaptation strategies and planning in the context of road- and rail-transportation systems, Wang et al. (2020) revealed the status quo and potential challenges associated with investing in public transportation, including climate risk assessment, transport asset management, climate planning and policy, and adaptation of transport infrastructure to climate change.

Green transportation investments are multifaceted and require supportive policies, technological innovation, and behavioral change. They encompass a wide range of strategies, from promoting EVs to enhancing public transportation and encouraging active transportation modes. These investments contribute to reducing GHG emissions and offer additional benefits such as improved air quality, reduced traffic congestion, enhanced accessibility, and potential cost savings for consumers.

Green Buildings and Infrastructure

The built environment sector contributes up to 40 percent of total GHGs as a result of the whole life-cycle carbon of the building. Embodied carbon is associated with the construction materials, major refurbishments, and waste in their production, the building process, and the fixtures and fittings inside, as well as from deconstruction and disposal at the end of a building's lifetime. The operations aspect, such as energy used to heat, cool, and light, also has an impact.

Green buildings and infrastructure investments are vital for a sustainable future and central to the global shift toward sustainability. Green buildings are designed to minimize their environmental footprint by using energy, water, and materials more efficiently and creating a healthier indoor environment. The first research on green building appeared for the first time in the United Kingdom in 1990 and became a development trend in the United States, Canada, and some developed countries. The green construction revolution has actively taken place in the construction–architecture industry in many developing countries worldwide in response to climate change. Green infrastructure refers to the ecological framework needed for environmental sustainability, including both natural systems and engineered solutions.

The integration of green buildings and infrastructure into urban planning and development is a complex but rewarding endeavor that requires collaboration, innovation, and a long-term commitment to sustainability. These investments focus on the development and retrofitting of buildings and infrastructure to reduce environmental impact, enhance energy efficiency, and promote overall sustainability. They align with global efforts to reduce GHG emissions, conserve resources, and enhance the quality of life.

1. Energy-Efficient Buildings: Investing in energy-efficient buildings involves supporting the construction or retrofitting of structures that prioritize energy conservation. Upgrading insulation, improving heating, ventilation, and air conditioning (HVAC) systems, installing energy-efficient lighting, and implementing smart building technologies can lead to substantial energy savings. Building energy

management systems (BEMS) solutions are gaining popularity as a means to optimize energy usage in buildings. These systems combine automation, data analytics, and control strategies to monitor and manage energy-consuming systems such as HVAC, lighting, and appliances. BEMS allow for real-time adjustments, demand response capabilities, and integration with renewable energy sources. Investments in BEMS providers offer opportunities to enhance building energy efficiency. Energy service companies (ESCOs) often facilitate energy performance contracts (EPCs) to finance and execute building retrofit projects, sharing the energy savings with the building owners. ESCOs and green building developers are potential avenues for investment in this sector. Energy-efficient buildings and sustainable infrastructure often result in cost savings over time, and they may also enhance property values and attract socially conscious investors and tenants. Notably, energy-efficient buildings offers potential strong financial performance and low risk (Joshi and Dash, 2023).

2. Renewable Energy Integration: Investments in green buildings can include the integration of renewable energy systems such as solar panels, wind turbines, or geothermal heating and cooling systems. Supporting renewable energy integration in buildings helps reduce reliance on fossil fuels and supports the transition to clean energy. Investing in renewable energy project developers or solar/wind installation companies can align with this objective.

3. Sustainable Materials: Green buildings prioritize the use of sustainable and environmentally friendly materials. Investing in companies that develop or supply sustainable construction materials, such as recycled content materials, low-emission paints, sustainable timber, or energy-efficient windows, can contribute to the greening of the construction industry.

4. Green Real Estate Investment Trusts (REITs): Green REITs focus on investments in environmentally responsible and energy-efficient properties. Investing in green REITs allows for diversified portfolios of green buildings and sustainable infrastructure projects while providing financial returns. Green REITs are managed by specialized investment firms or real estate developers with expertise in sustainable buildings.

5. Green Building Certifications: Green building certifications, such as Leadership in Energy and Environmental Design (LEED) or Building Research Establishment Environmental Assessment Method (BREEAM), are widely recognized standards for sustainable buildings. Investments can be made in companies that provide green building certification services or in properties seeking green building certification.

6. Smart Cities and Infrastructure: Cities are critical in climate actions as they constitute the main source of GHG emissions. Smart city initiatives integrate technology, data analytics, and intelligent infrastructure systems to enhance urban sustainability and livability. Investments in smart city projects, such as ITS, smart grids, or IoT-based infrastructure solutions, offer opportunities for sustainable urban development.

Climate-intelligent cities are digitally enabled cities that are climate first and climate compatible. Pee and Pan (2022) highlighted four information-research themes that can contribute to the development, including energy and resource optimization, climate-neutral digital economy, digital citizen engagement, and intelligent governance. Pee and Pan also suggested that all major streams of information research, ranging from information systems acceptance and information technology (IT) governance to fintech applications, can contribute meaningfully to mitigate climate change.

Using a quantitative and spatial analytical approach to assess whether interventions green-resilient-infrastructure protect social groups traditionally most at risk and/or least able to adapt to climate impacts, Shokry et al. (2020) found a strong negative association between green-resilient-infrastructure siting and increased minority population, and a strong positive association between green-resilient-infrastructure siting, gentrification, and reduced minority population.

Investing in green buildings and infrastructure represents a forward-thinking approach, focusing on generating economic returns and contributing to reducing carbon footprints, enhancing energy efficiency, and promoting the use of renewable resources. These investments are pivotal elements in the transition toward a more sustainable and environmentally conscious global economy. Investments in green buildings and infrastructure are expected to grow, supported by technological advancements, regulatory frameworks, and changing societal values.

Climate-Change Mitigation and Adaptation

Responding to climate change is usually presented in terms of *climate-change mitigation* (reducing and stabilizing the levels of heat-trapping GHGs in the atmosphere), or *climate-change adaptation* (adapting to the climate change already taking place), and increasing *climate-change resilience* (the ability of a system to anticipate, prepare for, respond to, and recover from adverse climate-related events). Investments in climate-change mitigation and adaptation focus on strengthening the capacity of communities and systems to withstand and bounce back from climate securities, and making adjustments to social, economic, and ecological systems in response to observed or expected changes in the climate. This investment theme focuses on long-term strategies to adapt to changing climatic conditions.

Climate-change mitigation and adaptation investments are becoming increasingly important as the effects of climate change become more pronounced. These investments can also reduce the vulnerability of economies to the adverse impacts of climate change, such as extreme weather events, rising sea levels, and shifting weather patterns.

1. Infrastructure Resilience: Investments in climate-resilient infrastructure focus on adapting existing infrastructure and designing new infrastructure to withstand climate-related risks. This includes investments in resilient buildings, flood management systems, coastal protection measures, and green infrastructure projects. Collaborating with infrastructure developers or investing in resilience-focused infrastructure projects can contribute to climate adaptation efforts.

2. Water Management and Resilience: Investments in water management and resilience aim to address the challenges of changing precipitation patterns, water scarcity, and flood risks. Opportunities include investments in water storage and distribution systems, stormwater management infrastructure, water conservation technologies, and

drought-resistant agricultural practices. Investing in companies that provide water management solutions or collaborating with water utilities can support climate resilience in the water sector.

3. Ecosystem Restoration and Conservation: Investments in ecosystem restoration and conservation contribute to climate resilience by preserving and restoring natural habitats, protecting biodiversity, and enhancing ecosystem services. This can involve investing in projects focused on reforestation, wetland restoration, coral reef conservation, or sustainable land management practices. Collaborating with conservation organizations or participating in ecosystem restoration initiatives can support climate adaptation efforts.

4. Climate-Resilient Agriculture: Investments in climate-resilient agriculture practices help farmers adapt to changing climatic conditions, reduce vulnerability, and enhance food security. Opportunities exist in investing in drought-tolerant crop varieties, precision agriculture technologies, soil conservation practices, and climate-smart farming methods. Collaborating with agricultural technology companies or supporting sustainable farming initiatives can drive climate resilience in the agricultural sector.

5. Insurance and Risk Transfer: Investments in insurance and risk transfer mechanisms, such as climate risk insurance or catastrophe bonds, help transfer climate-related risks from vulnerable communities, businesses, and infrastructure. These financial instruments provide support in the event of climate-related disasters and can enhance resilience by providing financial protection. Investing in insurance companies or participating in climate risk transfer markets can align with climate resilience objectives.

6. Climate Data and Analytics: Investments in climate data collection, analysis, and modeling enable better understanding of climate risks and inform adaptation strategies. Opportunities exist in investing in climate data platforms, satellite imagery analysis, and climate modeling technologies. Collaborating with climate data analytics companies or supporting research institutions can contribute to evidence-based decision making for climate resilience.

7. Urban Resilience and Adaptation: Investments in urban resilience focus on making cities more resilient to climate-related risks, such as

heatwaves, flooding, and sea-level rise. This can involve investments in urban green infrastructure, resilient building codes, climate-resilient urban planning, and smart city solutions. Collaborating with urban planning firms or investing in urban resilience projects can support climate adaptation in urban areas.

8. Community-Based Climate Adaptation: Investments in community-based climate adaptation initiatives empower local communities to develop resilience strategies and implement climate adaptation measures. This can include investments in community-driven projects, capacity building programs, and participatory planning processes. Collaborating with community-based organizations or investing in grassroots climate adaptation initiatives can drive resilience at the local level.

Climate-change mitigation and adaptation investments are essential for safeguarding communities, economies, and ecosystems against the growing threats posed by climate change, and contributing to a more sustainable and resilient future. Climate-change mitigation and adaptation investments require a multifaceted approach that includes risk assessment, infrastructure development, community engagement, policy support, and innovation.

The economy for the next 30 years is likely to be driven by the Paris Agreement and SDGs agendas and will have a strong base in a cluster of innovative technologies: renewable energy, energy efficiency, green buildings and infrastructure, circular economy technologies, and biophilic urbanism. Some are well underway, and the others will need interventions if not cultural changes and may miss being mainstreamed in this recovery but could still play a minor role in the new economy. Newman (2020) suggested that the resulting urban transformations are likely to build on COVID-19 through "global localism" and could lead to five new features: including relocalized centers with distributed infrastructure, tailored innovations in each urban fabric, less car dependence, symbiotic partnerships for funding, and rewritten manuals for urban professionals.

Investment Process and Engagement

This section delves into the nuanced and increasingly vital world of climate-conscious investing, focusing on three key areas: ESG integration, portfolios with purpose, and stewardship and engagement. This section is designed to provide readers with a comprehensive understanding of how ESG factors are intricately woven into investment policies and processes. These three areas of focus offer a holistic view of how climate-conscious investment practices are reshaping the investment landscape, balancing profit with purpose, and leading to a more responsible and impactful approach to managing investments.

ESG Integration

ESG integration, as an investment strategy, considers financially material ESG factors at each applicable step of the investment process. The United Nations Environment Programme Finance Initiative, along with legal firm Freshfields and the UN's *Principles for Responsible Investment (PRI)* conducted analysis across jurisdictions and argued that the fiduciary duties of investors require them to:

- Incorporate ESG issues into investment analysis and decision-making processes, consistent with their investment time horizons;
- Encourage high standards of ESG performance in the investees in which they invest; and
- Understand and incorporate beneficiaries' and savers' sustainability-related preferences, regardless of whether these preferences are financially material.

Societal pressure and investor demands have also led the ESG integration to become more mainstream. According to the 2023 MSCI survey, companies in the ESG index, which includes companies that have strong sustainability practices, outperformed the MSCI World Index by 2.5 percent per year from 2007 to 2016. Joshi and Dash (2023) also provided evidence that a portfolio of companies with high sustainability ratings outperformed a traditional portfolio by 6 percent over a 10-year period.

ESG integration can also lead to better risk-adjusted returns and portfolio efficiency. Using compliance and voluntary carbon offsets from around the world, Behr et al. (2023) showed that investment strategies that include such offsets broadly achieve higher Sharpe ratios than the diversified benchmark, with the long-short strategy performing the best. The results also suggest that compliance and voluntary carbon offsets are mostly net volatility and return spillover recipients, consistent from a macro perspective.

ESG Factors

Incorporating ESG criteria into asset evaluation and investment analysis involves evaluating companies based on their environmental impact, social responsibility, and governance practices. Under this framework, asset owners and asset managers prioritize investments in companies and sectors with strong ESG performance, and integrate these considerations throughout the investment process, where applicable.

Key environmental factors:

1. Climate Change: Carbon emissions, climate-change vulnerability, financing environmental impact, and product carbon footprint;
2. Natural Capital: Biodiversity and land use, raw material sourcing, and water stress;
3. Pollution and Waste: Electronic waste, packaging material and waste, and toxic emissions;
4. Environmental Opportunities: Opportunities in clean technology (CleanTech), opportunities in green building, and opportunities in renewable energy.

Asset owners and asset managers should conduct analysis at the company or project level, sector level, country level, or market level. At a company or project level, an assessment of material environmental risk factors will inform key financial metrics as monitored and disclosed in financial statements. As such, it is important to undertake an analysis of how well the company is managing these risks over time.

Environmental and climate-related factors have varying degrees of impact on different sectors. Some sectors have higher exposure to environmental risks (such as chemicals, energy, steel and cement, extractives, food or beverages, and transportation) or physical risk from natural disasters—for example, to buildings, production facilities, agricultural land, or urban infrastructure. Companies in these sectors tend to be influenced by an environmental risk premium, which may affect the discount rate used. Hence, these sectorwide considerations also need to be considered, and they should be overlaid on the company analysis.

A country's environmental regulations, emission targets, and enforcement may vary in emphasis across different jurisdictions. Often, investments may be multijurisdictional, and hence, several country-specific considerations and regulations will need to be factored into the valuation of a company based on the country in which it is located or where its operations lie. Consideration of marketwide impacts can further influence investors' investment strategy and decisions. In addition to environmental risk assessments, asset owners and asset managers conduct social and governance assessments.

Key social factors:

1. Human Capital: Human-capital development, diversity, equity, and inclusion (DEI), and employee health and safety;
2. Product Liability/Consumer Protection: Product safety, quality, health and demographic risks, and data privacy and security;
3. Stakeholder Opposition: Community relations and controversial sourcing;
4. Social Opportunities: Access to communications, finance, and health and nutrition;
5. Social and news media;
6. Animal welfare and microbial resistance.

A good starting point when implementing social factors in investment decision is to determine which social factors are most controversial or financially material in each industry. As a next step, asset owners or asset managers can assess how exposed certain companies are to these sector-specific social factors and if and how the company manages these risks. This might depend on their business models or on the nature and geographical location of their business operations. Then, where relevant, assess critical social factors in the supply chain.

It should be noted that the social elements that are considered to have the largest financial materiality depend on specific aspects mostly related to their field of industry. Social factors can also be categorized between those impacting external stakeholders (such as customers, local communities, and governments) and groups of internal stakeholders (such as the company's employees).

Key governance factors:

1. Corporate Governance: Shareholder rights, organizational structure, executive pay, audit, board independence, diversity, accountability, related-party transactions, and dual-class share structures;
2. Corporate Behavior: Business ethics, tax, and transparency.

Of the three ESG factors, governance is the one most often considered by traditional asset managers. *Corporate governance* is the process and structure for overseeing the business and management of a company. Governance failures lead to fines and additional liabilities, as well as litigation and other costs, and harm security values.

Different asset owners and asset managers integrate governance factors into their investment decision making in different ways. For many, it is a threshold assessment—a formal minimum criterion to consider before they will consider making an investment at any price. For others, it is a risk assessment tool, which may represent the level of confidence about future earnings or the multiple on which those earnings are placed in a valuation—or it may be reflected less in full financial models and more in a simple level of confidence in the valuation range or investment thesis.

If the analysis of corporate governance is specifically built into valuation models, this analysis is most typically done by recognizing negative governance characteristics by way of adding a risk premium to the cost of capital or raising the discount rate applied. Others regard weak governance as an engagement and investment opportunity—the logic being that governance can be improved through active dialogue with management and proxy voting. In almost every market, asset owners will be faced annually with voting decisions on matters such as accepting the report and accounts, board appointments, the appointment of the auditor, and executive remuneration. These can be directly addressed in the annual-general-meeting (AGM) agenda.

Qualitative ESG Analysis

ESG integration should be considered in light of two different investment strategies: qualitative ESG investment strategies and quantitative investment strategies. Qualitative ESG investment strategies most commonly take the form of a fundamental approach, often focusing on depth within a portfolio, manifested through a portfolio of few, more concentrated holdings. An asset owner or asset manager would work to complement bottom-up financial analysis alongside the consideration of ESG factors to reinforce the investment thesis of a particular holding.

> Step 1: Filter the investment universe based on ESG criteria. Asset owners and asset managers can use a materiality map that covers various ESG issues and span over their subsectors to identify ESG risks and opportunities that may have a material impact on financial outcomes. Materiality is typically measured in terms of both the likelihood and magnitude of impact;
>
> Step 2: Analyze ESG data to form an opinion on a selected company's ability to manage certain ESG issues;
>
> Step 3: Incorporate material ESG issues, factors, signals, risks, and opportunities into research to strengthen financial analysis;
>
> Step 4: Combine the opinion on the company's ability to manage ESG issues with financial analysis by linking specific aspects of the company's ESG risk-management strategy to different value drivers (e.g., costs, revenues, profits, and capital expenditure requirements);
>
> Step 5: Integrate this opinion in a quantified way into financial models by adjusting assumptions used in the model (e.g., growth, margins, or costs of capital).

The asset owner or asset manager would then work to understand the aggregate risk at the portfolio level across all factors to understand correlation and event risks and potential shocks to the portfolio. Certain qualitative techniques might be more suitable, or weighted differently, for different asset classes.

Quantitative ESG Analysis

Quantitative investment strategies are, broadly speaking, rules-based approaches employing the statistical application of financial and/or non-financial factors to drive security selection. Quantitative strategies generally seek to minimize the higher costs associated with discretionary active management. Quantitative strategies focus on breadth, using a much larger portfolio of holdings to target risk and volatility-adjusted returns. Quantitative investment strategies typically integrate ESG factors alongside other factors, such as value, size, momentum, growth, and volatility.

Step 1: Some quantitative factors can be from databases, models, or a mix of third-party data and internal proprietary data. This assessment is typically done with large datasets of stocks or bonds, rather than individual company assessment, though some asset managers create their own proprietary scores from individual company assessment. The data gathering is similar to that done in fundamental analyses but tends to be over larger datasets;

Step 2: Aggregate ESG data into an ESG score, which is added to the quant models. This could be a screen that creates the investment universe or a quant model used to adjust valuations based on several factors, including ESG;

Step 3: Include ESG data in the investment processes, which could result in upward or downward adjustments to the weights of securities, including zero.

Overall, ESG techniques can be considered quantitative or qualitative or have elements of both. Within ESG analyses of companies or securities, the elements of ESG integration typically include:

1. Adjust forecast financials and assumptions (e.g., revenue, operating cost, asset book value, capital expenditure);
2. Adjust valuation models or multiples (e.g., cost of capital, discount rates, terminal values, ratios);
3. Adjust credit risk and duration;
4. Managing risk, including exposure limits, scenario analysis, and value-at-risk models;

5. ESG factor tilts;
6. ESG momentum tilts.

Portfolios With Purpose

"Portfolio with Purpose" is an investment strategy that achieves financial objectives with a dedicated ESG focus. To implement this strategy, asset owners and asset managers often rely on various tools and resources, such as internal ESG research, company questionnaires and management interviews, watch lists, red-flag indicators, external ESG research, and checks with outside experts.

1. Internal ESG research: Asset managers perform proprietary ESG research and analysis, and provide output in scores, rankings, or reports. Research could consist of materiality frameworks, ESG-integrated research notes, research dashboards, SWOT analysis with ESG factors, scenario analysis, and relative rankings;
2. Company questionnaires and management interviews: This information is also used in parallel with regular company engagement meetings, where asset owners or asset managers, and investee companies meet to discuss the most material ESG issues;
3. Watch lists: These lists might include securities with high ESG risk added to a watchlist for monitoring, or securities with high ESG opportunities that are put on a watchlist for possible investment;
4. Red-flag indicators: Securities with high ESG risk are flagged and investigated further or excluded;
5. External ESG research: Sell-side, ESG specialists, and third-party databases issue these research reports and create materiality framework;
6. Checks with outside experts: Asset owners or asset managers might interview key industry thought leaders or other stakeholders of the company, such as customers, suppliers, and regulators.

For a strategy to be considered a "Portfolio with Purpose," asset owners or asset managers should do the following:

1. Complete the processes for ESG integrated strategies;
2. Complete describing the ESG focus of the strategy;

3. Follow policies on documentation and record keeping, establish any additional records required to demonstrate that the ESG focus is being measured and monitored;

4. Review the investment process and documentation procedures;

5. Review any material new operational processes, which can support the investment strategy, such as data sources, benchmarks, and instrument types;

6. Complete an annual certification that the "Portfolio with Purpose" and investment process as described remains in place.

ESG Scorecard

An ESG scorecard is created based on the self-assessment response with ESG factor scores ranging from zero to five. Scores of zero could make a company unattractive, and scores of five could lead to further investment work. High or low scores are then used in valuation or further assessment work. Alternatively, total scores of all factors in the scorecard are used in further assessment or valuation work. The scorecard can take a qualitative judgment of a factor and put a form of quantitative score on it.

Developing an ESG scorecard involves the following six steps:

Step 1: Identify sector- or company-specific ESG items;
Step 2: Break down issues into a number of indicators (e.g., policy, measures, disclosure);
Step 3: Determine a scoring system based on what good/best practices look like for each indicator/issue;
Step 4: Assess a company and assign a score;
Step 5: Calculate aggregated scores at the issue-, dimension-, or ESG level, or a total score level;
Step 6: Benchmark the company's performance against industry averages or peer group.

While there are philosophical similarities in identifying material ESG factors and then applying those to the analysis, the type of factors used can differ across asset classes, as can the type of integration techniques. Real assets, including vacant land, farmland, timber, infrastructure, intellectual property, commodities, and private real estate, carry certain advantages and challenges compared to the equities and corporate bonds asset classes.

In many cases, asset owners own the asset outright; majority or full ownership stakes offer them much greater control over the definition, application, and reporting of ESG data alongside or outside of existing reporting standards such as those of the GRI or the *Global Real Estate Sustainability Benchmark (GRESB)*. The materiality frameworks used might have philosophical similarities—as in material ESG factors—but the identification of those factors can differ.

ESG Ratings

ESG data and analytics providers can provide ESG data, ratings, screening, voting advisory, benchmarks, and controversies. ESG ratings are primarily based on historical company data and alternative data sources, such as media sources. ESG data and analytics providers or rating agencies synthesize these data to provide information on a company's behavior and policies regarding ESG criteria to inform investment decisions.

Morningstar, a popular investment and research platform catering to both retail and institutional investors, first introduced its sustainability rating to complement its core fund rating in 2016. In 2017, Morningstar started acquiring Sustainalytics to expand access to ESG research and analytics. The Morningstar methodology now reflects a company's ESG risks measured on the same scale across industries, and the overall fund rating shows the ESG risk embedded in the fund's portfolio.

Other major ESG data and analytics providers include MSCI, Bloomberg, Institutional Shareholder Services owned by Deutsche Börse, RepRisk, TruValue Labs by FactSet, the London Stock Exchange Group's Financial Times Stock Exchange (FTSE) Russell, Refinitiv, Moody's Vigeo Eiris, CDP, Real Impact Tracker, Mercer, and the World Bank Group. Asset owners and asset managers can use the raw ESG ratings or adjust them to reflect their own views, which can then be compiled for use in assessment or idea generation.

It is important to note that ESG metrics differ considerably across ESG data and analytics providers, and the choice of providers can have a fundamental impact on the ESG credentials of portfolios (Atta-Darkua et al. 2020). Popescu et al. (2021) found that carbon footprints, exposure metrics, and ESG ratings, while widely used, have several shortcomings. Popescu et al. suggested prioritizing open-source, science-based, and sustainability-driven assessment methods, and upgrading methods by incorporating measurement of positive impact creation and by adopting a life-cycle perspective.

When choosing data and analytics providers, consider the following:

- The number of companies covered;
- The length of history of datasets;
- The stability of methodology;
- The regularity of updates;
- Asset-class coverage;
- The quality of methodology;
- The range of datasets; and
- The range of tools and services offered.

Stewardship and Engagement

ESG integration should be complemented with stewardship and active engagement. *Stewardship* is typically used as an overarching term encompassing the approach that asset owners take as active and involved owners of the companies and other entities in which they invest through voting and engagement. Engagement is the way in which asset owners and asset managers put into effect the stewardship responsibilities in line with the PRI principle. Engagement is often described as purposeful dialogue with a specific objective in mind—that purpose often relates to improving companies' business practices, especially in relation to the management of ESG issues. Engagement is seen as complementary to the approaches to climate-conscious investing and as a way to encourage companies to act more responsibly.

Stewardship and engagement are beneficial because they enhance shareholder value and support asset managers in the execution of their fiduciary duty. When done well, stewardship and engagement encourage enhanced information flows between asset owners, asset managers, and investee companies as the parties discuss and debate issues. These exchanges allow them to learn from each other, build relationships, and, most importantly, encourage change as they communicate their perspectives on key issues that the company is facing.

Climate-conscious investing is influenced by the ability of investees to create social value, which plays a vital role in the interorganizational relationship between asset owners and investees (Agrawal and Hockerts, 2019). Agrawal and Hockerts (2019) found that an emphasis on communication, due diligence, and sector specialization increases the likelihood of investment, while social impact measurement, reporting, and frequent engagement increase the possibility of postinvestment alignment. Based on these findings, Agrawal and Hockerts argued that similar to industry specialization in for-profit investing, social sector specialization is equally relevant for alignment and returns.

Although the efficacy of engagement usually depends on the scale of ownership of the asset owner or the collective initiative, the success factors or characteristics of engagement approach typically include:

1. Objective(s) should be specific and targeted to enable clarity around delivery;
2. Objectives should be strategic or governance-led, or linked to material strategic and/or governance issues;
3. The engagement approach should be bespoke and tailored to the target company; and
4. The quality of the engagement dialogue and method used.

Asset owners and asset managers can achieve these goals by engaging to generate research insights and by engaging for action.

Engaging for Insight

Engagements for insight are to learn more about an ESG issue facing an investee. Engagement enhances research process, generating insight into investees' strategies and competitive positioning. It also reveals how management teams, as well as company boards, address and manage risks and opportunities, including material ESG considerations. By engaging, asset owners are able to better assess the quality of an investee's management, strategy, operations, and corporate governance structure.

A full assessment of operational performance must encompass financial and nonfinancial performance factors if they could materially affect long-term financial outcomes and relevant to the investee company's stakeholders. This valuable information should be integrated into security analysis and investment decisions—with the ultimate goal of generating enhanced risk-adjusted returns.

Engaging for Action

Engagements for action enables asset owners and asset managers to share ESG research assessment to engage investees to better address material ESG risks or take advantage of ESG opportunities. The goal is to encourage investees to make decisions with a long-term view that is in asset owners' best interest. Although vary by industry and business activities, the key areas of engagement for action include companies' disclosure, strategy, targets, governance, and transition plans.

1. Disclosure: Encourage companies to adopt standardized reporting frameworks, such as the *Task Force on Climate-related Financial Disclosures (TCFD)*, to provide clear, consistent, and comparable information on climate risks and opportunities. The TCFD takes the Paris Agreement's temperature target, and tries to operationalize it for the business world. TCFD's June 2017 Final Report urges companies to disclose against: (i) governance, (ii) strategy, (iii) risk management, and (iv) metrics and targets. The TCFD recommends that these disclosures are provided as part of the mainstream financial filings.

2. Strategy: Push investee companies to integrate climate considerations into their long-term business strategies, ensuring that they are aligned with global climate goals.

3. Targets: Advocate for companies to set clear, science-based targets for reducing GHG emissions.

4. Governance: Ensure that the investee company's board and management have the necessary expertise and oversight mechanisms to manage climate risks effectively.

5. Transition Plans: Encourage companies, especially those in carbon-intensive sectors, to develop and disclose transition plans toward a low-carbon business model.

Asset owners are using their influence to engage with companies and various stakeholders to reduce their carbon footprint, improve sustainability practices, and disclose climate-related risks and opportunities, in line with standardized reporting frameworks. Asset owners can encourage investee companies to improve their ESG practices via a company's AGM by formally expressing their views through voting on resolutions. Engagement can also happen outside this process, with an asset manager discussing ESG issues with the investee's board or management.

Asset owners and asset managers are expected to engage with leaders of public and private companies and noncorporate entities, or executives with whom asset owners or asset managers wish to share their perspectives or escalate concerns from talks with senior executives and management. For sovereign issuers, engage with key members of governments and regulatory agencies or departments. For securitized investments, consider engaging beyond the originators to the servicers and other third parties.

Typically, engagements can be via direct dialogue, shareholder resolutions, executing voting rights, and conducting collaborative engagement. All engagements should be conducted from a fiduciary perspective in accordance with relevant market regulations and frameworks.

1. Direct Dialogue: Initiate conversations with the investee company's management or board members to discuss concerns about climate risks and its approach to managing them.
2. Shareholder Resolutions: Propose resolutions at AGMs that call for specific actions or disclosures related to climate risk. Even if the resolution does not pass, it can draw attention to the issue and prompt the company to take action.
3. Voting Rights: Use voting rights to support proposals that promote better climate risk management and oppose those that do not align with climate goals.

4. Collaborative Engagement: Join forces with other shareholders or investor coalitions to amplify the message and put more pressure on the company.

Shareholder resolutions on environmental issues are becoming more common. Engagement can happen anywhere within the investment process—during research analysis, investment selection, portfolio construction, strategy implementation, while holding a position, and after divestment. These conversations are often ongoing, as we continue to revisit previous topics and discuss progress.

By pushing companies to address climate risks, asset owners can help protect their investments from potential value loss. Investees that proactively manage climate risks and seize related opportunities are likely to be better positioned for long-term success, benefiting asset owners. Engagement is an effective way to ensure that asset owners' investments align with their values and contribute to a more sustainable future. A sample carbon offsets engagement guide can be found in Appendix B.

Summary

Chapter 3 is a comprehensive chapter that delves into the evolving landscape of climate-conscious investment approaches. It highlights the growing importance of integrating climate considerations into investment decisions, reflecting a shift toward more sustainable and responsible financial practices. Climate-conscious investing refers to investing in investees that contribute to environmental sustainability, while thematic investing focuses on themes or assets specifically related to sustainability factors.

This chapter then delves into the investment processes that underpin climate-conscious investing. This section explains how ESG integration helps in identifying risks and opportunities that traditional financial analysis might overlook. It emphasizes that ESG integration is not just about excluding harmful industries but involves a nuanced understanding of how ESG factors can affect an investee's performance and risk profile. "Portfolio with Purpose" discusses the tools and resources asset owners and asset managers can use to reflect their personal values and ethical beliefs, without compromising on financial goals.

Lastly, the chapter covers the topic of stewardship and engagement, where asset owners use their influence to encourage investees to improve their ESG practices. This can involve dialogues with company management, voting at AGMs, shareholder resolutions, and collaborating with other asset owners for greater impact. Active engagement can happen anywhere during the investment process. Asset owners, policy makers, asset managers, investees, and regulatory bodies all play vital roles in advancing climate-conscious investing.

CHAPTER 4

Climate-Conscious Investment Instruments and Vehicles

In an era where climate change poses not just an existential threat to our environment but also a significant challenge to global economies, the role of finance in driving sustainable practices has never been more crucial. This chapter delves into the burgeoning world of green finance, exploring a range of innovative investment instruments and vehicles designed to support environmental sustainability while offering viable investment opportunities. Climate-conscious investment instruments and vehicles are financial tools specifically designed to align with climate goals, support sustainability, and contribute to the global effort to mitigate and adapt to climate change. These tools enable capital to flow toward projects, technologies, and practices that mitigate climate change, enhance resilience, and promote sustainable development.

Green bonds have emerged as a cornerstone of climate-conscious investing. These bonds are specifically earmarked to fund projects that have positive environmental benefits, ranging from renewable energy to sustainable waste management. While green bonds are explicitly environmentally focused, climate-aligned bonds offer a broader spectrum of investment in assets and projects that align with long-term climate goals. ETFs and mutual funds focused on sustainability criteria have democratized access to climate-conscious investments. These vehicles aggregate investments in companies and projects that meet specific environmental standards, allowing asset owners to contribute to a greener future. Impact-investing funds are designed for those who are intent on generating social and environmental impact alongside a financial return.

Venture capital (VC) focused on climate solutions is a critical driver of innovation in green technology. Green REITs offer asset owners the opportunity to invest in portfolios of properties that are developed or managed with sustainability as a core principle. Community investment notes allow for investing directly in community-level projects that have environmental and social benefits. Finally, public–private partnerships (PPPs), which often involve large-scale infrastructure projects, are structured to address climate change and are crucial in mobilizing resources from both public and private sectors for sustainable development.

This chapter aims to provide a comprehensive overview of the diverse range of climate-conscious investment vehicles, highlighting their unique features, potential impacts, and the role they play in steering the global economy toward a more sustainable future. The growth and diversification of climate-conscious investment options reflect the increasing recognition of climate risks and opportunities in the financial landscape, as well as the growing demand for responsible and impact-driven investment strategies.

Green Bonds: A Pathway to Sustainable Development

As a financial approach integrating the protection of the ecosystem into economic profits, green bonds are increasingly being applied to finance emissions reductions, sustainable development, and other cleaner production investments conducive to reaching the temperature target of the Paris Agreement. *Green bonds* are a type of fixed-income instrument specifically earmarked to fund projects that have positive climate and environmental benefits. The green-bond market has grown rapidly since the first green bond was issued by the World Bank Group in 2008.

Developed markets (DM) represent most countries that have issued green bonds (Alsmadi et al. 2023), and emerging markets (EM) are increasingly raising money for climate action by issuing green bonds. Countries such as Colombia, Egypt, India, and Indonesia are among 19 EM countries funding renewable energy and mass transit from the proceeds of green bonds. India, for instance, launched its first green bond in early 2023 to raise approximately US$2 billion for projects contributing to climate change mitigation, adaptation, environmental protection, resource and biodiversity conservation, and net-zero objectives.

- According to the Climate Bonds Initiative (CBI), the green, social, sustainability, sustainability-linked and transition (GSS+) debt reached US$204.8 billion for the first quarter of 2023. This was a 17 percent increase compared to the previous quarter, but a 21 percent year-on-year drop against the first quarter of 2022.
- By the end of March 2023, the CBI had recorded lifetime GSS+ of US$3.9 trillion since the market inception in 2007. The opening quarter of 2023 showed that bond volumes were recovering from the market trauma of late 2022.

Using a panel dataset of over US$300 billion in green bonds issued in 49 countries between 2007 and 2017, Tolliver et al. (2020) suggested that NDCs and other macroeconomic and institutional factors are driving growing green-bond issuances that will finance climate and sustainability investments through the future. Nonetheless, green bonds still represent a small fraction of the total global bond market. Ye and Rasoulinezhad (2023) recommended implementing operational plans to develop the green bonds market, promoting green foreign direct investment (FDI), efficient monetary policy to lower inflation rate, and enhancing digital green bonds, as practical policies.

Structure of Green Bonds

Green bonds can be issued by corporations, governments, supranational institutions, and financial institutions.

1. Corporations: Companies can issue green bonds as part of their financing strategy and commitment to sustainability.
2. Governments: National and local governments can issue green bonds to finance public environmental projects.
3. Supranational institutions: International institutions, such as the World Bank Group, issue green bonds as part of its climate support activities.
4. Financial institutions: Banks and other financial institutions can issue green bonds, often using the proceeds to finance green projects by their clients.

The proceeds from green bonds are typically tied directly to the financing of eligible green projects, such as renewable energy or energy-efficient technologies, green transport, sustainable water, waste water treatment, pollution prevention, and biodiversity conservation. Green bonds are typically asset linked and backed by the balance sheet of the issuing entity. That said, they usually carry the same credit rating as their issuer's other debt obligations.

The green bond market helps to address the fact that climate change, deforestation, pollution, and other environmental problems require large-scale capital solutions. Ye and Rasoulinezhad (2023) examined the effect of issued green bonds on the effectiveness of renewable natural resource utilization in 15 selected Asia-Pacific countries during 2012 to 2021. The results concluded that the issued green bonds have positive and statistically significant impacts on renewable natural resource utilization efficiency in both the short term and long term, and the magnitude of the impacts is more extensive in the long-term context.

Impact on Issuers

1. Diversifying Investor Base: Green bonds can attract a broader range of investors, particularly those with a focus on sustainability and ESG criteria.
2. Enhancing Reputation: Issuing green bonds can improve the issuer's reputation as a responsible entity committed to environmental sustainability.
3. Potential for Lower Cost of Capital: In some cases, green bonds can be issued at a slightly lower yield compared to conventional bonds, potentially reducing the cost of capital for issuers.
4. Reporting and Compliance: Issuers must commit to ongoing transparency and reporting, which can entail additional costs and administrative efforts.

Focardi and Fabozzi (2020) argued that bond investors offer more promise in forcing corporations to adopt policies to reduce carbon emissions than do equity investors by affecting funding costs. This can be done through carbon emission reduction covenants in corporate bond indentures and carbon policy performance bonds; the latter can be used to control government performance as well as corporate performance. On the financing side, green bonds can be used to fund carbon emission reduction projects.

With the use of matched bond-issuer data, Fatica and Panzica (2021) tested whether green bond issues were associated to a reduction in Scope 1 emissions of nonfinancial companies, and found that compared with conventional bond issuers with similar financial characteristics and environmental ratings, green issuers display a decrease in the carbon intensity of their assets after borrowing on the green segment. The results also suggest that the decrease in emissions is more pronounced, significant, and long-lasting when green bonds with refinancing purposes are excluded, which is consistent with an increase in the volume of climate-friendly activities due to new projects.

Impact on Asset Owners

1. Meeting ESG Objectives: Green bonds provide asset owners with an opportunity to contribute to environmental sustainability, aligning with their ESG investment goals.
2. Risk and Return Profile: The risk and return profile of green bonds is generally similar to that of traditional bonds from the same issuer, making them an attractive proposition for risk-averse investors seeking sustainability.
3. Transparency and Assurance: The certification and reporting requirements offer asset owners a higher degree of transparency and assurance that their funds are contributing to environmental projects.
4. Market Growth and Diversification: The growing green-bond market offers asset owners more options to diversify their portfolios within the fixed-income space.

Adding green bonds into the investment portfolios brings considerable diversification avenues for the asset owners who tend to take fewer risks in periods of economic stress and turbulence. Broadstock et al. (2022) investigated the comovements across and within the respective markets for green and traditional bonds in China, Europe, and the United States, with a particular focus on the connectedness during the COVID-19 pandemic. The results suggest that investing in green bonds results in more efficient portfolios. Broadstock et al. also showed that the minimum connectedness portfolio achieves the highest Sharpe ratio and significantly reduces the investment risk. Naeem et al. (2023) examined the hedge and safe-haven properties of the Sukuk and green bond for the stock markets pre- and during the COVID-19 pandemic period, and found that green bonds also provide hedges for various international stocks, as indicated by the hedge ratio and hedge effectiveness.

Certification Process

Before issuing a green bond, issuers often obtain an external review or verification from a third party, such as a sustainability rating agency. This review assesses the environmental sustainability of the proposed projects and the issuer's ability to track and report on the use of proceeds. Fatica and Panzica (2021) found a larger reduction in carbon emissions in case of green bonds that have external review, as well as those issued after the Paris Agreement.

The types of reviews can include second-party opinions, verification, certification, and green bond ratings. A popular certification is the Climate Bonds Standard (CBS), provided by the CBI. The Center for International Climate Research (CICERO) developed a "shades of green" methodology to provide second-party opinions that determine how a green or sustainability bond aligns with a low-carbon-resilient future.[1]

- Dark green: For projects and solutions that are realizations today of the long-term vision of a low-carbon and climate-resilient future. Typically, this will entail zero-emission solutions and governance structures that integrate environmental concerns into all activities.
- Medium green: For projects and solutions that represent steps toward the long-term vision, but are not quite there yet.
- Light green: For projects and solutions that are environmentally friendly but do not by themselves represent

or is part of the long-term vision (e.g., energy efficiency in fossil-based processes).

- Brown: For projects that are irrelevant or in opposition to the long-term vision of a low-carbon and climate-resilient future.

Tolliver et al. (2020) highlighted the need for broader examinations of the determinants of green-bond issuances for sustainable outcomes. After the bond is issued, ongoing reporting is required to update investors on the use of proceeds and the environmental impact of the projects. This reporting is typically done annually until the bond matures.

Regular reporting on the use of proceeds from green bonds and the environmental impact of the projects funded by these bonds is a critical component of the green-bond framework. The key components of reporting include the use of proceeds, project progress and milestones, environmental impact metrics (such as reduction in carbon emissions, amount of renewable energy generated, or improvement in energy efficiency), methodology used for tracking and reporting, third-party verification, as well as frequency and accessibility.

The *Green Bond Principles* (GBP), established by the International Capital Market Association (ICMA), provide voluntary guidelines on transparency, disclosure, and reporting in the green bond market. Adherence to GBP is often seen as a benchmark for green bond issuance. The ICMA continues to serve as the Secretariat to the GBP, providing support while advising on governance and other issues.

Regular reporting underpins the integrity and success of the green bond market. It aligns investor expectations with actual outcomes, drives market growth, and ensures that green bonds continue to be a powerful tool for achieving environmental objectives. The GBP recommends transparency and disclosure and promote integrity in the development of the green bond market. This transparency is not only essential for maintaining the credibility of the bond but also plays a significant role in the broader context of sustainable finance:

1. Transparency and Accountability: Regular reporting ensures that the funds raised are being used as intended, which is to finance or refinance projects with clear environmental benefits. This transparency

holds issuers accountable to their commitments, reinforcing investor trust.

2. Market Perception: Detailed and frequent reporting on how funds are used and the environmental impact achieved boosts asset owners' confidence.

3. Benchmarking and Impact Assessment: Reporting allows for the measurement and communication of the environmental impact, which is crucial for benchmarking against other climate initiatives and assessing the overall effectiveness of the green bond market.

4. Market Growth and Development: Consistent and reliable reporting helps in the development of the green-bond market by providing data and success stories that can attract more issuers and asset owners.

5. Regulatory Compliance: In many cases, regular reporting is not just a best practice but also a regulatory requirement, especially in markets where green bonds are subject to specific disclosure regulations.

Climate-Aligned Bonds: Beyond Green

Climate-aligned bonds are a type of standard bond issued to finance projects that contribute to a low-carbon and climate-resilient economy and SDGs. Climate-aligned bonds are similar to green bonds, but with a broader focus—while green bonds are typically used to finance specific green projects, the proceeds of climate-aligned bonds that are issued by corporations, financial institutions, and governments can be used to finance a wide range of climate-friendly activities.

Climate-aligned bonds often finance projects that align with environmental sustainability, such as renewable energy, clean transportation, or sustainable water management. By doing so, these bonds contribute to SDGs such as affordable and clean energy (SDG 7), clean water and sanitation (SDG 6), and sustainable cities and communities (SDG 11). By focusing on sustainability, climate-aligned bonds help mitigate environmental and social risks, aligning with the goal of peace, justice, and strong institutions (SDG 16).

In addition to financing sustainable projects, climate-aligned bonds may fund projects that, while not directly environmental, have indirect benefits. For example, bonds financing health care or education infrastructure can lead to more energy-efficient buildings and reduced carbon footprints, contributing to climate action (SDG 13). Climate-aligned bonds are an important tool for mobilizing the capital needed to transition to a low-carbon economy, while also earning a return on investments.

Climate-aligned bonds are identified via a proprietary methodology developed by the CBI, which continues to provide a comprehensive analysis of the global unlabeled climate-aligned bond market. The CBI has expanded its standard to include new sectors and activities, such as agriculture, basic chemicals, bioenergy, buildings, cement, electrical grids and storage, low-carbon transport, forestry, land conservation and restoration, geothermal energy, hydrogen, hydropower, marine renewable energy, shipping, solar energy, steel, waste management, and water infrastructure.

Climate-aligned bonds, through investing in sustainable projects, can also stimulate economic growth and create jobs in new and emerging sectors. This aligns with SDGs such as decent work and economic growth (SDG 8) and industry, innovation, and infrastructure (SDG 9). Moreover, by funding projects that promote efficient use of resources and sustainable practices, climate-aligned bonds support responsible consumption and production (SDG 12).

Beyond these, climate-aligned bonds promote social inclusion, facilitate market development for sustainability, and set standards and reporting. Many climate-aligned projects also have social components, like improving access to essential services for underserved communities, thus contributing to goals such as no poverty (SDG 1) and reduced inequalities (SDG 10). The issuance of climate-aligned bonds, even if not labeled green, helps develop the market for sustainable finance, raising awareness and setting precedents for future green and sustainability-linked financial instruments. Climate-aligned bonds often require issuers to follow certain standards and reporting practices; in this sense, these bonds can improve transparency and accountability in how companies and governments address sustainability.

However, worldwide, climate bonds were used less where the per capita use of fossil fuels was the highest, and the global amount of climate bonds was statistically negatively correlated with the per-capita emissions (Lucchetta, 2023). High-income countries are only recently decreasing their use of fossil fuels, while the total used by low-income countries has always been very low. Lucchetta (2023) argued that climate-aligned bonds should be allocated considering per-capita use of fossil fuels in coordination with the heterogeneity of population growth and of different macroregional economic development. EM countries, in particular, need more financial resources for an ethically acceptable green transition.

Green ETFs and Mutual Funds: Democratizing Climate Investment

Green ETFs specifically invest in stocks of companies with environmentally friendly practices. These ETFs invest in a range of sectors, including clean energy, EVs, and water resources. Green mutual funds specifically aim to invest in companies that are environmentally responsible. They use different strategies, including negative screening (excluding certain sectors or companies from their portfolio), positive screening (selecting companies for positive ESG performance relative to industry peers), and impact investing (targeting companies that aim to solve social or environmental challenges while generating a financial return). The underlying assets in green and sustainable ETFs and mutual funds are typically selected based on criteria that focus on ESG factors, sustainable impact, and thematic focus.

The performance of green and sustainable ETFs and mutual funds is influenced by these selection criteria, along with broader market trends and macroeconomic factors. Using monthly data between 2011 and 2019, Ji et al. (2021) studied 6,519 actively managed mutual funds in BRICS after sorting them into black, brown, and green categories based on their investment holdings. The comparative performance shows that green funds outperform their counterparts for the entire sample and within-country assessment. The findings also indicate that Chinese green funds perform better than those of other countries, which is attributed to the multiple ecologically friendly economic policies that China has adopted over the years.

Europe witnessed the most significant new sustainable open-ended mutual-fund and ETF launches. The growth of green and sustainable ETFs and mutual funds have been influenced by several macroeconomic factors, especially market trends, consumer sentiment, inflation, retail sales, economic activity, construction, and housing market:

- A favorable environment for stocks can positively impact green and sustainable ETFs and mutual funds;
- High consumer sentiment can influence market dynamics; however, the impact on green and sustainable ETFs and mutual funds depends on the broader economic setup;
- Developments in consumer prices can affect market expectations and investor sentiment, potentially influencing the performance of these funds;
- Retail sales data provide insights into consumer spending patterns, which can indirectly influence the market performance of these funds;
- Trends in the housing market can impact sectors related to sustainability and green technology.

Impact-Investing Funds: Intentional Change

Also known as social impact funds, *impact-investing funds* are a type of investment fund that seeks to generate both financial return and positive social or environmental impact, and they are one of the most appropriate ways for the financial system to contribute to sustainable development. The proceeds of impact-investing funds finance projects aiming to enhance forest management, sustainable agriculture, endangered species protection, ecosystem service provision, and nature-based solutions to climate change (Thompson, 2023).

Impact-investing funds differ from traditional investment funds by prioritizing impact as a core part of their investment strategy. Impact-investing funds often target sectors that are directly linked to significant social or environmental outcomes, such as renewable energy, sustainable agriculture, health care, education, financial inclusion, affordable housing, and CleanTech. These funds invest in companies, organizations, and funds with the intention to generate social and environmental impact, which is often outlined in their investment thesis. Investments are selected based on their potential to offer solutions to social or environmental challenges.

In reality, the balance they strike between impact and returns varies based on their specific investment strategy and the preferences of their investors. Some funds are "impact-first," prioritizing impact over financial return, while others are "finance-first," seeking to achieve market-rate returns while also delivering impact. Some impact funds use blended finance, combining capital with different risk appetites and return expectations, to make projects viable. Despite challenges such as high inflation, rising interest rates, and recession fears, global impact-investing funds hit nearly US$2.8 trillion at the end of June 2023. Europe witnessed the most significant impact-investing-fund launches.

The dual returns trade-offs originate in market failures and increase with positive externalities, and in practice, a key determinant of market failure and the size of returns trade-offs is the availability of intermediate public goods, which varies systematically across sectors and country-markets (Schmidt, 2023). Schmidt (2023) evaluated the effectiveness of impact-investing funds from the perspective of the market failures approach to business ethics and suggested that the effectiveness of impact investing depends on the interaction of the determinants of feasibility and the size of project trade-offs. Thompson (2023) examined impact investments in biodiversity conservation—specifically, debt finance in the form of conventional bonds and impact bonds, and scrutinized whether the dual goals of generating profit and environmental and/or social impact were achievable by evaluating the financial risks and impact risks. The results reveal that the risks stemmed from projects with vague cashflow forecasts, project sites with low or ambiguous threat statuses, and simplified impact metrics that might measure activities or outputs—rather than impact.

Impact-investing funds measure and report the social and environmental performance and progress of their investments. This is often done using standardized metrics such as the *Global Impact Investing Network's* IRIS metrics, which focuses on reducing barriers to impact investment by building critical infrastructure and developing activities, education, and research that help accelerate the development of a coherent impact-investing industry. Many impact-investing funds actively engage with their portfolio companies to enhance their impact and improve business performance.

Some of the largest and most well-known impact-investing funds include:

1. The Rise Fund: The Rise Fund is one of the largest impact-investing funds, focusing on investments that can make a positive social or environmental impact. It targets sectors such as education, energy, food and agriculture, health care, financial services, and technology.
2. Bain Capital Double Impact: Bain Double Impact fund focuses on middle-market companies where they can create significant social and environmental impact. The fund targets sectors such as health and wellness, sustainability, and community building.
3. The BlackRock Impact Opportunities Fund: BlackRock, the world's largest asset manager, has several impact-focused funds, including the Impact Opportunities Fund. This fund aims to invest in companies and projects that generate measurable social and environmental impact alongside a financial return.

The Green Climate Fund (GCF) is a significant and potentially innovative addition to the UNFCCC frameworks for mobilizing increased finance for climate-change mitigation and adaptation. Bowman and Minas (2019) analyzed the challenges with reference to the GCF's internal regulations and its agreements with third parties, and found that these features include linkages with UNFCCC constituted bodies, particularly the technology mechanism, and enhanced engagement with nonparty stakeholders, especially through its private sector facility. Bowman and Minas posited that deepening GCF interlinkages would increase both the coherence of climate finance governance and the GCF's ability to contribute to ambitious climate action in uncertain times.

Based on a comparative analysis of the primary financial mechanisms under the UNFCCC, including the Least Developed Country Fund, the Special Climate Change Fund, the Adaptation Fund, and the GCF, Kasdan et al. (2021) demonstrated an increasing emphasis on transformational adaptation across impact-investing funds over time, particularly the GCF. The analysis suggests that acknowledging tensions that arise with transformation in adaptation finance is critical because investment criteria and definitions of transformation impact the approaches to adaptation that countries take.

Community Investment Notes: Grassroots-Level Impact

Community investment notes are a type of fixed-income instrument that allows asset owners to invest in community-focused projects, often solutions for inequality and climate change and support local, national, and global projects focused on climate resilience and clean energy. These notes are designed to finance organizations that are creating positive social and environmental impacts in communities around the world.

The common types of organizations issuing large community investment notes are national community development financial institutions (CDFIs), community development banks and credit unions, and specialized funds. These organizations use the capital raised to fund various projects and green initiatives in underserved or low-income areas.

- National CDFIs: Larger, well-established community-development financial institutions that operate on a national scale are more likely to issue larger notes. These CDFIs have a broader reach and can engage in more significant or numerous projects.
- Community Development Banks and Credit Unions: Some community-focused banks and credit unions issue investment notes to fund their lending activities in underserved areas.
- Specialized Funds: Certain funds focus specifically on community development may issue large notes. These funds might target specific sectors such as affordable housing, green energy, or small business development in low-income areas.

The minimum investment amount can be relatively low, making them accessible to a broad range of investors. They pay interest to asset owners, usually on an annual or semiannual basis. At the end of the term, which is typically fixed, the principal is repaid to the investors, assuming the investments have performed as expected.

In terms of risk-return profile, the interest rates on community investment notes are generally modest, often slightly higher than traditional savings accounts, and these notes are often considered lower risk compared to other climate-conscious investment vehicles. This is partly because CDFIs have a strong track record of managing risk effectively; however, since these are not insured by the Federal Deposit Insurance Corporation, there is always a risk of default. In addition, community investment notes are typically illiquid, meaning investors should be prepared to commit their capital for the full term of the note.

Asset owners purchase community investment notes, effectively lending money to the issuing organization. By providing capital to underserved communities, community investment notes help stimulate economic growth, create jobs, and support small businesses. Many CDFIs also use the funds to develop or refurbish affordable housing, addressing a critical need in many communities. Some of these investments are directed toward green projects, such as renewable energy installations or energy-efficient building renovations, contributing to environmental sustainability. Some also fund projects with a direct social impact, such as health care centers, educational facilities, and community centers. By demonstrating the viability of community-focused projects, these notes can attract additional funding from other sources, amplifying their impact.

Calvert Impact Capital is a well-known player in the field of impact investing, and its community investment note is a prominent example of how investors can contribute to community development while potentially earning a financial return. The Calvert Community Investment Note is designed to channel capital into various community development initiatives. The funds raised are used to provide loans to nonprofits, social enterprises, and community development organizations to fund projects in areas such as affordable housing, environmental sustainability, small business development, and community services. These projects are aimed at creating positive social and environmental impacts, particularly in underserved communities. One of the notable features of the Calvert Community Investment Note is its accessibility to a wide range of investors, offering a relatively low minimum investment requirement.

The return on investment, while modest compared to more aggressive investment vehicles, reflects the social impact nature of the note.

Climate Venture Capital: Fueling Green Innovation

Climate VC is a growing field that offers both financial returns and the opportunity to address climate change by investing in innovative technologies and business models that aim to reduce GHG emissions and promote sustainability. Climate VC funds often structured as limited partnerships, primarily invest in early-stage companies that are developing technologies or business models related to clean energy, sustainable agriculture, water conservation, waste reduction, and other areas crucial for climate mitigation and adaptation. Climate VC fund managers conduct due diligence on potential investments to assess their feasibility, scalability, and potential impact on climate change. Investments are typically made in exchange for equity in the companies.

By providing capital and support to start-ups, climate VC funds help bring innovative climate solutions from the lab to the market. Many climate-related technologies are capital-intensive and risky, which can deter traditional investors. Climate VC funds fill this gap by taking on higher risk for potentially higher rewards. Moreover, investment by these funds can serve as a stamp of approval, attracting further investment and attention to the sector.

Besides providing capital, climate VC funds often take an active role in the investees, including providing strategic guidance, networking opportunities, and operational support to help them grow and succeed. The ultimate goal is to exit these investments through a sale or initial public offering, generating returns fund's investors.

VC is a significant funding source of climate-tech and deep-tech investments, according to World Economic Forum. Using different stages of VC fundings, Maiti (2022) examined if development in the VC investments could lead to green growth. The results showed that 1 percent increase in the seed capital on the national average would lead to an increase in the overall CO_2 productivity. On the other hand, 1 percent increase both in the early-stage and later-stage VC investments on the national average would lead to increases in the share of environmental-related technology innovations and renewable energy supply.

Many large corporations, particularly those in traditional energy sectors, are actively investing in climate tech through their venture arms. Public funding and incentives, often in partnership with private VC funds, played a significant role in supporting climate tech start-ups. While the United States and Europe remained hotspots for climate-tech investment, there is growing activity in Asia and other regions.

However, climate VC funds operate in a complex and evolving landscape that requires a unique blend of financial acumen, technological understanding, and a long-term commitment to sustainability. Investing in unproven technologies carries significant risk. Some innovations may not achieve commercial viability or may be outpaced by competing technologies. Moreover, climate tech often requires longer development and commercialization periods, which can challenge the traditional VC model that seeks quicker returns. The rapidly evolving nature of the climate-tech market, along with fluctuating public interest and economic conditions, adds to the uncertainty. Beyond these, quantifying the actual climate impact of an investment can be challenging, yet it is crucial for the credibility and mission alignment of the fund.

Notably, many climate-related markets are also heavily influenced by government policies and subsidies; changes in policy can significantly impact the viability of investments. Polzin and Sanders (2020) pointed out that large asset owners and lenders, such as pension funds and banks, in particular, were reluctant to invest in the renewable energy or grid infrastructure because of expected policy discontinuities.

Therefore, more VC and household investments are needed to finance low-risk small-ticket projects in the early stages of innovative clean energy technologies, to complement the abundantly available funds for large-scale investments. Maiti (2022) suggested encouraging VC investment at the aggregate country level to increase the share of green technology innovation and renewable energy supply.

Green-Real-Estate Investment Trusts: Sustainable Property Investment

The real-estate industry is moving beyond cyclical headwinds—the companies not only consider the traditional profitability and revenue growth aspects of their businesses, but also a more long-term future growth dimension (Autio et al., 2023). As an outcome, real-estate asset owners started basing their strategies on eight strategic themes, which are "innovation," "ESG," "marketing and sales," "financial management," "leasing management and tenant satisfaction," "competitive environment and portfolio management," "outsourcing and strategic partnerships," and "cost and operation optimization." The growing interest in green real estate is spurring innovation in sustainable construction practices and building technologies.

Green REITs are a type of REIT that focuses on investing in properties that are environmentally friendly or sustainable, or infrastructure projects related to clean energy. These properties often have features such as energy-efficient systems, renewable energy sources, water-saving fixtures, and other green-building practices. Green real estate investment requires low construction density, increased design- and construction-investment costs, and international organizations' high fees for green-building certification (Duong et al., 2023). Therefore, the typical criteria for green-real-estate investments include:

1. Energy Efficiency: Properties that use less energy for heating, cooling, lighting, and operating appliances.
2. Sustainable Building Materials: Using materials that are nontoxic, recycled, or sustainably sourced.
3. Water Efficiency: Implementing systems that reduce water consumption, such as low-flow fixtures, efficient irrigation systems, and water recycling systems.
4. Indoor Environmental Quality: Ensuring good indoor air quality, adequate natural lighting, and use of materials that do not emit volatile organic compounds.
5. Waste Reduction: Facilities for recycling and composting, and the use of construction methods that minimize waste.
6. Renewable Energy Sources: Incorporating renewable energy sources such as solar panels, wind turbines, or geothermal systems to reduce dependence on fossil fuels.
7. Location and Land Use: Preference for developments in areas with existing infrastructure, access to public transportation, and minimal environmental impact of the construction.

8. Green Certification: Properties that have been certified by recognized standards such as LEED, BREEAM, or ENERGY STAR.

Green Street, a leader in real-estate analysis and research, has introduced metrics to provide a comprehensive view of the environmental costs and impacts across the commercial-real-estate sector. These metrics consider regulatory risks, compliance costs, grid greenness, and energy and emissions intensity (Yunus, 2020).

- Factoring E into commercial-real-estate underwriting has emerged as an increasingly important valuation input for asset owners;
- Most European property sectors are more E-sensitive or greener due to more stringent regulations on the continent than in the United States;
- The datacenter and tower sectors are the most E-sensitive, while the self-storage and manufactured home sectors are the least E-sensitive.

Green Street approach to rank E-sensitivity is to take a variety of inputs, including regulations and emissions intensity, and compare them across sectors with as little subjective input as possible. The weights represent what they consider the most meaningful E-sensitivity factors. Green Street also points out that REIT portfolios tend to be greener than privately held real estate—REIT assets are 60 percent less energy intensive than the private market average across all sectors and geographies.

Energy and water efficiency lead to significant savings in utility costs, making green properties financially attractive in the long term. Green properties often command higher sale prices and rental rates due to their lower operating costs and increasing desirability among tenants and buyers. Green properties may be seen as less risky investments over time, as they are more likely to comply with future regulations and less likely to become obsolete. Beyond financial returns, green-real-estate investments contribute to broader social and environmental goals, like reducing carbon emissions and improving public health. The findings of Duong et al. (2023) indicate that green-real-estate projects bring effective results despite specific difficulties and obstacles of economic benefits for both investors and users.

Public–Private Partnerships: Collaborative Efforts for Sustainability

PPPs for sustainability represent a collaborative model where the public sector (government entities) and the private sector (businesses and asset owners) join forces to achieve sustainable development goals. When the public entity identifies a need or opportunity that aligns with sustainability goals but requires expertise, innovation, or funding beyond its capacity, it can engage private-sector entities that have the necessary resources and expertise. The specific structure can vary depending on the project's nature, but PPPs usually involve long-term commitments, with many projects spanning several years or even decades.

A PPP is formalized through agreements that outline each parts roles, responsibilities, financial contributions, and expected outcomes. One of the key aspects of PPPs is the sharing of risks between public and private sectors, which can make complex projects more viable and attractive to both parties. The public-sector partner may provide funding, facilitate policies, and have the capacity to regulate and provide protections; the private-sector partner often takes on the construction, operation, and management of a project, mobilizing capital and fostering innovation. By combining strengths, PPPs can achieve more significant environmental and social impacts than either sector could achieve alone.

PPPs can stimulate local economies, finance, and build infrastructure projects that mitigate climate change and help communities adapt. The key areas of focus of PPPs are renewable energy projects, sustainable infrastructure, urban development, conservation and biodiversity, and climate-change mitigation and adaptation.

- Renewable Energy Projects: PPPs are commonly used to develop and manage renewable energy projects such as wind farms, solar parks, and bioenergy facilities;

- Sustainable Infrastructure: Including transportation, water management, and waste management systems designed to be environmentally friendly and resource-efficient;
- Urban Development: Sustainable urban development projects, such as green buildings and smart city initiatives, often use PPP models;
- Conservation and Biodiversity: PPPs aimed at protecting natural habitats, restoring natural environments that sequester carbon, promoting biodiversity, and sustainable land use are increasingly common;
- Climate Change Mitigation and Adaptation: Projects that focus on reducing GHG emissions or adapting to climate change impacts are often suited to PPP models.

PPPs investments in these projects are crucial to sustainable development (de Lange, 2023; Mundonde and Makoni, 2023; Sun et al., 2023). Other examples of climate-conscious PPPs include:

- R&D: PPPs can promote the development and commercialization of new climate-friendly technologies. The government can provide funding and other support for R&D, while the private sector can bring technologies to market and scale them up;
- Climate Data and Risk Assessment: Public and private entities can collaborate to develop more comprehensive and accessible data on climate risks, which can help companies, investors, and communities make more informed decisions;
- Education and Training Programs: PPPs can provide education and training to build the skills needed for a low-carbon economy.

Using a sample of 300 transportation firms across 28 countries, de Lange (2023) pointed out that coordination across sectors was needed to reduce transportation-related GHG emissions. de Lange argued that if more sustainable transportation is to be constructed to address climate change and other public interests, policy makers may need to rethink PPPs to adapt to the needs of transportation firms.

Summary

In this chapter, the section on green bonds highlights these as debt instruments specifically designed to fund projects that have positive environmental or climate benefits. Green bonds are a rapidly growing segment of the bond market, offering a way to contribute to environmental sustainability while receiving a fixed income. This section explains the criteria and certification processes for green bonds, emphasizing their role in financing renewable energy, pollution prevention, sustainable water management, and other ecofriendly projects.

Climate-aligned bonds are another focus of the chapter. Unlike green bonds, which are explicitly labeled and used for green projects, climate-aligned bonds include a broader range of bonds issued by organizations that are significantly engaged in climate-friendly activities. This section discusses how these bonds help finance companies and projects indirectly contributing to climate mitigation or adaptation, even if the bonds proceeds are not directly earmarked for green projects.

The chapter then delves into green ETFs and mutual funds. These investment vehicles pool money from multiple asset owners to invest in portfolios of companies that are selected based on their environmental sustainability. The section explains how these vehicles offer diversification and professional management, making it easier for asset owners to access sustainable investments across different sectors and regions.

Impact-investing funds are covered extensively, emphasizing their goal of generating social or environmental impact alongside financial returns. These funds invest in companies, organizations, or projects committed to addressing climate change. The section outlines how impact-investing funds measure and report their impact, providing transparency to asset owners.

Community-investment notes are introduced as fixed-income instruments that support community development. These notes finance projects with social and environmental benefits, such as affordable housing, renewable energy, and small business development in underserved communities. The section discusses the risk and return profiles of these notes and their role in promoting inclusive and sustainable development.

In the alternative asset-class space, climate VC is presented as a high-risk, high-reward investment avenue, focusing on start-ups and early-stage companies developing innovative solutions to climate change. The section discusses the role of VC in driving technological advancements in key areas. Green REITs are highlighted as a way to invest in portfolios of properties that are environmentally sustainable. These REITs focus on properties with energy-efficient designs, sustainable materials, and reduced carbon footprints. This section explains how green REITs combine the benefits of real estate investment with a commitment to environmental sustainability.

Finally, the chapter explores PPPs as a mechanism for financing large-scale infrastructure projects with climate-conscious objectives. This section highlights the risk-sharing aspect of PPPs, which makes complex projects more viable. These partnerships between government entities and private companies can fund projects such as public transportation systems, energy-efficient public buildings, and water conservation infrastructure.

Despite the growing interests in these innovative climate-conscious investment instruments and vehicles, more investments are needed, especially to finance low-risk small-ticket projects to complement the abundantly available funds for large-scale investments. Moreover, the world needs to act as a single community and divert its resources toward different climate investment themes to control climate change and accomplish the SDGs (Sun et al., 2023). The investment instruments and vehicles presented in this chapter have different risk- and return profiles and liquidity characteristics, and their suitability will depend on individual circumstances, risk tolerance, and investment goals.

CHAPTER 5

Climate-Conscious Portfolio Construction and Management

Portfolio management is confronting climate change—risks arising from the transition from a brown, carbon-based to a green, low-carbon economy need to be integrated into portfolio and risk management. This chapter delves into the intricate process of integrating climate considerations into portfolio construction, a practice that is rapidly moving from a niche interest to a mainstream imperative in the investment world.

The foundation of any investment portfolio lies in strategic asset allocation (SAA). The SAA section will explore how traditional asset allocation (AA) models are being redefined to incorporate climate risks and opportunities, and how to balance the trade-offs between financial returns and environmental impact. Screening is a critical tool in the climate-conscious asset owners' arsenal. This part will cover the methodologies and criteria used in different screening approaches.

Building a climate-conscious portfolio requires a robust framework. This chapter will then introduce a comprehensive integrated portfolio framework. The "Portfolio Implementation" section addresses the practical aspects of implementing a climate-conscious portfolio. The process outlined in this chapter can help readers establish specific goals, evaluate potential options, and decide on an appropriate climate-conscious portfolio approach based on personalized criteria and trade-off considerations.

Strategic Asset Allocations

For asset owners and asset managers, AA represents the most important, top-down decision that carry wide-ranging implications, depending on the exposure to asset classes and investment strategies. SAA is the process in which an asset owner or asset manager chooses to allocate capital across asset classes, sectors, and regions based on their need for return and/or income and their risk appetite. Evidence suggests that SAA policy may account for as much as 90 percent of the variability in investment returns of a typical investment portfolio over time (Elsayed et al. 2020).

Risk Factors and Scenarios

Climate-conscious SAA is a forward-looking investment approach that integrates climate-related risks and opportunities into the process of determining the mix of asset classes in a portfolio. The goal is to achieve long-term investment objectives while also aligning with climate goals and promoting sustainability.

Two key questions shape the overall climate-conscious SAA:

1. Are asset-owner-related factors a risk management tool or a source of investment advantage?
2. Which aspects of the climate-related factors most matter from the perspective of the asset owner?

Different asset owners and asset managers integrate climate-related factors in different ways, which can be integrated (i) as a threshold requirement before investment can be considered; (ii) as factors that inform the valuation or provide a quant basis for adjusting or tilting exposures; (iii) as a risk assessment that offers a level of confidence in the valuation; (iv) as a basis for stewardship engagement; or (v) as a combination of two or more of these methods, which is very often the case.

As recommended by the TCFD framework, climate scenario analysis is as important in the wider AA process as it is in understanding the micro-, macro-, and ESG sensitivities within a single investment portfolio, whereby asset owners and asset managers would work to sensitize the portfolio against different warming scenarios using the 1.5°C (2.7°F) as promoted in the Paris Agreement of 2015 as a baseline. Different scenarios should stress test different asset classes across regions, sectors, time periods, and temperature assumptions to understand the risks that are formally characterized as physical risks and transition risks.

Asset owners are inherently exposed to varying degrees of both physical and transition risks in their investment portfolios. SAA is particularly useful in determining where these risks lie across different asset classes and investment strategies over time. Depending on the extent of asset reallocation, some of these choices may require near-term versus long-term trade-offs. Climate-conscious SAA can be more suitable to asset owners that have longer investment horizons, given the time it might take for certain technologies to mature or for regulatory landscapes to evolve. Some climate investments, like private equity (PE) in green-tech start-ups, might have longer lock-up periods.

Asset Sensitivity

Equities can be classified by industries, sectors, investment styles (e.g., growth versus value), capitalization (e.g., large-, mid-, small-cap), and trading techniques (long versus short positions). Traditional AA to equities focuses on hedge against inflation, which can result from supply shocks and high government spending. Equities are also sensitive to economic growth and macroeconomic performance. Climate-conscious SAA assumes that equities are sensitive to climate impacts on macroeconomic performance.

Fixed-income instruments usually include sovereign, municipal, and corporate (investment-grade versus high-yield) bonds. Fixed-income instruments are sensitive to interest rates, but they typically have lower volatile returns. Under the climate-conscious SAA, fixed-income instruments are sensitive to fiscal policy related to climate challenges. They are also sensitive to climate-related impacts on issuers' creditworthiness, many of which fall within the tenor of long-term bonds.

Alternative investments include REITs, commodities, currencies, PE, VC, derivatives, hedge funds, and more. Alternative investments are attractive for diversification, for their low or inverse correlation to market returns, and their heterogeneous and wide-ranging risk/return profiles. Under the climate-conscious SAA, diversification offered by alternative investments may allow for greater hedging of climate risks. The development of climate-conscious investment instruments and vehicles, as detailed in Chapter 4, offers asset owners and asset managers novel ways to hedge against climate risks or directly invest in climate solutions. On the other hand, climate risk exposure may be concentrated, opaque, or difficult to assess.

Deciding how much of an investment portfolio should be allocated to climate investments is a strategic decision that depends on an asset owner's financial goals, personal values, risk tolerance, and investment horizon. Asset owners should also carefully consider factors such as volatility and liquidity. Generally, maintaining a balance between traditional and climate-conscious investments helps manage the risk-return trade-off effectively.

Specific Percentage Approach Versus Incremental Approach

Determining the SAA to climate-conscious investments could be a specific percentage. Asset owners or asset managers can allocate a fixed percentage of a portfolio to climate investments. This could be a conservative 5 to 10 percent or a more aggressive 20 to 30 percent, depending on their situation.

This specific percentage approach is clear-cut and easy to implement and monitor. By allocating a fixed percentage, asset owners or asset managers can ensure a significant and consistent impact aligned with their climate goals. This approach allows for a straightforward risk assessment and management, as the impact of climate investments on the overall portfolio is more predictable; however, this approach might be less flexible and might not fully capitalize on the investment opportunities as they arise.

Alternatively, asset owners or asset managers can use an incremental approach and start with a smaller allocation, say 5 percent, and gradually increase it over time as they become more comfortable and familiar with the climate investment landscape. This incremental approach is more dynamic and can be aligned with evolving market conditions and climate investing standards.

The incremental approach allows asset owners and asset managers to adjust their climate-conscious SAA based on market performance, changes in ESG reporting and standards, capitalize on emerging opportunities in climate investment themes, and reduce exposure in response to changing risks. Importantly, the incremental approach can be aligned more closely with the evolving climate goals of asset owners and asset managers. In rapidly evolving markets, the flexibility of the incremental approach can be advantageous; however, this approach requires more active management and a deeper understanding of the climate investment landscape, which can be more resource-intensive.

Investment Selection

Screening remains one of the oldest, simplest, and most widely used approach to implement a climate-conscious investment policy. Building a portfolio that aligns with climate goals requires selecting assets that meet specific criteria related to sustainability, emissions, and resilience to climate change; therefore, the goal of screening is to evaluate potential investments based on specific ethical, sustainable, and governance criteria, whether they actively contribute to positive environmental outcomes, and how they are prepared to handle the risks associated with climate change.

Positive/Best-in-Class Screening

Positive screening involves selecting companies or investment vehicles that meet specific ESG criteria. In the context of climate investing, this means selecting companies that are actively working to reduce their carbon footprint, invest in renewable energy, high energy efficiency, or take other measures to combat climate change. Positive screening can also include companies from sectors that might be considered "controversial" such as oil and gas, as long as they demonstrate the best ESG credentials in their area of business. Positive screening can be seen as the opposite of negative screening, where asset owners or asset managers exclude companies that do not meet certain ethical or environmental standards.

In the positive-screening process, asset owners or asset managers typically begin by identifying an issue where they want to have a positive impact, such as climate change. They then determine the best way to measure the performance of a company or investment vehicle against specific criteria, such as carbon footprint. Some asset owners and asset managers may also invest in companies that might not currently score high on

ESG credentials but have the potential to improve through mechanisms, such as shareholder engagement.

Best-in-class selection is a method that focuses on investing in companies that perform better than their peers in terms of ESG performance. Best-in-class investment involves selecting only the companies that overcome a defined ranking hurdle, established using ESG criteria within each sector or industry. In the context of climate investing, best-in-class selection involves choosing companies that are industry leaders in reducing emissions, innovating in clean energy, or implementing sustainable practices.

In the best-in-class selection, companies are usually scored on a variety of factors that are weighted according to the sector. The portfolio is then constructed with the list of qualified companies. It is important to note that not all best-in-class companies or investment vehicles are considered "RI."

Owing to its all-sector approach, best-in-class investment is commonly used in investment strategies that try to maintain certain characteristics of an index. In these cases, security selection seeks to maintain regional and sectorial diversification along with a similar profile to the parent market-cap index while targeting companies with higher ESG ratings.

Positive screening and best-in-class selection are powerful tools in the context of climate investing. These two approaches can be used together to create a robust climate-conscious screening method. By first applying a positive screening to include companies that meet basic climate and environmental standards, and then using the best-in-class selection to choose the top performers within that group, asset owners or asset managers can create a portfolio that aligns with their ethical values and preferences, and potentially offers competitive returns.

Negative/Exclusionary Screening

Negative or exclusionary screening is one of the oldest methods of ESG screening. It involves identifying specific criteria that an asset owner or asset manager wants to avoid and deliberately excluding sectors, companies, practices, or business activities from a portfolio based on specific

ESG criteria. These criteria can be based on ethical beliefs, social considerations, environmental concerns, or a combination of these factors. Common examples of exclusion criteria are involvement in tobacco production, weapons manufacturing, fossil fuels, and human rights violations. According to the statistics maintained by the Global Sustainable Investment Alliance, exclusions-based approaches remain the largest portion of dedicated, ESG-screened assets under management (AUM).

Universal exclusions represent exclusions supported by global norms and conventions, such as the UN Global Compact, UN Declaration of Human Rights, International Labor Organization standards, Organization for Economic Cooperation and Development (OECD) Guidelines for Multinational Enterprises, and those from the World Health Organization. These can be referred to as "controversy screens" when companies engage in unethical behavior source. It could be argued that controversial arms and munitions, nuclear weapons, tobacco, and varying degrees of exposure to coal-based power generation or extraction all qualify as universally accepted, given normative support and the growing AUM they represent. However, since there is no single institution or authority determining a breach, whether an issuer is breaching international norms is subjective.

Negative or exclusionary screening allows asset owners and asset managers to align their investments with their values by avoiding companies or industries that engage in practices they find objectionable. Negative or exclusionary screening also provides a clear and transparent approach to climate-conscious investing, making it easy for asset owners and asset managers to understand what is and is not included in their portfolios.

In the negative or exclusionary screening process, once the exclusion criteria are identified, asset owners or asset managers screen potential investments to ensure that they do not engage in the identified practices. This can involve a combination of in-depth fundamental research and analyses and leveraging third-party data to understand the activities and practices of potential investments. In-depth fundamental research enables asset owners and asset managers to fully analyze a wide range of information and properly assess the risk at an issuer-specific level. If an investment involves a security where a major third-party research provider has deemed an issuer to be the violation of international norms, asset owners or asset managers should research, validate, and document the nature of the breach. This research should be updated annually thereafter, as long as the position continues to be held and continues to be in violation of international norms according to the third party. Ongoing monitoring and assessment are required to ensure that the investments continue to meet the exclusion criteria over time.

One notable disadvantage of negative or exclusionary screening is, excluding certain investments can influence the composition and risk-return profile of a portfolio. This screening process may lead to over-exposure to certain sectors or industries, underexposure to others, and reduced diversification. Excluding certain sectors or industries may also limit investment opportunities and potentially impact returns. The results of Folqué et al. (2021) indicate that, on average, funds that only apply negative filters achieve worse ESG risk scores and show worse carbon risk.

Negative or exclusionary screening can be used in conjunction with other methods to create a comprehensive and aligned investment strategy. By implementing negative or exclusionary screening and best-in-class selection, asset owners and asset managers can gain a desired level of carbon risk exposure, although sometimes at hidden costs (Görgen et al. 2021). Exclusions and engagement are also often employed as complements to each other, which can be advantageous (Atta-Darkua et al. 2020).

ESG Screening Across Asset Classes

Public and Private Equities

Public equities represent the most developed asset class in terms of ESG integration. Equities have various advantages relative to other asset classes—notably, the greatest amount of transparency owing to its capital structure where creditors and shareholders coexist, albeit in a relationship that subordinates shareholders. The listed nature of equities and their ownership structure provide shareholders with the ability to exercise their view through their voting rights on many aspects of operational and strategic direction of the company, including its board of directors. Shareholder rights and voting are one of the most prominent manifestations of stewardship, where asset owners increasingly address nonfinancial objectives alongside financial issues.

Hedge-fund or long/short investment strategies are increasingly embedding ESG factors into portfolio construction and management. Hedge funds are alternative investment vehicles that employ leverage to enhance returns and hedging strategies to manage net risk and produce alpha. Shorting or short selling involves borrowing a security generally on margin, hence the leverage component in hedge funds, and then selling it into the market to be bought later. A successful short sale means that the asset owner or hedge-fund manager is able to cover or buy back the security at a lower price than that which they initially paid to borrow it.

ESG integration in PE, like private credit and private real assets, faces several challenges, foremost being the lack of public transparency, established reporting standards, regulatory oversight, and public-market expectations around ESG. The lack of compulsory nonfinancial reporting regulations, such as the EU's Nonfinancial Reporting Directive for large European companies, severely limits a general partner (GP)'s ability to leverage ESG data for relative ranking and scoring comparability.

In addition, smaller private companies are often capacity-challenged by ESG reporting requirements. The quality, consistency, and continuity of strong integrated reports published by many public companies represent a high hurdle for smaller companies to achieve. Early-stage companies also tend to operate with a much greater degree of freedom than more mature, public companies. Consequently, GPs will have to weigh a company's ESG trajectory against the trajectories of more mature companies. This extends to how the business or asset operates and to the board-level-devised strategy.

In some cases, GPs and limited partners (LPs) must negotiate against a strong founder or founding team. Early and significant shareholders are often strategic and long-term oriented, creating a powerful incentive to establish a strong set of ESG key performance indicators (KPIs) early in the company's life cycle. It may be in the interest of GPs to establish specific, portfoliowide metrics as a means to support the overall portfolio strategy and communicate portfolio alignment to the LPs.

Like in other asset classes, GPs and LPs may certainly impose exclusionary screening on any number of criteria to restrict investment in certain sectors, either normatively or ethically defined. However, they do not have the benefit of the breadth and diversity of indexes and benchmarks of the public equities space, limiting opportunities for peer comparability analysis or portfolio optimization efforts around ESG criteria. In practice, GPs and LPs can benchmark segments of the portfolio against smaller investment universes, even including public companies, if data comparability exists.

Hence, it is more likely that the GPs may apply some form of positive screening or thematic focus within their respective investment charter. Because of the nonpublic nature of PE as asset class, LPs are increasing their expectations for GPs to integrate ESG analysis beyond screening in more robust forms. In addition, they may establish minimum-threshold ESG scoring for portfolio inclusion, or formally establishing an ESG program that institutes in-depth, predeal ESG due diligence, and ESG review for portfolio companies.

Corporate Bonds, Green Bonds, and Green Securitization

Generally speaking, ESG integration in fixed income has experienced a good deal of catch up relative to public equities. The bonds issued by a single corporate or sovereign, and for that matter, often represents multiple credit-risk profiles across bond issuances. These bond issuances represent different maturities, which refer to the payment date of a loan. The temporal dimension across multiple debt maturities and credit-risk profiles arguably lends itself to a more granular comprehension of ESG issues and their materiality. In contrast, companies issuing equities generally issue one common share class. Therefore, corporate bonds are now enjoying greater levels of ESG integration, despite there is still significant differentiation across the subasset classes.

Green securitization is an emerging area within fixed income, driven by several central banks, including the Bank of England (BoE). Green securitization represents the mutualization of illiquid, green assets or a series of assets into a fixed-income instrument. Green collateralized loan obligations, for which data that can be easily quantified and screened exists, constitute one such mutualized form of green securitization. The Green Finance Study Group defines sustainable assets as "sustainable loans, sustainable debt, and sustainable bonds as specific financial products or debt linked to assets or investments that target environment and social sustainability." Green securitization leverages the momentum and research behind the green-bond market.

Sovereign Bonds

ESG integration approaches that lend themselves well to public equities and corporate bonds run into a number of difficulties when applied to sovereign bonds. The number of governments issuing sovereign bonds represents a much smaller investable universe than the number of corporates that issue corporate bonds. Should their credit profile be strong enough, any listed corporates could issue some form of credit, from investment grade to high yield. While there is no limit to the creation of new corporate entities that issue debts, the pool of governments that issue debt is small by comparison and essentially finite. Credit-rating agencies represent an important component for sovereign-debt asset managers, thus should be leveraged at both the issuer and the portfolio levels.

Many climate-conscious sovereign-bond asset managers begin by building and integrating a framework based on the World Bank Group's Worldwide Governance Indicators. This dataset considers a country's governance score, and its rankings on political stability, voice and accountability, government effectiveness, rule of law, regulatory quality, and control of corruption. Although this dataset is slow-moving, it offers a near 20-year time series and a means for asset owners and asset managers to identify improving or deteriorating trends across these metrics.

Real Assets

Real assets, like real estate and infrastructure, carry certain advantages and challenges compared to the equities and corporate bonds investment universe. In many cases, real-asset owners are majority owners or own the asset outright, which offers them much greater control over the definition, application, and reporting of ESG data alongside or outside existing reporting standards, like that of the GRI. Managing a portfolio of real assets requires building a picture of what the aggregate risk looks like as well as the correlation risk among all the underlying assets.

GRESB's full benchmark report provides a composite of:

- Peer-group information;
- Overall portfolio KPI performance;
- Aggregate environmental data in terms of usage and efficiency gains;
- A GRESB score that weighs management, policy, and disclosure;
- Risks and opportunities, monitoring, and environmental management system;
- Environmental impact reduction targets; and
- Data validation and assurance.

Nonetheless, this report depends heavily on companies, investment products, and assets participating in the GRESB reporting assessment process. For portfolios where a significant percentage of their holdings do not participate in the GRESB assessment, asset managers will need to supplement with their own ESG scoring. As reporting data and standards improve for real assets, asset managers should work toward a stronger link between ESG considerations and their financial implications.

Asset owners with significant real-estate exposure are increasingly leveraging the analytical modeling capabilities and historical datasets of insurance companies to understand weather risk generally and climate risk more specifically. Munich Re, one of the world's largest reinsurers, produces climate-risk assessments that model potential property-impact scenarios based on a broader set of 12 natural hazard types, including earthquakes, volcanic eruptions, tsunamis, tropical cyclones, extratropical storms, hail, tornadoes, lightning, wildfires, river floods, flash floods, and storm surges.

In climate-conscious investment selection, it is essential to note that ESG screening methodologies and criteria, particularly for environmental factors, are diverse and can be tailored to align with the specific values and goals of the asset owner. The weighting given to different factors in ESG screening can vary, as the relevance of certain environmental criteria varies by sector. For instance, water usage is a critical factor for the agriculture and beverage industries, while carbon emissions are a key concern for the energy sector.

Integrated Portfolio Framework

The Paris Agreement, the development of RI, and the emergence of net-zero emission policies considerably change portfolio frameworks of both passive and active investment strategies. The endgame for integrating climate goals at the portfolio level is the combination of top-down analytics and underlying ESG analyses to produce a more complete picture of climate-conscious exposure and risk at the portfolio construction and management levels.

In this respect, integrating climate goals within portfolio management requires a different manner of explanatory power than integration at the individual-security level. Evidence suggests that in climate-conscious investing, commonly used portfolio construction mechanisms fail to demonstrate consistency with asset-owner-impact objectives, as does little to reallocate capital that would incentivize companies to contribute to the climate transition (Amenc et al. 2022). For asset managers, adopting a total portfolio management approach is the most adequate strategy to align fiduciary duty and mission, and resolve the ethical tension (Zolfaghari and Hand, 2021).

Macro Variables

Macro variables will be different in a world that is transitioning to a sustainable future. Climate change has a profound impact on everything that goes into forming a view on long-term asset-class returns, including economic growth, employment, inflation, interest rates, trade, exchange rates, and fiscal policy. The following section delves into the sophisticated interplay between macroeconomic variables, risk premia, and fundamental analyses, all within the context of a changing climate.

Economic Growth

Climate change can impact agricultural output and productivity. Many crops are highly sensitive to temperature changes and extreme weather conditions such as droughts, floods, and storms. Climate change can disrupt growing seasons, reduce crop quality, and lower overall agricultural productivity and yields. Warmer temperatures can lead to the proliferation of pests and diseases that affect crops, requiring more resources for pest control and potentially leading to greater use of pesticides. Changes in rainfall patterns and increased evaporation rates can also lead to water scarcity, further challenging agricultural output.

Increased frequency and intensity of extreme weather events such as hurricanes, floods, and wildfires can impact economic growth. These events can cause significant damage to infrastructure, including roads, bridges, and buildings. Coastal infrastructure is particularly at risk due to rising sea levels, leading to the need for significant investment in adaptation measures. All these impacts can slow down economic growth.

Extreme weather events and rising temperatures can also reduce labor productivity, particularly in outdoor and manual labor industries, such as construction, agriculture, and manufacturing. Climate change can lead to higher absenteeism and reduced workforce efficiency. The need to adapt to and mitigate the effects of climate change can redirect capital from other economic activities. The increase in production costs and the relative prices of carbon-intensive goods and services negatively affects real wages, consumption, investment and, ultimately, output (McKibbin et al. 2017).

Meanwhile, rising temperatures can lead to an increase in heat-related illnesses, putting a strain on health care systems. Changes in climate can expand the range of certain vector-borne diseases, such as malaria and dengue fever, increasing health care burdens. Extreme weather events can also have a profound impact on mental health, leading to long-term psychological and social issues. The increasing frequency and severity of natural disasters can eventually lead to higher insurance premiums and greater uninsured losses.

Employment

Climate change has a significant impact on employment, leading to job losses in sectors that are negatively impacted (e.g., fossil-fuel industry, agriculture, and manufacturing and heavy industry) and job gains in sectors that are positively impacted (e.g., renewable energy, energy efficiency, sustainable agriculture, and environmental protection and restoration). Gaikwad et al. (2022) showed that people who reside in coal-producing regions prefer compensation for lost jobs. The general public privileges diffuse redistribution mechanisms and investments, discounting compensation to targeted groups. Those who are both physically and economically vulnerable have cross-cutting preferences, and there is considerable support for policies that compensate different coalitions of climate-vulnerable citizens.

Inflation

Climate change significantly impacts commodity prices and supply chains, leading to broader economic consequences, including inflationary pressures. Extreme weather events and variability can lead to fluctuations in the prices of essential food commodities, affecting global food markets. The increasing frequency of extreme weather events can also disrupt the production and distribution of energy commodities, such as oil and natural gas. Additionally, the transition to renewable energy sources in response to climate change can also influence energy prices.

As extreme weather events can damage infrastructure, this disruption can lead to delays, increased transportation costs, and costs of services, contributing to inflationary pressures. Factories and production facilities are also vulnerable to climate-related events, which can halt a business' production processes, leading to supply shortages and increased costs for finished goods. These disruptions can eventually lead to cost-push inflation, as the business raise prices to maintain profit margins.

While in some cases, climate change can also contribute to demand-pull inflation. For example, if consumers anticipate future shortages or price increases in certain goods, such as food or energy, they might increase their current demand, further driving up prices. McKibbin et al. (2017) found that more volatile prices pose greater challenges to central banks than more predictable prices, all else equal, in part because they complicate the forecasting of inflation and other economic variables that central banks use to benchmark their policies. McKibbin et al. argued that in addition to impacting prices and output levels, climatic disruption can affect central banks' ability to forecast and manage inflation.

Interest Rates

The integration of sustainability and climate-related risks into the economic assessments and monetary-policy decisions by central banks and regulators is a significant development in response to the economic impacts of climate change. This integration can lead to adjustments in interest rates. McKibbin et al. (2017) argued that in a carbon-constrained and climatically disrupted world, there are important linkages between the climate-change and monetary-policy regimes, and the two jointly influence macroeconomic outcomes.

Central banks often adjust interest rates to control inflation. Since climate change can lead to inflationary pressures, as discussed earlier, central banks might counteract by raising interest rates. If climate change is expected to slow economic growth, a central bank might lower interest rates to stimulate investment and consumption, and stabilize the economy. Some central banks are also considering policies to support green financing, such as lower interest rates for sustainable projects or higher capital requirements for carbon-intensive investments.

The adjustments in interest rates, in turn, have important implications for asset valuation, as interest rates are a key component in the discount rates used for valuing assets. Lower interest rates generally increase the present value of future cash flows, making assets more valuable, while higher rates have the opposite effect. For the broader financial market, changes in interest rates affect the cost of debt for businesses and governments. Lower rates can reduce borrowing costs, potentially encouraging investment in sustainable projects.

Meanwhile, changes in interest rates can influence investment decisions across various asset classes. For instance, lower rates might make equities more attractive compared to bonds. Interest-rate changes also directly impact mortgage rates, influencing the housing market and real-estate investments. In general, ambitious climate policy can affect output, both in aggregate and disproportionately in select emissions-intensive sectors. Optimal climate policy frameworks could make monetary policies more efficient and effective (McKibbin et al. 2017).

Trade

The transition to a sustainable future has the potential to significantly alter global economic power and trade dynamics. This transition can affect the comparative advantage of countries in various goods and services, leading to shifts in trade patterns. Countries that invest heavily in sustainable technologies and infrastructure, such as renewable energy, EVs, and green manufacturing, may emerge as new economic leaders.

Likewise, countries with abundant renewable energy resources, such as solar, wind, and hydroelectric power, could gain a new comparative advantage in the global market. Nations that lead in green technology innovation and production, such as battery technology or sustainable agriculture techniques, may also find themselves with a competitive edge. Countries that excel in resource efficiency and low-carbon manufacturing processes could become preferred trading partners.

There will be an increased global demand for sustainable goods and services, benefiting countries that specialize in these areas. Conversely, economies heavily reliant on fossil fuels or industries with high carbon footprints may experience a decline in their economic influence unless they adapt to the new paradigm.

From another perspective, the introduction of carbon tariffs and environmentally focused trade policies could redirect trade flows. Countries with lower carbon footprints might enjoy preferential trade terms. That countries and companies reconfigure supply chains to be more sustainable, resilient, and compliant with new environmental standards will also shift trade networks.

The transition to a sustainable future also has geopolitical implications. Countries may shift toward energy independence through domestic renewable energy sources, altering the geopolitical dynamics associated with oil and gas dependency. The global response to climate change could lead to both increased international collaboration in areas, such as technology sharing and joint environmental initiatives, and potential conflicts over resources such as rare earth metals crucial for technology.

Exchange Rates

The interplay of interest rates, trade patterns, and investment flows is a crucial aspect of the global financial system, impacting currency values and, by extension, international economic dynamics. Higher interest rates in a country typically increase the return on investments denominated in that country's currency, making it more attractive to foreign investors. This increased demand can boost the currency's value.

Conversely, lower interest rates can decrease the attractiveness of a currency but might be used to stimulate economic growth. The impact on the currency's value depends on how investors and asset managers view the balance between growth stimulation and lower returns. High inflation can devalue a currency, so effective inflation control by central banks through interest rate adjustments can support a currency's value.

Changes in trade patterns affect currency values. A country with a strong export economy and a trade surplus, where exports exceed imports, typically sees stronger demand for its currency, as foreign buyers need the currency to pay for the country's goods and services. This demand can increase the currency's value. Changes in global demand for certain goods and services can affect trade balances.

For instance, a surge in demand for renewable energy technology might strengthen the currencies of leading exporters in that sector. New trade agreements or changes in trade policies can also impact trade flows and, consequently, currency values. Tariffs, quotas, and trade wars can significantly alter currency demand.

In the context of investment flows, high levels of foreign direct investment into a country can increase demand for its currency, as foreign companies and investors convert their funds into the local currency to invest. International portfolio investments in stocks, bonds, and other financial assets can also influence currency values. If a country's financial markets are seen as attractive, the inflow of foreign capital can raise the value of its currency. Currency values can also be affected by speculative capital flows, where investors move money in and out of countries based on short-term expectations of currency movements, interest rates, and economic conditions.

Fiscal Policy

The challenges posed by climate change necessitate significant action from governments, including increased spending on adaptation and mitigation efforts and potentially the introduction of new taxes to incentivize sustainable practices. Governments may need to invest heavily in upgrading infrastructure to withstand the impacts of climate change, such as extreme weather events. This includes strengthening flood defenses, building more resilient transportation networks, and upgrading buildings and public spaces.

Increased frequency and severity of natural disasters due to climate change will likely require more government spending on disaster relief and preparedness, including emergency services, rebuilding efforts, and support for affected communities. Funding for conservation efforts, such as reforestation, wetland restoration, and biodiversity protection, is also essential for mitigating climate change and protecting natural ecosystems. Carbon pricing and other climate policies, which will be detailed in Chapter 7, may be introduced to incentivize sustainable practices.

The characteristics of climate risks, that is, deep uncertainty, nonlinearity and endogeneity, challenge traditional approaches to macroeconomic and financial risk analysis. Battiston et al. (2021b) argued that the financial ecosystem falls short of methodologies that allow for the successful analysis of the risks that climate change poses to financial stability. Battiston et al. proposed embedding climate change in macroeconomic and financial analyses using innovative perspectives for a comprehensive understanding of the macrofinancial relevance of climate change.

Risk Premia

The evolving landscape of climate change is poised to bring about significant changes in risk premia across various asset classes. A *risk premium* refers to the extra return that asset owners require to compensate for the risk of holding a particular asset. As climate change alters the risk profiles of different assets, asset owners can expect corresponding adjustments in their risk premia.

Finance theory and empirical evidence suggest that asset owners may prefer "green" over "dirty" assets for both financial and nonfinancial reasons and may thus demand higher returns from environmentally harmful investment opportunities. Assets that are aligned with the climate goals, such as the Paris Agreement, may be perceived as less risky, leading to changes in risk premia.

Equity Risk Premium

1. Sectoral Shifts: Climate change can disproportionately impact certain sectors. For instance, industries heavily reliant on fossil fuels may face increased risks due to policy changes and shifting consumer

preferences, potentially leading to a higher equity risk premium for these sectors.

2. Sustainability Premium: Companies that are aligned with climate goals, proactively adopt sustainable practices, or contribute to climate mitigation might be perceived as lower risk, leading to a lower equity risk premium. Conversely, companies that are not aligned with climate goals may face higher risk premia.

3. Market Volatility: Increased frequency of extreme weather events and uncertainty regarding climate policies could lead to a greater market volatility, influencing the overall equity risk premium.

Carbon beta is priced in the cross-section of equity returns. The results of Huij et al. (2023) indicate that returns to stocks with high carbon betas are lower during months in which climate change is more frequently discussed in the news, in which temperatures are abnormally high, and during exceptionally dry months. Huij et al. also found that variation in carbon betas correlates with green patent issuance and forward-looking measures of climate risk.

Fixed-Income Risk Premium

1. Sovereign Bonds: Climate change can affect the economic stability of countries, particularly those heavily reliant on climate-sensitive sectors such as agriculture. This might lead to a reevaluation of sovereign risk and, consequently, the risk premium of government bonds.

2. Municipal Bonds: The risk premium on municipal bonds could be affected by how climate change impacts local economies and infrastructure needs.

3. Corporate Bonds: Companies in high-risk sectors might face higher borrowing costs and wider spreads, reflected in higher risk premia for their bonds. Conversely, green bonds and the bonds issued by companies that are committed to climate goals may see a lower risk premium, leading to tighter spreads, due to their perceived lower risk and growing market demand.

Commodity Risk Premium

1. Supply and Demand Fluctuations: Climate change can cause significant fluctuations in the supply and demand of various commodities,

particularly agricultural products, leading to changes in their risk premia.

2. Transition to Renewable Resources: Commodities that are central to the transition to a sustainable future may see changes in their risk premia due to increased demand and strategic importance. For instance, the risk premium for fossil-fuel commodities might increase due to the heightened risk of stranded assets and regulatory changes.

Real Estate Risk Premium

1. Location-Specific Risks: Real estate in areas prone to climate-change impacts like sea-level rise or extreme weather events might see an increased risk premium.
2. Green Buildings: Conversely, properties that incorporate sustainable design and resilience against climate risks might attract a lower risk premium.

Beyond these, breakthroughs in climate tech can create new investment opportunities and disrupt existing industries. This can lead to significant shifts in asset-class returns and risk premia. That governments' introduction of new regulations to promote sustainability can also directly impact asset valuations and risk premia.

The impact of climate change on risk premia reflects a broader reassessment of risk in the investment world, as asset owners are increasingly factoring in environmental risks and sustainability considerations into their investment decisions. This shift necessitates a more nuanced understanding of risks across asset classes and underscores the importance of integrating climate risk into investment analyses and portfolio management.

Fundamentals

Climate change and the ensuing policies designed to address the challenges are reshaping the business landscape, exerting a profound influence on companies' fundamentals and profitability across a wide range of sectors. Industries are compelled to adapt to new environmental regulations, shifting market demands, and the evolving risks associated with climate-related events. This dynamic scenario compels businesses to innovate and rethink their strategies. From energy production to agriculture, transportation to real estate, and beyond, the ripple effects of climate change are prompting a significant transformation in how companies operate and strategize for future growth and sustainability.

Energy Sector

- Traditional Energy Companies: As governments push for a reduction in carbon emissions, fossil-fuel-based industries may face challenges. Companies in oil, natural gas, and coal may face declining demand and increased regulation, leading to potential decreases in profitability.
- Renewable Energy: Companies in solar, wind, and other renewable sources may benefit from increased investment and favorable policies.

Automotive and Transportation

- Changes in weather patterns can disrupt transportation routes, leading to increased costs and delays.
- Traditional Automakers: May face challenges due to stricter emissions regulations and a shift toward EVs.
- EV and Alternative Fuel Companies: Likely to benefit from policies promoting cleaner transportation options.

Agriculture and Food Production

- Changes in weather patterns can affect crop yields. Some regions might benefit from warmer temperatures, while others could see a decline in production. This can disrupt supply chains and lead to volatility in food prices and impact the profitability of agricultural enterprises.
- Companies focusing on sustainable and resilient agricultural practices may gain a competitive edge.

Real Estate and Infrastructure

- Rising sea levels and increased frequency of extreme weather events can increase the risk of property damage and affect the value of coastal properties and infrastructure. There might be increased costs associated with building resilient infrastructure.

- There will be growing demand for sustainable and energy-efficient buildings.

Financial Services

- As extreme weather events become more common, insurance claims related to natural disasters could rise, impacting the profitability of insurance companies.
- Banks and financial institutions that have significant exposures to high-risk sectors might face challenges. There could be an increase in nonperforming assets if companies in these sectors face financial distress.
- Potential growth in green financing and investment in sustainable projects.

Technology and Innovation

- Opportunities in developing technologies for energy efficiency, climate monitoring, and sustainable practices.
- Increased demand for data analytics and software solutions for climate risk management.

Consumer Goods

- Changes in climate can affect the availability and cost of raw materials, impacting the profitability of consumer goods companies.
- Shift toward sustainable and ecofriendly products.
- Potential regulatory impacts on production processes and supply chains.

Tourism and Hospitality

- Certain tourist destinations, especially those reliant on natural beauty, might see a decline in visitors due to the effects of climate change.

- Opportunities in promoting sustainable and ecofriendly tourism.

Companies that are heavily reliant on fossil fuels or are not prepared for the transition to a low-carbon economy might face credit downgrades. This can increase their borrowing costs and affect their overall financial health. As certain sectors or companies become more vulnerable to climate-related risks, the likelihood of credit defaults might increase. Companies might also face regulatory risks if they fail to comply with climate-related disclosures or if they are not in line with national or international climate goals.

New Return Expectations

In light of the potential changes in assets' financial and economic well-being, valuation models need to be adjusted to account for climate risks and opportunities. These adjustments can significantly impact the key financial metrics of businesses or assets.

A general guide on how these adjustments can be integrated into valuation models:

Cost of Capital

- Risk Premia: Incorporate climate-related risk premia into the cost of equity. Companies with higher exposure to climate risks may face a higher cost of equity.
- Debt Financing: Assess how climate risks impact a company's creditworthiness and, consequently, its cost of debt. Companies in high-risk sectors might face higher borrowing costs.

Cash-Flow Projection

- Revenue Adjustments: Estimate how climate change can affect demand for products and services. For instance, companies in renewable energy might see increased demand, while those in fossil fuels might experience a decline.

- Cost Implications: Factor in potential increases in operational costs due to climate-related regulations, carbon pricing, or necessary investments in adaptation and mitigation strategies.
- Insurance and Compliance Costs: Account for potentially higher insurance premiums and compliance costs related to environmental regulations.

Asset Valuation

- Physical Asset Risk: Adjust the value of physical assets by considering their vulnerability to climate-related events such as floods, storms, or rising sea levels.
- Stranded Assets: Identify assets that might become stranded or obsolete due to climate policies or market shifts, such as fossil-fuel reserves in the energy transition context.

Discount Rate

- Adjust discount rates to reflect the increased uncertainty and risks associated with climate change impacts.

Long-Term Projection

- Extend the time horizon of financial projections to capture the long-term impacts of climate change, which might not be evident in short-term analyses.

Sensitivity Analysis

- Conduct sensitivity analyses to understand how changes in climate-related factors, such as carbon prices or temperature increases, could impact the valuation.

Scenario Analysis

- Incorporate various climate-related scenarios (e.g., a 2°C scenario, a business-as-usual [BAU] scenario) into the

valuation models to understand how different outcomes
might affect the company's financials.

By integrating these factors and considerations into valuation models,
asset owners and asset managers can more accurately assess the fundamentals of a company or asset. This approach helps in identifying investees that are not only managing risks effectively but also capitalizing on
the opportunities arising from the transition to a more sustainable, low-
carbon economy.

To derive new return expectations, a step-by-step guide is summarized
for reference as follows:

Step 1: Estimate Corporate Earnings Consistent With Green Transition Scenario

To arrive at estimates, first assess the sensitivity of earnings to carbon
pricing, which, whether through a carbon tax or a cap-and-trade system,
directly affects the cost structure of companies, especially those in carbon-intensive industries.

By understanding how sensitive a company's earnings are to changes
in carbon pricing, asset owners and asset managers can estimate the
potential impact on profitability as carbon prices rise or as stricter carbon
pricing mechanisms are implemented. This requires a deep dive into the
company's operations, supply chain, and energy sources.

Step 2: Assess the Impact of Climate Risks

Assess the impact of climate risks on different sectors. The definitions and
financial implications of these risks were detailed in Chapter 1.

Then score sectors on how exposed they are to climate change.
To determine the exposure of a sector to climate change, consider the
following factors:

1. Physical Exposure: Evaluate the direct physical risks posed by climate
   change to the sector. For instance, agriculture might be exposed to

changing rainfall patterns, while coastal real estate might be exposed to rising sea levels.

2. Regulatory Exposure: Some sectors might face stricter regulations in the future as governments push for a greener economy. For example, the fossil-fuel industry might face stricter emission standards.

3. Supply Chain Exposure: Consider how climate change might affect the supply chains of industries. For instance, industries reliant on certain raw materials might face shortages if those materials become scarcer due to climate impacts.

4. Consumer Demand: Assess how changing consumer preferences in response to climate awareness might affect the sector. For example, there might be increased demand for EVs and decreased demand for gasoline-powered cars.

Step 3: Determine Risks/Opportunities

The next step is to determine whether such exposure to climate change represents a risk or an opportunity for the sector. Risks are generally associated with stranded assets, increased costs, and reputational damage, while sectors that are committed to green transition, innovation, and sustainable products or services will have more opportunities.

Risks

- Stranded Assets: Some sectors might have assets that become obsolete or nonperforming due to the green transition. For instance, coal mines might become stranded assets as demand for coal decreases.
- Increased Costs: Regulatory changes or the need to adapt to physical changes might increase operational costs for some sectors.
- Reputational Damage: Sectors that are seen as not doing enough to combat climate change might face reputational risks.

Opportunities

- Green Transition: Sectors that are at the forefront of the green transition might see growth opportunities. For example, renewable energy sectors stand to benefit from increased investments in green technologies.
- Innovation: Sectors that innovate and adapt to the changing landscape might find new revenue streams. For instance, automotive companies investing in EVs.
- Market Demand: As consumers become more climate-conscious, sectors that offer sustainable products or services might see increased demand.

This framework allows for systematically monitoring key metrics and the evolution of the green transition. This framework also explicitly accounts for uncertainty, which is highly relevant for climate change that will have varying but highly uncertain impacts. By following these steps, asset owners and asset managers can create a matrix that provides a clear picture of which sectors are most vulnerable to climate change and which ones stand to benefit from the green transition.

To enhance and maintain the effectiveness of this framework over time, consider the following steps:

1. Diversification: As the green transition evolves, some sectors or assets might become more attractive, while others might face challenges. Ensure that the investments are diversified to mitigate risks and capitalize on opportunities.
2. Scenario Analysis: Incorporate scenario analysis to model different potential outcomes of the green transition. This can help understand the best-case, worst-case, and most-likely scenarios for different sectors and investments.
3. Technology Utilization: Leverage advanced technologies such as artificial intelligence (AI) and machine learning (ML) to analyze vast amounts of data, identify patterns, and make predictive analyses.
4. Dynamic Data Integration: Ensure that the framework can seamlessly integrate real-time data from various sources. This includes data on

carbon emissions, regulatory changes, technological advancements, and market trends.

5. Regular Reviews: Schedule regular reviews of the framework to assess its effectiveness and make necessary adjustments. It is crucial to stay ahead of emerging trends, risks, and opportunities, ensuring that the investments are aligned with the evolving realities of the green transition.

6. Feedback Loop: Create a feedback loop where the insights and learnings from monitoring are fed back into the framework, allowing for continuous improvement.

7. Stakeholder Engagement: Engage with stakeholders, including industry experts, policy makers, and community leaders, to gain insights into the on-the-ground realities of the green transition.

8. Transparency: Maintain transparency in the methodology and findings. This can provide clarity on the approach.

9. Collaboration: Consider collaborating with research institutions, nongovernmental organizations (NGOs), and other organizations that are focused on the green transition. Such collaborations can provide valuable insights and resources.

The integration of climate-related adjustments into valuation models marks a pivotal shift in the approaches to investment analyses and return expectations. Embracing these refined models better equips asset owners and asset managers to navigate the complexities of a transitioning global economy, setting new benchmarks for return expectations. By meticulously accounting for the multifaceted impacts of climate risks and opportunities on cost of capital, cash flows, and asset values, asset owners and asset managers pave the way for a more nuanced and forward-looking financial perspective.

Repricing

As asset owners prioritize sustainability in their investment strategies, there is an increasing demand for climate-conscious investments. Changing investor preferences will spur a climate-change-led repricing due to the falling cost of capital for such assets. Consequently, climate-conscious investments are expected to generate higher returns than their traditional counterparts, at least in the short-to-medium term. These assets are also seen as less risky in a world increasingly affected by climate change.

However, as with any asset class, the repricing of climate-conscious investments is a phase. Once the market fully recognizes the value or advantages of these sustainable assets and prices them accordingly, the differential in returns between climate-conscious and traditional assets might normalize, and the returns from this "green premium" will start to narrow.

On the other hand, while the immediate benefits of climate-conscious investments might diminish once the market adjusts, the long-term benefits remain. These assets are better positioned to navigate the challenges of a changing climate, stricter regulations, and shifting consumer preferences. That said, even if the "green premium" in terms of returns diminishes, the resilience and potential for consistent long-term growth of climate-conscious investments make them attractive for long-term investors. For asset owners who recognize this trend early, there is an opportunity to capitalize on the repricing phase and achieve superior returns.

Scenario Analysis and Stress Testing

Scenario analyses and stress testing are increasingly important components of climate-conscious investment portfolios. A *scenario analysis* in the context of climate change involves creating and evaluating a range of plausible future scenarios based on different assumptions about GHG emissions, regulatory changes, technological advancements, and other factors affecting climate change and the transition to a low-carbon economy. The main goal of conducting a scenario analysis is to understand how different climate-related scenarios could impact investment returns, asset values, and overall portfolio risk.

Scenarios might include a BAU trajectory, a scenario where global warming is limited to well below 2°C (in line with the Paris Agreement), and more aggressive climate action or extreme climate scenarios. Asset owners can use these scenarios to assess the resilience of their portfolios under different climate futures, helping them to identify potential risks and opportunities.

In climate scenario analyses, the key variables associated with emissions pathway generally include the following, according to the framework of the Energy Transition Accelerator (ETA):

1. Target Temperature Over Preindustrial Levels: The temperature above preindustrial levels with which the scenario is consistent, in most cases, this is a constraint reflected in the carbon budget and so the pathway, or an outcome of assumptions.

2. Probability of Achieving Temperature Target: The probability of achieving a particular temperature outcome. This is a critical datapoint, as the uncertainties within climate science can lead to wide ranges of outcomes meeting that a probabilistic presentation is useful.

3. Carbon Emissions Budgets: Global warming is fundamentally linked to the absolute concentration of GHGs in the atmosphere. To stabilize global temperature at any level versus preindustrial, there is then a finite number of emissions that can be released before net emissions need to reach zero—for CO_2 emissions, this can be referred to as a carbon budget.

4. Scenario Start Year: The year the analysis of the particular scenario model starts.

5. Emissions Peak: The year at which emissions peak.

6. Year Temperature Target is First Reached: The year when the temperature target is first reached.

7. Net-Zero Year: The year where globally there are zero net emissions, which means any residual direct emissions are offset by carbon dioxide removal (CDR) (e.g. negative emissions technologies [NETS], including bioenergy with CCS [BECCS]).

8. Overshoot: The degree of temperature overshoot above the set target of the scenario. Overshoot can occur during the pathway time frame.

9. Return Year: The year when the temperature returns again to target after overshoot.

10. Scenario Transition Modeled End Year: The last year of the detailed modeling in the scenario. At this point, the temperature target may not be stable, and further assumptions are required to establish that.

11. Emissions Reduction on Base Year (%): The percentage reduction of emissions highlighted in the scenario at its end year measured against

its base year, which is not always the first year of the scenario model. This needs to be put in the context of a pathway—the slope of this curve shows timing of impact.

According to the ETA, the associated key economic and financial variables typically include:

1. Geography and Sector: The more granularity, the more useful for investment analysis.
2. Geographic Jurisdictions: Countries and regions in scope of analysis.
3. Key Sectors Covered: The range of sectors included in the scenarios. This includes any references to sectors at any point on the supply chain, thus including end-use sectors as well as primary producers.
4. Key policy drivers.
5. Carbon Prices: Carbon pricing is the most cited policy method to optimize the shift of capital from high to low carbon assets and, because it can be added to the asset level.
6. Key Economics and Financial Variables: This is what drives the economic results of the scenario. They are both inputs and outputs.
7. Technology Trajectories/Demand Profiles: These are not a single data point but are a series of signposts and datapoints that define how various technologies are developing. These, in effect, set out production profiles and so reflect expected demand in the economy.
8. Asset Level: For asset owners and investees, granular real-asset data and financial data is needed to apply economic results to portfolios and in engagement with companies.
9. Associated Capital Investment: The amount of capital required to achieve the various demand/production/emissions targets.
10. Stranded Assets: Stranded assets are now generally accepted to be those assets that at some time prior to the end of their economic life are no longer able to earn an economic return (i.e., meet the company's internal rate of return (IRR) as a result of changes associated with the transition to a low-carbon economy.
11. Associated Commodity Demand and Prices: Energy scenarios in particular have implications for the broad commodity-level analysis in terms of demand/supply and price.

12. Other Policy Levers: The types of policy needed to incentive invest-ment in new technologies or assets to achieve various emissions reduction targets. In some models, these in turn are proxied by a carbon price.

13. Other Key Technology Variables to Identify: These inputs/assump-tions make a substantive difference to the investment outlook in a scenario.

14. CCS/Carbon Capture, Utilization, and Storage (CCSU): CCS describes the capture of CO_2 and the subsequent geological storage of those gases. CCSU extends this to using carbon in various tech-nologies.

15. NETS/CDR: NETS describe any technology or series of processes where there is a reduction in emissions by either capturing the emis-sions at the point of process of physically extracting the emissions from the atmosphere.

16. BECCs: Describes capturing CO_2 from bioenergy applications and sequestering it through CCS.

In practice, many asset owners consider long-term horizons (typi-cally 10–30 years) to capture the full extent of climate impacts. Based on the interior risk-adjusted performance of the carbon-intensive indus-tries in the North American stock market, Fang et al. (2019) presented a scenario-based framework for building sustainable portfolios under the climate change scheme. Focardi and Fabozzi (2020) explained how build-ing future scenarios for assessing the climate consequences of more- or less-stringent actions and regulations would be challenging because doing so requires integrated assessment models that integrate climate science with economic data and predictions.

Stress testing involves assessing the resilience of an investment portfolio under extreme but plausible adverse conditions. In the context of cli-mate change, this might involve physical-risk stress testing, which focuses on examining the impact of severe weather events or long-term changes in climate patterns on portfolio assets. By contrast, transition-risk stress testing evaluates the impact of rapid policy shifts toward a low-carbon economy, such as the introduction of a carbon tax or a sudden decline in fossil-fuel demand. The objective of stress testing is to understand the potential vulnerabilities in a portfolio and to take proactive steps to mitigate these risks. Scenario analysis and stress testing approaches help understand and manage the risks associated with climate change, which can have significant financial implications.

The findings of Feridun and Güngör (2020) suggested that major regulatory and supervisory expectations could be categorized into four key areas: (a) board-level attention to climate risks and integrating them into internal governance frameworks; (b) embedding climate risks into strategies and overall risk-management frameworks; (c) identifying climate-related material exposures and disclosure of relevant key metrics; and (d) assessing capital impact from climate risk through scenario analysis and stress testing.

Portfolio Implementation

The nuanced process of portfolio implementation emphasizes the critical roles of diversification and the ongoing necessity of monitoring and rebalancing in the context of a rapidly evolving global climate landscape. Evidence suggests that investment portfolios that prioritize sustainability factors have shown resilience and competitive returns (Bender et al. 2019; Irfani and Sudrajad, 2023). By considering both financial metrics and sustainability factors, asset owners can construct portfolios that align with their sustainability objectives while optimizing risk and return.

Using the Markowitz model on the Sri-Kehati index, an esteemed sustainable investment index, and leveraging historical financial data and reliable ESG metrics, Irfani and Sudrajad (2023) developed optimized portfolios that strike a balance between risk and return while adhering to the sustainability criteria of the index. Bender et al. (2019) proposed a framework for building climate-conscious investment strategies within public equities, which rests on both mitigating the impact of climate risks and adapting to climate risk in the future, and demonstrated that this "mitigation and adaptation framework" has enough flexibility to build portfolios at different levels of concentration, tracking error, and climate risk exposure.

Two types of idiosyncratic belief shocks are (i) instances when asset owners experience local extreme weather events that are known to shift climate change beliefs, and (ii) instances when they change the language in shareholder disclosures to express concerns about climate risks. Using observed portfolio changes around such idiosyncratic belief shocks, Alekseev et al. (2022) showed that a portfolio that is long stocks that asset owners tend to buy after experiencing negative idiosyncratic climate belief shocks, and short stocks that they tend to sell, appreciates in value in periods with negative aggregate climate news shocks.

Diversification

A key pillar of climate-conscious portfolio implementation is diversification, both across sectors and geographies. Sector diversification in this context goes beyond traditional risk management; it is about understanding and engaging with sectors that are pivotal in the transition to a low-carbon economy. Geographical diversification, on the other hand, involves spreading investments across different regions, acknowledging that the impacts of climate change and the effectiveness of response strategies vary globally. This dual-diversification strategy is essential for mitigating risks and capturing a broad spectrum of opportunities presented by the global response to climate change.

Sector Diversification

As a fundamental concept in portfolio management, sector diversification serves as a key tool for managing risk and optimizing returns. Its application, however, takes on different nuances when viewed through the lenses of traditional risk management and climate-conscious investing. Sector diversification in the context of climate-conscious investing involves balancing investments across various industries, with an added focus on how different sectors contribute to, or are impacted by, and are responding to, climate change.

That said, asset owners should effectively allocate investments across renewable energy, sustainable agriculture, green technology, and other sectors poised for growth in a low-carbon economy, while also considering traditional sectors that are successfully adapting to these environmental imperatives. Meanwhile, reduce exposure to sectors that are highly vulnerable to climate risks. Asset owners could reduce ex-post risk by lowering the weightings of some fossil-fuel stocks with corresponding higher weightings in lower risk fossil-fuel stocks and/or in the stocks of companies active in energy efficiency markets. Benedetti et al. (2021) suggested that the financial costs of such derisking strategy are statistically negligible in risk-return space. Benedetti et al. developed a model to capture the potential impact of carbon pricing on fossil-fuel stocks, and used it to inform Bayesian portfolio construction methodologies, which were then used to create "Smart Carbon Portfolios."

Using newly developed low-carbon and carbon-intensive indexes for the EU, United States, and global stock markets, Monasterolo and de Angelis (2020) found that after the Paris Agreement, the correlation among low-carbon and carbon-intensive indexes dropped, and the overall systematic risk for the low-carbon indexes decreased consistently. The results of Dai et al. (2023) indicate that from the perspective of net spillover index, new energy is the largest net volatility transmitter and WTI is the largest net volatility receiver. When new energy is a long (short) position, the hedging efficiency of the portfolio with new energy vehicles using the hedging ratio strategy is the greatest. When new energy is long, taking a short position in new energy vehicles is the most effective hedging strategy, but the most expensive hedging strategies are found in resource-related sectors.

Geographic Diversification

Although climate change is a global phenomenon, its impacts and the responses to it vary widely across different regions. Geographical diversification in a climate-conscious portfolio involves spreading investments across various global markets, considering both the risks and opportunities presented by different countries' environmental policies, technological advancements, and exposure to climate risks. This approach not only helps in managing risk but also in tapping into diverse growth potentials offered by different economies at the forefront of climate action.

Monitoring and Rebalancing

A climate-conscious portfolio requires ongoing vigilance and adaptability. Regular monitoring ensures that the portfolio remains aligned with the latest climate science, regulatory landscapes, and market developments. Although asset owners and asset managers traditionally employed ESG integration for risk mitigation, many are growing more comfortable with framing ESG as a means to generate alpha. Yet, one of the challenges that remains is how to measure ESG-attributed performance, not just risk, at a portfolio level.

Current evidence for ESG as a performance enhancer often comes in the form of single-security or single-asset case studies. They may highlight innovative approaches for embedding ESG in valuation techniques or demonstrate new stewardship tactics when engaging company management on ESG issues; however, a case study represents a single anecdote and was most likely chosen because of selection bias, and it does not explain ESG returns in formal attribution terms for the overall portfolio.

Large asset owners typically apply two popular approaches toward decomposing performance attribution: Brinson attribution and risk factor attribution. Attribution models serve to quantify and demonstrate the effects of AA and investment-selection decisions on investment returns. Brinson attribution decomposes performance returns based on a portfolio's active weights. For a given time series, this generally represents performance returns attributed to regional, sector, and stock-specific exposure.

There are efforts to embed ESG within risk factor analysis. A risk-based performance approach measures investment returns based on a portfolio's active factor exposures. These can be well-established Fama–French style factors or less-established factors such as liquidity, low volatility, and currency carry. Where the Brinson model emphasizes stock-specific attribution, which generally makes it popular for discretionary managers, risk factor attribution emphasizes both factor and security-specific exposures.

Periodic rebalancing of the portfolio is equally crucial, as it allows asset owners and asset managers to adjust their holdings in response to shifting market dynamics and climate-related developments. This process is integral to maintaining the desired AA and risk-return profile of the portfolio while staying committed to climate-conscious objectives over time. Focusing on the European Central Bank (ECB)'s asset purchase program and how greenness can be combined with other investment criteria to construct corporate bond portfolios, Bressan et al. (2022) found evidence that portfolio rebalancing leads to a 10 percent reduction of exposure to climate transition risk. Bressan et al. also studied the relationship between bonds' rebalancing and issuers' ESG characteristics and GHG emissions. The results suggest that bonds issued by firms with low (high) ESG risk and GHG emissions are more likely to be bought (sold) in the rebalancing.

Summary

This chapter is very informative that aims to equip readers with the framework, insights, and tools needed to construct portfolios that not only yield financial returns but also contribute positively to the global fight against climate change as the investment landscape evolves. The chapter begins by discussing SAA, emphasizing the importance of incorporating climate risks and opportunities into the long-term AA process. It highlights how traditional models are evolving to include climate-related factors, which can significantly impact the risk and return profiles of asset classes. This chapter then moves on to investment selection with ESG screening. It explains different screening methods and underscores how they can be effectively used to mitigate climate risks.

Next, the "Integrated Portfolio Framework" section provides a comprehensive guide for asset owners looking to navigate the complexities of integrating climate considerations into their investment strategies. It begins by examining macro variables, highlighting how global economic and environmental trends are increasingly intertwined, and underscores the importance of understanding these dynamics in investment decision making.

The discussion on risk premia is pivotal, emphasizing the need to adjust traditional risk assessments to account for climate-related risks, which can significantly alter expected returns. A deep dive into fundamentals reveals how climate change impacts valuations, necessitating a reevaluation of asset worth in light of environmental factors. This leads to a recalibration of return expectations, where asset owners are encouraged to develop new benchmarks that reflect the realities of a climate-impacted world. The section on repricing delves into how market perceptions and valuations are shifting in response to climate awareness, influencing the investment landscape. The importance of scenario analyses and stress testing is highlighted, illustrating how these tools are essential for assessing the resilience of investments under various climate-related scenarios.

Finally, the chapter concludes with portfolio implementation, and addresses the ongoing monitoring and rebalancing of portfolios in response to evolving climate science and policy landscapes, ensuring that the portfolios remain aligned with both financial objectives and climate goals. Throughout, the chapter emphasizes the need for asset owners to be proactive and forward-thinking in considering climate change as a central factor in investment decision making.

CHAPTER 6

Case Studies: Successful Climate-Conscious Investments

This chapter serves as a beacon, illuminating the path forward in the realm of climate-conscious investment, showcasing a diverse array of success stories that not only yield financial returns but also drive significant climate action. Each case study presented here is a testament to the power and potential of investments that are acutely aware of their environmental impact, offering valuable insights into how financial strategies and investment decisions can effectively mitigate physical climate risks.

From innovative funding mechanisms to groundbreaking projects, these narratives provide a comprehensive understanding of how asset owners, policy makers, asset managers, investees, and regulatory bodies are collaboratively shaping a more sustainable and resilient future. As delving into these real-world examples, readers will gain a deeper appreciation of the intricate interplay between the financial ecosystem and environmental stewardship, and how this synergy is crucial for addressing the pressing challenges of climate change.

Success Stories in Green Financing

This section delves into seven compelling case studies that epitomize the triumphs and transformative potential of environmentally focused financial initiatives. Each story is a unique mosaic, piecing together innovative strategies, visionary leadership, and sustainable practices that have not only achieved financial success but have also made significant contributions to environmental conservation and climate action. These cases span a diverse range of industries and geographies, offering a panoramic view of how green financing is being effectively implemented across the globe.

The Green Bond Revolution: European Investment Bank

The European Investment Bank (EIB)'s issuance of the world's first green bond in 2007, known as the Climate Awareness Bond, marked a significant milestone in sustainable finance. The bond was designed to raise capital specifically for projects that address climate change, primarily focusing on renewable energy and energy efficiency. This was a pioneering step in creating a financial instrument that links asset owners' funds directly to environmentally beneficial projects.

Impact: Funding Renewable Energy and Energy Efficiency

1. Capital Allocation: The funds raised through these bonds have been allocated to various projects across Europe, focusing on renewable energy sources such as wind, solar, and hydroelectric power, as well as on improving energy efficiency.
2. Boosting Green Projects: The availability of dedicated funding has been crucial in advancing numerous green projects, which might have struggled to find financing otherwise.
3. Market Growth: The success of the EIB's Climate Awareness Bond has spurred the growth of the green bond market globally, encouraging other entities to issue similar bonds.

Lessons Learned: Transparency and Accountability

1. Transparency: One of the key lessons from the EIB's green bonds is the importance of transparency in how the funds are used. Asset owners increasingly demand clear evidence that their money is being used for genuinely green projects.
2. Reporting Standards: The EIB set a precedent for reporting standards in green-bond issuances. Regular reporting on the impact of funded projects is crucial for maintaining trust and supporting the growth of the green-bond market.
3. Certification and Standards: The development of standards and certifications for green bonds, like the CBS, was partly influenced by the need for accountability and transparency seen in these early issuances.

4. Market Confidence: Ensuring that the funds raised are used for their intended purpose has been vital in building and maintaining market confidence in green bonds as a financial instrument.

The EIB's initiative acted as a catalyst and significant precedent in the financial world, encouraging other institutions to consider how financial instruments can effectively support environmental objectives while offering viable investment opportunities. The success of green bonds has also influenced policy and corporate behavior, highlighting the role of financial ecosystem in addressing environmental challenges. The lessons learned from this initiative have shaped the evolution of green bonds and sustainable finance more broadly.

Scaling Solar Power: The International Finance Corporation

The International Finance Corporation (IFC), a member of the World Bank Group, launched the "Scaling Solar" initiative to accelerate the roll-out of competitively priced, utility-scale solar power in developing countries, with Zambia being one of the early adopters. The initiative combined competitive auctions for solar projects with a package of risk management tools. This approach aimed to attract private investors by reducing the complexities and risks typically associated with solar power projects in EM countries.

Impact: Affordable Clean Energy and Private Investment

1. Low-Cost Solar Power: In Zambia, the initiative led to some of the lowest tariffs for solar power in Sub-Saharan Africa, making renewable energy more affordable.
2. Attracting Private Investment: By mitigating risks and simplifying the process, the initiative succeeded in attracting significant private investment in Zambia's solar energy sector, a market that had previously been challenging for asset owners in private assets.
3. Capacity Building: The initiative also helped build local capacity for managing and implementing solar energy projects.

Lessons Learned: Role of Multilateral Institutions

1. Catalyzing Private Sector Investment: One of the key lessons is the vital role multilateral institutions like the IFC can play in catalyzing private sector investment in renewable energy, especially in markets perceived as high risk.
2. Risk Mitigation: The use of risk-management tools and competitive auctions demonstrated how perceived risks can be mitigated, making investments in renewable energy more attractive to the private sector.
3. Standardization and Simplification: The initiative showed the importance of standardizing and simplifying processes for project development and procurement. This approach can significantly reduce the time and cost of deploying solar energy projects.
4. Partnership Approach: The success of "Scaling Solar" in Zambia highlighted the effectiveness of a partnership approach, involving governments, multilateral institutions, and private investors, in achieving sustainable energy goals.
5. Replicability: The model developed under this initiative has proven to be replicable in other countries, demonstrating a scalable approach to expanding solar energy in EM countries.

The "Scaling Solar" initiative by the IFC in Zambia is a prime example of how innovative financing and risk management strategies can be employed by multilateral institutions to boost renewable energy projects, attract private investment, and achieve SDGs in challenging markets. "Scaling Solar" provided a one-stop-shop for governments to rapidly mobilize privately funded grid-connected solar projects, offering templates for contracts, financing, and risk management.

Green Loans for Sustainability: BBVA's Sustainable Loan to Iberdrola

Banco Bilbao Vizcaya Argentaria (BBVA), a major Spanish bank, extended a green loan to Iberdrola, one of the world's largest electricity utilities. This loan was specifically earmarked for financing various sustainable energy projects. The funds were intended for the development, expansion, and improvement of renewable energy projects, including wind, solar, and hydroelectric power plants. The loan was structured in accordance with the Green Loan Principles (GLP), which ensure that the funds are used for genuinely sustainable and environmentally friendly projects.

Impact: Renewable Energy Capacity and Emission Reduction

1. Expansion of Renewable Energy: The loan significantly contributed to Iberdrola's capacity to invest in and expand its renewable energy projects. This expansion is in line with the company's broader strategy of increasing its renewable energy portfolio.
2. Reduction in GHG Emissions: By funding renewable energy projects, the loan played a role in reducing GHG emissions, contributing to the global effort to combat climate change.
3. Demonstration Effect: The success of these projects can serve as a model for other utilities and companies looking to expand their renewable energy capabilities.

Lessons Learned: Green Loans in Corporate Sustainability

1. Effective Financing Tool: Green loans like this one demonstrate the potential of targeted financial instruments to support large-scale sustainability projects in the corporate sector.
2. Attracting Investment: This case shows that there is a growing appetite among asset owners and asset managers for green financing opportunities, especially when they are aligned with clear environmental objectives.
3. Transparency and Accountability: The importance of adhering to principles like the GLP is highlighted, ensuring that the funds are used as intended and that their environmental impact is measurable.
4. Market Confidence: Such successful green loans build confidence in the market, showing that sustainable investments can be both environmentally beneficial and financially viable.
5. Catalyzing Change in the Energy Sector: The loan to Iberdrola underscores how financial institutions can play a crucial role in the energy sector's transition toward more sustainable practices.

The BBVA–Iberdrola green-loan case exemplifies how financial mechanisms can be effectively utilized to support and accelerate the transition to sustainable energy, demonstrating the synergy between environmental sustainability and financial viability in the corporate sector.

Community-Based Green Financing: SolarCity's Solar Bonds

SolarCity, a company specializing in solar energy services, introduced solar bonds as a way to finance solar installations. These bonds were offered directly to the general public, allowing individuals to invest in solar projects. The bonds were designed to be accessible to a wide range of asset owners, with relatively low minimum investment amounts compared to traditional investment bonds. The funds raised through these bonds were used to finance the installation of residential and commercial solar power systems.

Impact: Democratization of Green Investment and Solar Expansion

1. Broadening Investment Opportunities: SolarCity's solar bonds allowed a broader segment of the population to participate in green investments, democratizing access to renewable energy financing.
2. Expansion of Residential Solar Power: The funds raised significantly contributed to the expansion of residential solar power in the United States, making solar energy more accessible to homeowners.
3. Public Engagement in Renewable Energy: By investing in solar bonds, individuals could directly contribute to the growth of renewable energy, fostering a sense of participation and ownership in the transition to greener energy sources.

Lessons Learned: Direct-to-Consumer Bonds in Renewable Energy

1. Mobilizing Small-Scale Investments: SolarCity's model showed that direct-to-consumer bonds could effectively mobilize small-scale investments, tapping into a new source of funding for renewable energy projects.
2. Market Viability: The success of these bonds demonstrated the market viability of renewable energy investments and the public's growing interest in environmentally sustainable projects.

3. Educational Aspect: Offering these bonds also had an educational aspect, increasing public awareness about solar energy and its benefits.

4. Risk and Return Considerations: For asset owners, these bonds offered a way to diversify their portfolios with investments that have a different risk-return profile compared to traditional securities.

5. Regulatory Environment: The initiative highlighted the importance of a supportive regulatory environment for innovative green financing mechanisms.

SolarCity's solar bonds initiative exemplifies how innovative financing mechanisms can play a crucial role in expanding renewable energy, offering an effective way to mobilize investment from a broad base of individuals. It underscores the potential of community-based financing models in supporting sustainable energy projects and the transition toward a greener economy.

Transition Bonds: Cadent Gas Ltd's Transition Bond

Cadent Gas Ltd, a major gas distribution network in the United Kingdom, issued a transition bond to finance projects that reduce carbon emissions, such as the development of hydrogen infrastructure and the integration of hydrogen and renewable natural gas into the gas network.

Impact: Supporting Sustainable Transition

1. Facilitating Change in Traditional Industries: The bond played a crucial role in supporting Cadent Gas' transition from a traditional gas utility to adopting more sustainable practices.

2. Investment in Green Technologies: The proceeds from the bond were used to invest in emerging green technologies, particularly hydrogen, which is seen as a key component in the future energy mix.

3. Reducing Carbon Footprint: The projects financed by the bond contribute to reducing the carbon footprint of the gas sector, aligning with broader climate goals.

Lessons Learned: Transition Bonds in Sustainable Finance

1. Filling a Financing Gap: Transition bonds like Cadent Gas' offer a way to finance companies in carbon-intensive industries that are looking to shift toward greener operations but are not yet fully green.

2. Market Acceptance: The successful issuance of such bonds indicates a growing market acceptance and investor appetite for financing the transition to a low-carbon economy.

3. Importance of Credibility: For transition bonds to be effective, it is crucial that the financed projects have a clear and credible pathway to reducing carbon emissions. Transparency and reporting are key to maintaining investor trust.

4. Broader Application: The concept of transition bonds can be applied to various industries, offering a flexible financing tool for companies at different stages of their sustainability journey.

5. Complementing Green Bonds: Transition bonds complement green bonds by providing financing solutions for companies that are in the process of transitioning but are not yet operating in fully sustainable sectors.

Cadent Gas' transition bond highlights the evolving nature of sustainable finance and the emergence of innovative financial instruments designed to support the transition of traditional industries toward more sustainable practices. Transition bonds represent a key tool in financing the shift to a greener economy, especially for sectors where the path to sustainability is complex and gradual.

Green Financing in Emerging Markets: ACWA Power's Noor Energy 1

ACWA Power is a developer, investor, co-owner, and operator of a portfolio of power generation. Its Noor Energy 1 is part of the Mohammed bin Rashid Al Maktoum Solar Park in Dubai, one of the world's largest solar power projects. The project involved a mix of public and private funding, showcasing a collaborative approach to financing. This included international banks, regional lenders, and export credit agencies. The project utilized various financing instruments, including loans and possibly green bonds, to secure the necessary capital.

Impact: Contribution to Renewable Energy Goals

1. Boosting Renewable Capacity: Noor Energy 1 significantly contributes to the United Arab Emirates' renewable energy targets, helping diversify the energy mix away from fossil fuels.
2. Carbon-Emission Reduction: By increasing solar power capacity, the project plays a crucial role in reducing carbon emissions, aligning with global efforts to combat climate change.
3. Economic Development: The project also supports economic development in Dubai and the broader region, creating jobs and fostering technological innovation in renewable energy.

Lessons Learned: Renewable Projects in Emerging Markets

1. Feasibility of Large-Scale Projects: Noor Energy 1 demonstrates the feasibility of executing and financing large-scale renewable energy projects in emerging markets.
2. Collaborative Financing: The project underscores the importance of collaborative financing structures, combining public, private, and international resources.
3. Risk Management: Managing risks in such large projects is crucial, and a mix of funding sources can help mitigate these risks.
4. Policy Support: Strong governmental support and favorable policies are key enablers for such ambitious projects.
5. Replicability: The success of Noor Energy 1 provides a model that can be replicated in other emerging markets looking to expand their renewable energy capabilities.
6. Long-Term Investment Perspective: Investors in such projects often need to take a long-term perspective, given the scale and duration of the return on investment.

ACWA Power's Noor Energy 1 project in Dubai is a landmark in green financing for emerging markets, illustrating how large-scale renewable energy projects can be successfully financed and implemented. It highlights the potential of EM countries in the global transition to renewable energy and the critical role of innovative and collaborative financing structures in this journey.

Innovative Green Financing: The New York Green Bank

The New York Green Bank was established as a state-sponsored financial entity to reduce New York State's carbon footprint and support clean energy and energy efficiency project.

Impact: Leveraging Private Sector Investment

1. Mobilization of Private Capital: One of the most significant impacts of the New York Green Bank has been its ability to attract and leverage private sector investment. By providing a range of financial products and reducing perceived investment risks, it has successfully drawn substantial private funds into renewable energy and energy efficiency projects.
2. Reduction in GHG Emissions: The bank's investments have directly contributed to the reduction of GHG emissions in New York State. By financing renewable energy projects, it has helped in significantly lowering the state's carbon footprint.
3. Economic Growth and Job Creation: The projects have not only been environmentally beneficial but have also spurred economic growth and job creation in the green energy sector, contributing to a more sustainable and resilient economy.
4. Demonstration Effect: The success of the New York Green Bank has served as a model for other states and countries, demonstrating the viability and effectiveness of green banks in promoting environmental sustainability through market-based solutions.

Lessons Learned: Role of Public Sector Entities

1. PPPs are Key: One of the primary lessons from the New York Green Bank is the importance of PPPs in green financing. The bank's

ability to leverage public funds to attract private investment has been crucial in its success.

2. Risk Mitigation to Encourage Investment: The bank's strategies in mitigating financial risks have been instrumental in encouraging private asset owners to invest in traditionally riskier green projects. This approach can be replicated in other markets to stimulate similar investments.

3. Flexibility and Innovation in Financial Products: The New York Green Bank's use of innovative and flexible financial products has been essential in addressing the specific needs of green projects and investors, highlighting the need for tailored financial solutions in green financing.

4. Measurable Impact Is Crucial: The ability to demonstrate tangible environmental and economic impacts has been vital for the bank's credibility and success. This underscores the importance of having robust mechanisms for measuring and reporting the impact of green investments.

5. Scalability and Replicability: The model of the New York Green Bank shows that with the right approach, green-financing initiatives can be scaled and replicated in different geographic and economic contexts, offering a pathway for global efforts in sustainable development.

This compelling case study showcases how a public investment entity can effectively catalyze private-sector investment in green projects, and illustrates how the New York Green Bank effectively bridged the gap between environmental sustainability and economic growth, leveraging innovative financial mechanisms. Its success offers valuable insights and lessons for global efforts in combating climate change through strategic investments.

Impact Investing Driving Climate Action

This section presents seven case studies that showcase how impact investing has been a driving force in climate action. These real-world examples highlight the effectiveness of targeted investments in generating positive environmental impacts alongside financial returns. The case studies cover a range of sectors and geographies, illustrating the diverse ways in which impact investing can contribute to combating climate change.

The Norwegian Government Pension Fund Global: Divesting From Fossil Fuels

The Norwegian Government Pension Fund Global, one of the world's largest sovereign wealth funds, made a landmark decision to divest billions from coal and other fossil fuels. The divestment focused on companies involved in coal mining, coal-fired power generation, and other fossil-fuel activities that are considered to be high in carbon emissions. This move was part of a broader strategy to reduce the fund's exposure to assets that are heavily impacted by climate-related risks.

Impact: Carbon Footprint Reduction and Investment Trends

1. Reducing Carbon Footprint: By divesting from fossil fuels, the fund significantly reduced its carbon footprint, aligning its investment portfolio more closely with global efforts to combat climate change.
2. Influencing Global Markets: The fund's decision sent a powerful signal to global markets, highlighting the growing financial risks associated with fossil-fuel investments.
3. Encouraging Sustainable Practices: This move has influenced other asset owners and funds to reconsider their investments in fossil fuels and to explore more sustainable alternatives.

Lessons Learned: Large Asset Owners and Divestment Strategies

1. Driving Change: The fund's decision demonstrates the power of large asset owners to drive change in the market through divestment strategies.
2. Risk Management: Divesting from sectors with high climate risks is increasingly seen as a prudent long-term risk management strategy.
3. Market Influence: Large asset owners have the ability to influence market trends and corporate behaviors, pushing for a transition toward more sustainable and environmentally friendly practices.

4. Catalyst for Policy Change: Such moves can also act as a catalyst for policy change, encouraging governments and regulators to implement more stringent environmental regulations.

5. Communication and Transparency: The fund's approach highlights the importance of clear communication and transparency in implementing and explaining divestment strategies.

The Norwegian Government Pension Fund Global's divestment from fossil fuels underscores the significant role that large asset owners can play in promoting sustainable investment practices. It demonstrates how investment decisions can align with environmental stewardship while also addressing long-term financial risks associated with climate change. This move has been influential in shaping global investment trends and encouraging a broader shift toward sustainability in the financial ecosystem.

Tesla's EV Revolution

Tesla's EV revolution represents a pivotal moment in the automotive industry, marked by significant advancements in green technology and a shift toward sustainable transportation. Tesla's growth was fueled by a combination of private investments, public funding (including government loans and incentives), and public stock offerings. These investments were crucial in the early stages when Tesla was developing its technology and scaling production. Tesla focused on developing high-performance EVs and, later, more affordable models. Its approach combined advancements in battery technology, electric powertrains, and software integration.

Impact: Contribution to Carbon Emission Reduction
and Market Acceleration

1. Reducing Carbon Emissions: By popularizing EVs, Tesla has contributed significantly to reducing carbon emissions in the transportation sector, traditionally dominated by fossil-fuel-powered vehicles.

2. Market Transformation: Tesla's success has accelerated the EV market globally, prompting traditional automakers to increase their investment in EVs and related technologies.

3. Battery Technology and Infrastructure: Tesla's innovations in battery technology and the development of charging infrastructure have been pivotal in making EVs more practical and appealing to a broader market.

Lessons Learned: Visionary Leadership and High-Risk Investments

1. Visionary Leadership: Elon Musk's role as a visionary leader was instrumental in Tesla's success. His commitment to the idea of EVs, even when it was not mainstream, set the course for the company.
2. High-Risk, High-Reward: Tesla's journey underscores the high-risk, high-reward nature of investing in disruptive technologies. The company faced numerous challenges and skepticism, but its success has had a substantial payoff.
3. Innovation as a Driver: Continuous innovation in product design, technology, and customer experience has been key to Tesla's market dominance.
4. Importance of Branding and Marketing: Tesla's branding and marketing strategies, often unconventional, played a significant role in its popularity and market penetration.
5. Ecosystem Approach: Tesla's approach to creating an entire ecosystem, including cars, charging stations, and energy storage, has been a critical factor in its success and in driving the industry forward.

Tesla's journey in the EV revolution highlights the transformative power of innovation, visionary leadership, and strategic investments in green technologies. It demonstrates how a single company's approach to disruptive technology can catalyze an entire industry's shift toward sustainability.

The Green Climate Fund's Investment in Renewable Energy in Developing Countries

The GCF, a key entity in international climate finance, was established to assist developing countries in their efforts to combat climate change, with a significant focus on financing renewable energy projects. The GCF provides grants, loans, equity, and guarantees to support projects in renewable energy, among other areas related to climate change mitigation and adaptation. Projects range from large-scale renewable energy infrastructure, such as wind and solar farms, to smaller, community-based renewable energy systems.

Impact: Access to Clean Energy and Sustainable Development

1. Enhancing Energy Access: GCF's investments have facilitated access to clean, affordable energy in many underserved regions, which is crucial for reducing reliance on fossil fuels and improving living standards.
2. Economic Development: By funding renewable energy projects, the GCF also promotes sustainable economic development, creating jobs and fostering local industries related to renewable energy.
3. Environmental Benefits: These projects contribute significantly to reducing GHGs and advancing global environmental goals.

Lessons Learned: International Cooperation in Climate Action

1. Importance of Funding: Adequate funding is crucial for climate action in developing nations, where resources for such initiatives are often limited.
2. Leveraging Private Sector Investment: GCF funding acts as a catalyst, attracting additional private and public sector investments in renewable energy projects.
3. Capacity Building: Beyond financial support, capacity building in local communities and governments is essential for the sustainable management and expansion of renewable energy projects.
4. Tailored Approaches: Projects need to be tailored to local contexts, considering the specific environmental, economic, and social conditions of each region.
5. Collaboration and Knowledge Sharing: International cooperation, including knowledge sharing and collaborative approaches, is key to addressing global climate challenges effectively.

The GCF's investment in renewable energy in EM countries underscores the critical role of international funding and cooperation in supporting climate action where it is needed most. This initiative not only contribute to environmental sustainability but also foster economic and social development, demonstrating the interconnected nature of climate action and development goals.

BlackRock's Climate-Change Fund

BlackRock, the world's largest asset manager, launched a climate-change fund specifically targeting companies that are either directly involved in sustainable practices or have strong environmental policies. The fund selects companies based on their performance in environmental metrics, including carbon footprint, energy efficiency, and sustainability practices. The fund includes a diverse portfolio of companies across different sectors that are contributing to or benefiting from the transition to a low-carbon economy.

Impact: Corporate Practices and Capital Allocation

1. Steering Capital Toward Sustainability: By directing investments toward sustainable businesses, the fund plays a role in steering overall capital flows in the market toward more environmentally friendly practices.
2. Influencing Corporate Behavior: The fund's focus on environmental metrics puts pressure on companies to improve their sustainability practices to attract investment.
3. Market Signal: The launch of such a fund by a major player like BlackRock sends a strong signal to the market about the growing importance of environmental sustainability in investment decisions.

Lessons Learned: Thematic Funds and Market Influence

1. Market Behavior Shaping: Thematic funds like BlackRock's climate-change fund have the potential to shape market behavior, encouraging more companies to adopt sustainable practices.
2. Risk and Opportunity: Thematic funds highlight the increasing recognition of climate change as both a risk and an opportunity in the investment world.

3. Investor Demand: The success reflects a growing demand among asset owners for opportunities that align with their environmental values.

4. Corporate Transparency: The focus on environmental metrics underscores the need for greater corporate transparency and reporting on sustainability practices.

5. Long-Term Perspective: Investing in climate-change-focused funds often requires a long-term perspective, considering the gradual nature of the transition to a low-carbon economy.

The launch of BlackRock's fund exemplifies how thematic investment funds can influence corporate strategies and market trends, highlighting the growing integration of environmental considerations in investment decisions. This approach reflects a broader shift in the financial sector toward recognizing and addressing the risks and opportunities presented by climate change. As the largest asset manager in the world, BlackRock's decision could represent a new paradigm in the investment industry in which the integration of material climate-related factors is mainstream.

The Blue Orchard Microfinance Fund

The Blue Orchard Microfinance Fund represents a unique approach to addressing climate change and promoting sustainable development, particularly in emerging markets. The fund invests in microfinance institutions that are dedicated to climate-change mitigation and adaptation efforts, especially in EM countries. By focusing on microfinance, the fund aims to empower local communities and small-scale entrepreneurs, providing them with the financial means to engage in sustainable practices. Investments typically support a range of projects, from renewable energy and energy efficiency to sustainable agriculture and water management.

Impact: Empowering Communities and Building Resilience

1. Local Empowerment: The fund helps local communities, often in vulnerable regions, to access financial resources necessary for implementing sustainable solutions.

2. Climate Resilience: By funding projects related to climate-change adaptation, the fund contributes to building resilience against the impacts of climate change in these communities.

3. Economic Development: The investments also support economic development by fostering small businesses and entrepreneurship in sustainable sectors.

Lessons Learned: Microfinance in Climate Action

1. Grassroots Impact: The Blue Orchard Microfinance Fund demonstrates the effectiveness of microfinance in driving climate action at the grassroots level.
2. Sustainable Development: The approach shows how financial inclusion and sustainable development can be integrated, addressing both economic and environmental challenges.
3. Risk Management: Investing in a diverse range of microfinance institutions and projects helps manage risks associated with microfinance in emerging markets.
4. Community Engagement: The success of such initiatives often hinges on strong community engagement and understanding local needs and contexts.
5. Scalability and Replicability: The model provides a scalable and replicable approach to funding sustainable development in various regions.

The Blue Orchard Microfinance Fund showcases how microfinance can be a powerful tool in addressing climate change and promoting sustainable development, especially in emerging markets. By focusing on small-scale, local initiatives, the fund demonstrates that empowering communities financially can lead to significant environmental and social benefits.

The Danish Climate Investment Fund

The Danish Climate Investment Fund represents a strategic approach to financing climate-related projects, particularly in emerging markets, while aligning with Danish business interests. The fund is a PPP, involving the Danish government and private investors, aimed at financing climate-related projects. The primary focus is on projects in emerging markets that contribute to the reduction of GHG emissions. A unique aspect of the fund is its alignment with Danish business interests, supporting projects that involve Danish technology or expertise.

Impact: GHG Reduction and Renewable Energy

1. Emission Reduction: The fund has been successful in contributing to the reduction of GHG emissions through its investments.
2. Renewable Energy Projects: Significant investments have been made in renewable energy projects, such as wind, solar, and biomass, which not only reduce emissions but also support sustainable energy development in emerging markets.
3. Energy Efficiency: The fund also focuses on improving energy efficiency, which is a key component in reducing overall carbon footprints.

Lessons Learned: Public Funds and Private Investment

1. Leveraging Public Funds: One of the key lessons is the effectiveness of using public funds to attract private investment. The involvement of the Danish government provides a level of security and credibility, encouraging private investors to participate.
2. Synergy Between Public and Private Sectors: The fund demonstrates how the synergy between public objectives (i.e., climate mitigation) and private interests (i.e., business opportunities) can lead to successful outcomes.
3. Market Development: Investments in emerging markets not only aid in climate-change mitigation but also help in developing these markets, creating new opportunities for sustainable technologies.
4. Risk Management: The PPP model helps in managing risks associated with investing in emerging markets, making it more attractive for asset owners with private-market investments.
5. SDGs: The fund's activities contribute to the achievement of multiple SDGs, including affordable and clean energy, climate action, and economic growth.

The Danish Climate Investment Fund showcases how the strategic use of PPPs can effectively mobilize resources for climate action in emerging markets. By aligning public funding with private-sector investment and

Danish business interests, the fund demonstrates a model that balances economic development with environmental sustainability.

Conservation International's Carbon Fund

The Carbon Fund by Conservation International is designed to invest in forest conservation projects around the world. The primary goal is to reduce carbon emissions through the preservation of forests, which are vital carbon sinks. The fund employs a strategy that includes protecting existing forests, restoring degraded ones, and supporting sustainable forestry practices. The fund combines donations, grants, and possibly investments that provide financial returns based on carbon credits or other ecosystem service valuations.

Impact: Forest Preservation and Carbon Sequestration

1. Ecosystem Preservation: The fund's activities contribute to the preservation of critical forest ecosystems, which are essential for biodiversity, water regulation, and local communities.
2. Enhanced Carbon Sequestration: By maintaining and restoring forested areas, the fund enhances the ability of these natural environments to sequester carbon, a key factor in mitigating climate change.
3. Community Benefits: Many forest conservation projects also bring socioeconomic benefits to local communities, often involving them in conservation efforts and sustainable livelihoods.

Lessons Learned: Natural Capital in Climate-Change Mitigation

1. Value of Natural Capital: The Carbon Fund underscores the immense value of natural capital, particularly forests, in the global fight against climate change.
2. Integrating Ecosystem Services: The initiative highlights the importance of recognizing and integrating ecosystem services into economic and environmental policies.
3. Holistic Approach: Successful forest conservation requires a holistic approach that considers ecological, social, and economic factors.

4. Community Engagement: Engaging local communities in conservation efforts is crucial for the sustainability of these projects.

5. Market-Based Mechanisms: The use of market-based mechanisms like carbon credits can provide a viable financial model for conservation initiatives.

Conservation International's Carbon Fund exemplifies how targeted environmental initiatives can contribute significantly to climate-change mitigation. By focusing on forest conservation, the fund not only aids in reducing carbon emissions but also preserves biodiversity and supports local communities, showcasing the interconnected nature of ecological and human well-being.

Investments Mitigating Physical Climate Risks

Investments that focus on mitigating physical climate risks are increasingly important in the context of global climate change. These investments are typically aimed at reducing the impact of climate-related physical risks such as extreme weather events, rising sea levels, and changing weather patterns. This section presents seven case studies that illustrate different approaches to this kind of investment.

Renewable Energy Projects

Renewable energy projects, particularly solar and wind energy farms, have become pivotal in the global transition toward sustainable energy sources. These projects involve the installation of solar panels and wind turbines to harness natural energy sources—the sun and wind, respectively. The scale of these projects can vary widely, from small, community-based installations to large, utility-scale farms.

Location: Global Spread

1. Geographical Diversity: Solar and wind energy projects are being developed globally, with significant installations in countries such as the United States, China, Germany, India, and Spain.

2. Site Selection: The location of these farms is critical and is often determined by the availability of sunlight and wind resources. For instance, solar farms are prevalent in regions with high solar irradiance, while wind farms are located in areas with consistent wind patterns.

Objective: Reducing Fossil-Fuel Reliance

1. Energy Transition: The primary objective is to transition from fossil-fuel-based energy generation to renewable sources, thereby reducing GHG emissions.
2. Sustainability: These projects aim to create a sustainable energy supply that can meet current needs without compromising the ability of future generations to meet their own needs.

Outcome: Clean Energy Generation and Emission Reduction

1. Clean-Energy Contribution: Solar and wind farms have successfully generated significant amounts of clean energy, contributing to the diversification of energy sources.
2. Carbon-Emission Reduction: By replacing fossil-fuel-based power generation, these projects have contributed to a reduction in carbon emissions, aiding in the fight against climate change.
3. Economic Viability: With technological advancements, the cost of producing solar and wind energy has decreased, making them increasingly cost-effective compared to traditional energy sources.
4. Job Creation: The development of renewable energy projects has also created jobs, contributing to economic growth in various regions.
5. Energy Security: These projects enhance energy security by reducing dependence on imported fossil fuels.

Solar and wind energy farms represent a significant stride in the global effort to transition to cleaner, more sustainable energy sources. Their success is a testament to the potential of renewable energy to contribute effectively to environmental goals while also offering economic and social benefits. Ongoing technological advancements are crucial for increasing the efficiency and reducing the costs of renewable energy.

Green Infrastructure

Green infrastructure projects, particularly urban green spaces and green roofs, are increasingly recognized as essential components of sustainable urban development. These projects involve the development of green spaces such as parks, gardens, and green corridors, as well as the installation of green roofs on buildings.

Location: Global Implementation

1. Cities Worldwide: Urban green spaces and green roofs are being implemented in cities around the world, with notable examples in Singapore, known for its "City in a Garden" vision, and Toronto, which has a green roof bylaw.
2. Adaptation to Local Contexts: The design and implementation of these projects vary depending on local climates, urban layouts, and cultural contexts.

Objective: Enhancing Urban Resilience and Biodiversity

1. Combatting Urban Heat Island Effect: One of the primary objectives is to mitigate the urban heat island effect, where urban regions experience higher temperatures than their rural surroundings.
2. Stormwater Management: These green spaces help in managing stormwater, reducing the risk and impact of flooding.
3. Biodiversity and Ecosystem Services: They also aim to enhance urban biodiversity and provide ecosystem services such as air purification and carbon sequestration.

Outcome: Environmental and Social Benefits

1. Temperature Regulation: Urban green spaces and green roofs have been effective in lowering local temperatures, making cities more comfortable for residents.
2. Improved Air Quality: These projects contribute to improved air quality by filtering pollutants and producing oxygen.

3. Stormwater Management: They play a significant role in absorbing and managing stormwater, thereby reducing the strain on urban drainage systems.

4. Recreational and Aesthetic Value: Green spaces provide recreational areas for residents, improving mental health and overall quality of life.

5. Habitat for Wildlife: They create habitats for various species, thereby supporting urban biodiversity.

Urban green spaces and green roofs are excellent examples of how green infrastructure can contribute to making cities more sustainable, resilient, and livable. They demonstrate the potential of integrating nature into urban environments to address environmental challenges while enhancing the quality of urban life. Incorporating green infrastructure is becoming a crucial element of sustainable urban planning.

Coastal Protection Investments

Investments in coastal protection, particularly through projects such as mangrove restoration and sea wall construction, are crucial in mitigating the impacts of climate change and protecting coastal communities. Mangrove restoration involves replanting and conserving mangrove forests, which are vital ecosystems along coastlines. Mangroves act as natural buffers against storms and are crucial for biodiversity. Building sea walls is a more traditional approach to coastal protection, designed to prevent erosion and flooding caused by rising sea levels and storm surges.

Location: Global Coastal Regions

1. Indonesia: Known for its extensive mangrove restoration projects, Indonesia has one of the world's largest mangrove ecosystems, which are critical for its coastal protection.

2. The Netherlands: Famous for its advanced sea wall systems, the Netherlands has a long history of land reclamation and coastal defense.

Objective: Coastal Protection and Climate Resilience

1. Mitigating Climate-Change Impacts: The primary objective is to protect coastal areas from the adverse effects of climate change, such as rising sea levels and increased frequency of extreme weather events.
2. Ecosystem Preservation: Particularly for mangrove restoration, there is also a focus on preserving and restoring vital coastal ecosystems.

Outcome: Environmental and Community Benefits

1. Coastal Erosion Reduction: Both mangrove restoration and sea walls have been effective in reducing coastal erosion, thereby protecting land and property.
2. Biodiversity Protection: Mangroves provide habitats for a wide range of species, thus contributing to biodiversity conservation.
3. Natural Barriers Against Storms: Mangroves, in particular, serve as natural barriers against storm surges and tsunamis, reducing the impact of these events on coastal communities.
4. Flood Prevention: Sea walls are crucial in preventing flooding in low-lying areas, especially in regions prone to high tides and sea-level rise.
5. Socioeconomic Benefits: These projects also provide socioeconomic benefits, such as fisheries enhancement in mangrove areas and tourism opportunities.

Coastal protection investments such as mangrove restoration and sea wall construction are essential in building resilience against the impacts of climate change. They demonstrate how a combination of natural and engineered solutions can effectively protect coastal regions while providing ecological and socioeconomic benefits. These initiatives highlight the importance of sustainable coastal management practices.

Sustainable Agriculture

Sustainable agriculture, particularly through the adoption of regenerative farming practices, is increasingly recognized as a crucial component in addressing environmental and food security challenges. Regenerative farming includes a set of agricultural practices aimed at restoring soil health, enhancing water retention, and increasing biodiversity. Key practices include no-till farming, cover cropping, crop rotation, and integrated pest management.

Location: Global Implementation

1. The United States: In the United States, regenerative agriculture is gaining traction among both small-scale farmers and larger agribusinesses.
2. Europe: European farmers are increasingly adopting these practices, often supported by EU agricultural policies and incentives.
3. Africa: In Africa, regenerative practices are being adapted to local conditions, focusing on improving soil fertility and crop diversity.

Objective: Enhancing Environmental Sustainability

1. Soil Health: A primary objective is to improve soil health, which is crucial for nutrient retention, water absorption, and overall fertility.
2. Biodiversity: These practices aim to increase biodiversity both in the soil and above ground, supporting a wider range of plant and animal life.
3. Carbon Footprint: By enhancing the soil's ability to sequester carbon, regenerative farming helps reduce agriculture's overall carbon footprint.

Outcome: Environmental and Agricultural Benefits

1. Improved Soil Health: Regenerative practices have led to healthier soils, which are more resilient to erosion and degradation.
2. Increased Carbon Sequestration: Healthier soils can store more carbon, helping to mitigate climate change.
3. Crop Resilience: Farms using these practices often report better crop resilience against climate extremes, such as droughts and heavy rains.
4. Yield Stability: While initial transitions to regenerative practices can be challenging, many farmers report stable or increased yields over time.

5. Ecosystem Services: These practices enhance ecosystem services, such as pollination and natural pest control.

Regenerative farming practices represent a significant shift in agricultural paradigms, emphasizing sustainability, soil health, and ecological balance. These practices offer a promising path toward more sustainable and resilient food systems, addressing both environmental and food security challenges. Transitioning to regenerative agriculture can be economically viable for farmers, especially when supported by appropriate policies and market mechanisms.

Water Resource Management

Water resource management, especially through the implementation of advanced irrigation and water conservation systems, is crucial in regions facing water scarcity. These projects involve the use of advanced technologies and practices to optimize water use. This includes drip irrigation, sensor-based irrigation systems, water recycling, and efficient urban water-management practices.

Location: Arid and Water-Stressed Regions

1. Israel: Known for its pioneering work in drip irrigation and water conservation, Israel has become a global leader in efficient water management in agriculture.
2. California: Facing periodic droughts, California has been implementing advanced water-management systems in both agricultural and urban settings.

Objective: Optimizing Water Use

1. Agricultural Efficiency: In agriculture, the goal is to maximize crop yield per unit of water used, reducing overall water consumption while maintaining or improving crop productivity.
2. Urban Water Conservation: In urban areas, the objective is to reduce water waste and promote the reuse and recycling of water.

Outcome: Sustainable Water Management

1. Reduced Water Waste: These technologies and practices have significantly reduced water waste, making water use more efficient and sustainable.

2. Agricultural Productivity: In agriculture, the use of advanced irrigation systems has led to higher productivity and better crop quality, even with limited water resources.

3. Resilience to Water Scarcity: Regions using these systems have improved their resilience to water scarcity and drought conditions.

4. Environmental Benefits: Efficient water use also helps in preserving aquatic ecosystems and reducing the energy footprint associated with water pumping and treatment.

5. Economic Benefits: While the initial investment in these technologies can be high, the long-term economic benefits include reduced water costs and increased agricultural yields.

Advanced irrigation and water-conservation systems represent a critical advancement in managing water resources more sustainably, particularly in arid and drought-prone regions. These initiatives demonstrate how technology and efficient practices can significantly contribute to sustainable water management, agricultural productivity, and environmental conservation. Lessons learned from successful implementations in Israel, California, and other regions can be adapted and applied globally, especially in water-stressed areas.

Climate-Resilient Infrastructure

Climate-resilient infrastructure, particularly in the form of flood-resistant bridges and roads, is increasingly crucial in a world where extreme weather events are becoming more frequent and severe. These projects involve the design and construction of bridges and roads that are capable of withstanding flooding and other related impacts of extreme weather events. These projects incorporate advanced engineering techniques, such as elevated structures, improved drainage systems, and materials that can endure flood conditions.

Location: Global Implementation in Flood-Prone Areas

1. Worldwide Scope: Such infrastructure projects are being implemented globally, particularly in regions that are prone to flooding or have experienced significant flood damage in the past.
2. Localized Design: The design and construction of these projects are tailored to local geographic and climatic conditions.

Objective: Enhancing Infrastructure Resilience

1. Withstanding Extreme Weather: The primary objective is to build infrastructure that can resist damage from floods and continue to function during and after such events.
2. Minimizing Disruption: Another key goal is to minimize the disruption to transportation and communication networks during floods, which is crucial for emergency responses and maintaining economic activities.

Outcome: Improved Resilience and Reduced Impact

1. Enhanced Transportation Network Resilience: Flood-resistant bridges and roads have significantly improved the resilience of transportation networks in flood-prone areas.
2. Economic Benefits: By reducing the damage and disruption caused by floods, these projects help in minimizing the economic impact associated with rebuilding and repair.
3. Social Benefits: Reliable infrastructure during floods is crucial for ensuring the safety and well-being of communities, as well as for effective emergency response and recovery efforts.
4. Long-Term Sustainability: These projects contribute to the long-term sustainability of infrastructure, reducing the need for frequent repairs and rebuilds.

Flood-resistant bridges and roads are key examples of how infrastructure can be adapted to meet the challenges posed by climate change. These projects not only enhance the resilience of transportation networks but also play a crucial role in safeguarding economies and communities from the impacts of floods. Investing in climate-resilient infrastructure is increasingly seen as a necessity rather than an option, given the rising frequency of extreme weather events.

Investment in Climate Technology Start-Ups

VC funds globally are increasingly investing in start-ups that focus on CleanTech, which encompasses a wide range of products and services aimed at reducing carbon emissions and enhancing environmental sustainability. Investments cover various sectors, including renewable energy, energy storage, CCS, smart grid technology, EVs, and energy efficiency solutions.

Location: Global Reach

1. Worldwide Scope: CleanTech start-ups attracting VC investments are located around the world, with significant activity in North America, Europe, Asia, and increasingly in emerging markets.
2. Silicon Valley and Beyond: While Silicon Valley remains a hub for tech start-ups, CleanTech ventures are also thriving in regions such as Europe (notably Scandinavia and Germany), China, and Israel.

Objective: Driving Climate-Change Innovation

1. Innovation in Climate Solutions: The primary objective is to foster innovation in technologies that directly address climate-change challenges.
2. Scaling Up Solutions: VC investment is crucial for scaling up promising technologies, moving them from the development stage to commercial viability.
3. Diversifying Clean Energy Portfolio: These investments aim to diversify the range of available clean energy technologies, ensuring a more robust approach to tackling climate change.

Outcome: Development of Scalable Climate Solutions

1. Advancements in Carbon Capture: VC investments have accelerated the development of innovative carbon-capture technologies, which are essential for reducing GHG emissions from industrial sources.

2. Renewable Energy Storage: Breakthroughs in energy storage technologies, such as advanced batteries, are crucial for the wider adoption of renewable energy sources such as solar and wind.

3. Enhanced Energy Efficiency: Start-ups have developed various technologies and solutions that significantly improve energy efficiency in buildings, transportation, and industry.

4. Economic Growth and Job Creation: The growth of CleanTech start-ups contributes to economic growth and job creation in the green technology sector.

5. Attracting Further Investments: Success stories in the CleanTech space attract further investments, creating a positive cycle of innovation and growth.

Investment in climate-tech start-ups through VC is a key element in driving forward the technological innovations needed to combat climate change. This trend not only fosters the development of new solutions but also contributes to building a sustainable and resilient global economy. VC investment in CleanTech not only involves high risks but also the potential for high rewards, both financially and in terms of environmental impact.

These case studies demonstrate a range of strategies for mitigating physical climate risks through investment. They encompass both direct interventions in at-risk areas and broader efforts to reduce the overall pace of climate change. As the effects of climate change become more pronounced, such investments are likely to play an increasingly crucial role in global efforts to adapt to and mitigate these changes.

Summary

This chapter delves into the realm of climate-conscious investing, showcasing a series of case studies that highlight the successful integration of environmental sustainability into investment portfolios. It emphasizes how green financing, impact investing, and strategies mitigate physical climate risks, drive positive environmental outcomes, and offer viable financial returns.

Success Stories in Green Financing examines instances where green bonds, sustainable loans, and other forms of green financing have been effectively utilized. The section demonstrates how these investment instruments have funded renewable energy projects, energy-efficient infrastructure, and low-carbon transport solutions. It highlights the growing market acceptance and demand for green financing solutions.

The section on "Impact Investing Driving Climate Action" explores case studies of impact investments that have directly contributed to climate action. This section showcases investments in companies focused on innovative climate solutions. It underscores the role of impact investing in bridging the gap between financial returns and environmental impact.

The section on "Investments Mitigating Physical Climate Risks" presents examples of investments aimed at reducing the impact of physical risks. The section covers a range of strategies, from coastal protection projects to climate-resilient infrastructure. It illustrates how these investments not only safeguard against climate risks but also offer long-term financial stability and growth. These case studies serve as compelling evidence that climate-conscious investing can lead to substantial environmental benefits while still achieving financial objectives.

CHAPTER 7

Evolving Regulatory Landscape

This chapter delves into the dynamic and increasingly complex world of environmental regulation, a critical aspect for financial-market participants, investees, and policy makers in the era of climate change. This chapter is structured to provide a comprehensive understanding of the key regulatory areas shaping the response to environmental challenges. This chapter begins by exploring the intricacies of disclosure requirements, emphasizing the importance of transparency and accountability in environmental reporting. Next, it delves into the mechanisms of carbon pricing and other climate policies, examining how economic tools are being employed to incentivize reductions in GHG emissions. The section on climate stress testing addresses the need for robust risk management strategies in the face of climatic uncertainties, highlighting the evolving practices in this area. This chapter aims to provide readers with a clear understanding of how regulatory landscapes are adapting and driving change in the face of global environmental challenges.

Disclosure Requirements

The intricacies of disclosure requirements in environmental reporting represent a pivotal aspect of contemporary corporate governance, reflecting an increasing global emphasis on sustainability and environmental stewardship. These requirements, while varying across jurisdictions and industries, share common goals: enhancing transparency and ensuring accountability in how organizations impact the environment. Disclosure requirements often mandate that companies and investments report on a range of environmental metrics, including GHG emissions, energy usage, waste management, and water consumption.

The depth and breadth of these reports are critical to asset owners, as they provide a comprehensive view of a company's environmental footprint and how companies are positioned in the face of climate-related challenges and opportunities for assessing the sustainability and long-term viability of investments. Transparent disclosures boost market confidence, informing policymaking and advocacy.

Transparent reporting also benefits investees. It helps them identify and manage risks, potentially averting future crises or regulatory penalties. They can build stronger trust with consumers and the public, enhancing their brand reputation. Effective disclosure requirements also encourage investee companies to adopt more sustainable practices.

Mandatory climate-risk disclosures represent a significant step toward a more transparent and resilient financial system. The global initiatives for CSR have had important roles in leveraging companies to become more actively involved in environment-related disclosure, in which climate-risk reporting is central to evaluating whether and to what extent a company and its operations are friendly to the environment.

On the other hand, climate-conscious asset owners' requirements and company disclosures suffer from a lack of standardization (Dye et al. 2021). With the emergence of various reporting frameworks like the GRI, Sustainability Accounting Standards Board (SASB), and TCFD, there is a growing push toward standardization. This ensures that disclosures are comparable across companies and industries, facilitating easier analysis and decision making.

Task Force on Climate-Related Financial Disclosures

Along with the growth of the UN's PRI in 2005, one of the most recent global initiatives that has been formed is the TCFD, which has considered the climate-related financial-disclosure recommendations of G20 finance ministers. The TCFD sets out recommendations for companies to disclose climate-related financial information, which are structured around four thematic areas: (i) governance, (ii) strategy, (iii) risk management, and (iv) metrics and targets.

An increasing number of countries and organizations are adopting the TCFD recommendations, either on a voluntary or mandatory basis.

European financial institutions have been leading the way in requiring companies to define their climate risk, set targets, measure performance, show improvement, and connect to strategy (Dye et al. 2021).

Sustainable Finance Disclosure Regulation

The Sustainable Finance Disclosure Regulation (SFDR) requires financial-market participants in the EU to disclose how they integrate sustainability risks in their investment decisions and the adverse impacts of their investments on sustainability factors. The SFDR is part of the EU's action plan on sustainable finance. Article 6, 8, and 9 funds are the three classifications that are applied to all investment products sold within the EU under the SFDR, in effect since 2022. They compel asset managers to reveal the differing levels of sustainability integration that an investment strategy contains.

Article 6

Article 6 covers funds that do not integrate any kind of sustainability into the investment process. While these will be allowed to continue to be sold in the EU, provided they are clearly labeled as nonsustainable, they may face considerable marketing difficulties when matched against more sustainable funds.

Article 8

Article 8 covers "light green" investment products that promote, among other characteristics, environmental or social characteristics, or a combination of those characteristics, provided that the companies in which the investments are made follow good governance practices.

Article 9

Article 9 covers investment products that are "dark green" or have sustainable investment as its objective and an index has been designated as a reference benchmark.

The reliability of environmental reporting is paramount. This often necessitates third-party verification or auditing to ensure the accuracy and honesty of the disclosed information, thereby bolstering stakeholder trust. Tröger and Steuer (2021) studied the design features of disclosure regulations and found that transparency obligations stipulated in green finance regulation could be categorized as either compelling the standardized disclosure of raw data, or providing quality labels that signal desirable green characteristics of investment products based on a uniform methodology. Both categories of transparency requirements can be imposed at activity, issuer, and portfolio level.

The European Commission has published the Regulatory Technical Standards (RTS) under the SFDR. The RTS complement the provisions of SFDR applying from March 10, 2021, by providing detailed guidance on disclosures relating to principal adverse impacts on sustainability factors at the financial-market participants' level and precontractual, periodic, and website disclosures of Article 8 and Article 9 products. The RTS are composed of the RTS text and five separate annexes that contain the standardized disclosure templates. The RTS text (and annexes 1, 2, 3, 4, 5) specify the exact content, methodology, and presentation of the information to be disclosed with the aim to improve the quality and comparability of reporting, as well as to address greenwashing.

EU Taxonomy for Sustainable Activities

The EU taxonomy for sustainable activities is a classification system established by the EU to determine whether an economic activity is environmentally sustainable. It aims to provide clarity on which investments are sustainable, helping to prevent greenwashing. Policy makers see it as vital in steering the private sector participating in the funding of the *European Green Deal* (EGD) (Sikora, 2021).

The EU taxonomy sets performance thresholds for economic activities that make a substantive contribution to one of six environmental objectives:

1. Climate-change mitigation
2. Climate-change adaptation

3. Sustainable and protection of water and marine resources
4. Transition to a circular economy
5. Pollution prevention and control
6. Protection and restoration of biodiversity and ecosystems

The elements of the EU taxonomy screening include (i) substantially contribute to at least one of the six environmental objectives as defined in the regulation; (ii) do no significant harm to any of the other five environmental objectives as defined in the proposed regulation; and (iii) comply with minimum safeguards.

Other Developments

- The U.S. Securities and Exchange Commission (SEC) Proposals in the United States: The SEC has been considering rules to enhance and standardize climate-related disclosures for asset owners. This includes requiring companies to disclose their GHG emissions and how climate risks affect their business.
- Global Reporting Standards: Efforts are underway to develop global standards for sustainability reporting. Organizations like the International Financial Reporting Standards Foundation are working on creating a global baseline of high-quality sustainability disclosure standards to meet the information needs of asset owners.
- National Regulations: Various countries are developing their own regulations and guidelines for climate-related disclosures, often building on frameworks like the TCFD.

While some disclosures are mandated by regulations, many companies engage in voluntary reporting to demonstrate CSR and appeal to climate-conscious asset owners. The balance between regulatory compliance and voluntary initiatives reflects a company's commitment to environmental stewardship beyond mere legal obligations. Many countries are moving toward mandatory disclosure of climate-related risks by companies.

Meanwhile, large asset owners are driving CSR performance and demanding more comprehensive and standardized climate-related disclosures, especially long-term-oriented asset owners, as they are more inclined to affect CSR engagement through improving businesses' information transparency, internal control, and making more site visits (Xiong et al. 2022). This is driving regulatory changes and influencing corporate reporting practices.

Asset-owner-led market discipline can benefit from mandatory transparency requirements and their rigid (public) enforcement, because these requirements prevent an underproduction of standardized high-quality information. Based on the data on Chinese-listed companies during 2010 to 2018, Xiong et al. (2023) found that this positive relationship was more profound for state-owned enterprises, politically connected companies, and companies with low financial constraint.

Using the impact metric of the amount invested into securities, bonds, and stocks, issued by fossil-fuel companies, Mésonnier and Nguyen (2020) investigated the real effects of mandatory climate-related disclosure by financial institutions on the funding of carbon-intensive industries. A French law, which came into force in January 2016 in the aftermath of the Paris Agreement on climate change, was unique in Europe at that time, and it requires institutional asset owners (e.g., insurance companies, pension funds), and asset-management companies, but not banks, to report annually on both their climate-related exposure and climate-change mitigation policy. Mésonnier and Nguyen compared the portfolio choices of French institutional asset owners with those of French banks and financial institutions located in other countries, and evidenced that French asset owners, subject to the new disclosure requirements, curtailed their financing of fossil-energy companies compared to other asset owners in the euro area. Dye et al. (2021) argued that industry failure to respond to evolving disclosure requirements can lead to divestment, and contended that oil and gas companies that do not acknowledge climate risk and outline energy-transition strategies tied to their business models and reputations potentially sacrifice access to capital.

Sanderson et al. (2019) presented a stepwise blueprint on climate-risk assessment and financial disclosures that support companies on reorienting capital flows toward more sustainable investments and with their disclosure process to foster transparency and long-termism in financial and economic activity in line with the action plan on sustainable finance adopted by the European Commission in March 2018 to achieve sustainable and inclusive growth.

Popescu et al. (2021) argued that given the need to anchor sustainability assessments in the reality, the compatibility of investment products with science-based targets for sustainable development should become a central element of reporting requirements. Horan et al. (2022) recommended an issuer reporting framework that supports portfolio reporting and evaluation as well as an ESG product template that focuses on nonfinancial investment objectives, process elements, and measurable outcomes.

Carbon Pricing

Government support moderates significantly among investment strategies, financial knowledge, and organizational profitability (Yang and Liu, 2022). Many countries have implemented national climate policies to accomplish pledged NDCs and to contribute to the temperature objectives of the Paris Agreement on climate change.

Carbon pricing has emerged as a pivotal tool for countries aiming to reduce GHG emissions in line with global climate goals. Carbon pricing, in the shape of *carbon taxes* and *cap-and-trade* schemes, is often seen as the main, or essential climate policy instrument, based on theoretical expectations that this would promote innovation and diffusion of the new technologies necessary for full decarbonization. By assigning a cost to the emission of CO_2 and other GHGs, these economic tools aim to internalize the cost of carbon emissions, incentivizing companies and consumers to reduce their carbon footprint.

Many regions and countries have begun implementing or are considering carbon pricing mechanisms, such as carbon taxes or cap-and-trade systems, including the EU, Canada, and parts of the United States. Many regions are also either implementing new systems or expanding existing ones. In 2021, over 40 percent of GHG emissions were covered by carbon prices, up from 32 percent in 2018, with average carbon prices from emissions trading systems (ETS) and carbon taxes more than doubling to reach €4 per ton of CO_2e over the same period (OECD, 2022).

Carbon pricing provide incentives, which radiate up and down supply chains and potentially across entire economies, delivering emissions reductions where they make sense. Carbon pricing can generate useful public revenue during the transition to the green economy, a period in which it may be particularly useful given the high level of public investment that will be required. When the resulting revenues are sensibly deployed, carbon pricing can be part of a system that is overall progressive, rather than regressive.

The evolving landscape of the carbon-pricing mechanisms plays a significant role in climate investing and has significant implications for carbon-intensive industries. This incentive to "retrofit the economy" can lead to investments, including in R&D that can spur economic growth, especially in periods of inadequate aggregate demand.

Studies have found that carbon pricing can have a huge influence on the development and growth of renewable energy and new technologies (Bento et al. 2021; Joshi and Dash, 2023). By putting a price on carbon emissions, governments can incentivize businesses to adopt cleaner technologies and practices. Joshi and Dash (2023) found that a carbon price of US$40 per ton of CO_2 would lead to a threefold increase in investment in clean energy technologies. On the other hand, carbon prices alone will not be enough. Hepburn et al. (2020) suggested that implicit carbon prices could be designed to be inversely correlated to international oil prices, smoothing out prices faced by consumers.

Countries adapt their emission-reduction strategies to their specific circumstances, with some relying on carbon pricing more than others (OECD, 2022). Carbon taxes and cap-and-trade systems are two primary market-based mechanisms used by governments and regulatory bodies to reduce GHG emissions and combat climate change. Both systems aim to reduce emissions efficiently by providing economic incentives, encouraging businesses to reduce their carbon footprint.

Carbon Tax

A carbon tax directly sets a price on carbon by levying a fee on the production, distribution, or use of fossil fuels based on their carbon content. The tax is typically set per ton of CO_2 emitted. This tax incentivizes companies to reduce emissions to save costs. Carbon taxes provide predictable costs for carbon emissions, making it administratively easier for businesses to implement and invest in reducing emissions.

The revenue generated from carbon taxes can be used by governments for various purposes, including funding renewable energy projects, lowering or offsetting other taxes (revenue-neutral approach), and supporting social programs. Several countries, including Canada, Sweden, and Switzerland, have implemented carbon taxes. The rate of the tax and how it is implemented varies by jurisdiction.

While different forms of environmental taxation can discourage environmentally harmful activities and generate revenue that can be used for sustainability initiatives, a carbon tax raises price levels, thereby lowering the real wage, further decreasing the incentive to work and exacerbating the existing distortions in the labor market (McKibbin et al. 2017). This "tax interaction effect" can be potentially quite large, suggesting the benefits of using the carbon tax revenue to reduce other tax rates may be significant.

Cap-and-Trade

Cap-and-trade systems set a cap on the total amount of GHG emissions allowed. Within this cap, companies receive or buy emission allowances that they can trade with each other. The cap is gradually lowered over time, reducing the total emissions. Companies that can reduce their emissions at a lower cost can sell their excess allowances to those facing higher reduction costs, incentivizing cost-effective emission reductions.

In cap-and-trade systems, the market determines the carbon price, leading to an efficient allocation of resources. Companies with lower abatement costs can profit from selling allowances, while those with higher costs have a financial incentive to innovate. On the other hand, this mechanism can lead to price volatility, which can be challenging for businesses planning long-term investments. The EU ETS is the largest multicountry, multisector GHG ETS in the world.

Gugler et al. (2021) quantified the effectiveness of climate policies in the form of pricing carbon and subsidizing renewable energies for

Germany's and the United Kingdom's power sectors. While Germany relies on heavy subsidies for renewables but on a weak price for carbon certificates (EU Allowances [EUA]) from the EU ETS, its emissions hardly declined. To underpin the low EUA price, the United Kingdom introduced a unilateral tax on power sector emissions, the Carbon Price Support, and within only five years, carbon emissions declined by 55 percent. The results of Gugler et al. (2021) demonstrate that in the power sector, even a modest carbon price ($\sim$€30/t CO_2) can induce significant abatement at low costs within a short period as long as "cleaner" gas plants exist to replace "dirty" coal plants. Based on these results, Gugler et al. argued that carbon pricing is superior to subsidizing wind or solar power in Germany and the United Kingdom.

The impact of carbon taxes and cap-and-trade systems extends beyond environmental policy, influencing economic decisions, corporate strategies, and investment trends worldwide. The choice between carbon taxes and cap-and-trade systems often depends on political, economic, and environmental considerations specific to each region. Some systems combine elements of both, like the linkage between California's cap-and-trade system and Quebec's. A cap-and-trade system might also include a price floor or ceiling to prevent the price of allowances from going too low or too high. Bento et al. (2021) evaluated how national carbon pricing policies influenced company-level internal carbon pricing and corporate-emission targets, and found that company-level internal carbon prices were significantly higher in countries explicitly pricing carbon through tax and/or cap-and-trade programs.

Other Climate Policies

In addition to carbon-pricing mechanisms, governments around the world have implemented a variety of other climate policies to combat climate change and reduce GHG emissions. These policies are diverse and cater to different aspects of environmental protection and sustainable development. Renewable energy mandates, energy efficiency standards, and subsidies for green technology are key policy tools used by governments worldwide to promote sustainable energy practices along with conservation strategies and technological innovations.

Renewable Energy Mandates

Renewable energy mandates are regulations that require a certain percentage of a country's energy production or consumption to come from renewable sources. Examples include the Renewable Portfolio Standards in the United States where states set targets for the proportion of electricity that must come from renewable sources, and Feed-in Tariffs (FiTs) where renewable energy producers are guaranteed a certain price for the energy they feed into the grid. FiTs have been widely applied to encourage the application of renewable energy, which is demonstrated successfully in different countries (Lu et al. 2020).

Renewable energy targets could have a huge influence on renewable energy industry growth and the development of new technologies (Joshi and Dash, 2023). Based on a public policy database and a multimodel scenario analysis, Roelfsema et al. (2020) showed that implementation of the existing renewable energy mandates policies leaves a median emission gap of 22.4 to 28.2 $GtCO_2eq$ by 2030 with the optimal pathways to implement the well below 2°C and 1.5°C Paris Agreement goals. The results suggest that if NDCs would be fully implemented, this gap would be reduced by a third. Roelfsema et al. also indicated that countries would need to accelerate the implementation of policies for renewable technologies, especially EM countries and fossil-fuel-dependent countries.

Hille et al. (2020) showed a consistently positive impact of FiTs and does not detect technology-specific differences in the effectiveness of this policy instrument. Painuly and Wohlgemuth (2021) illustrated that renewable energy targets, promotion measures, and support mechanisms such as FiTs, auction, renewable energy certificates, renewable portfolio standards, and net metering could address the barriers that renewables face to achieve their full potential.

Energy Efficiency Standards

Energy efficiency standards are designed to reduce energy consumption and increase efficiency in various sectors, which can apply to:

1. Buildings: Setting requirements for insulation, heating, and cooling systems to reduce energy use.

2. Appliances and Electronics: Mandating that products such as refrigerators, air conditioners, and televisions meet certain energy efficiency criteria.

3. Industrial Processes: Encouraging or requiring industries to adopt more energy-efficient technologies and practices.

Financial incentives for green buildings are a major component of energy policy planning and play a vital role in the promotion of sustainable development and carbon-mitigation strategies. Lu et al. (2020) presented a review on sustainable energy policy for promotion of renewable energy by introducing the development history of energy policy in five countries: the United States, United Kingdom, Germany, Denmark, and China. The results indicate that energy efficiency standard is one of the most popular strategies for building energy saving, which is dynamic and renewed based on the current available technologies. Lu et al. suggested that building energy performance certification schemes be enhanced in terms of reliable database system and information transparency to pave the way for future net-zero energy building and smart cities.

Rana et al. (2021) found that financial incentives for buildings in Canada can be distributed into tax, loans, grants, and rebates. Among these, rebates from utility providers are the most common and are administered in all provinces. In addition to these, special incentives are available for three end users, including low-income, aboriginal people, landlords and tenants, and for three types of buildings, including heritage, nonprofit, and energy rated. By contrast, financial incentives are offered in three regulatory regimes—federal, provincial, and municipal. Alberta, British Columbia, Ontario, and Quebec are leading in green-building efforts.

Subsidies for Green Technology

Subsidies are part of the policy landscape—governments provide financial support and incentives to encourage the development and adoption of renewable energy technologies. Painuly and Wohlgemuth (2021) showed that fiscal incentives and government support mechanisms could address the barriers that renewables face to achieve their full potential. Subsidies for green technology can take various forms:

1. Tax Credits and Rebates: For individuals and businesses that install renewable energy systems such as solar panels or wind turbines. Incentives are also being provided for the adoption of EVs and the development of hydrogen fuel cell technologies. These incentives can include tax rebates, lower registration fees, and grants.
2. R&D Grants and Support: Governments are funding R&D in green technologies. This support can come in the form of direct funding for research projects, tax incentives for R&D activities, or PPPs to develop new technologies. Some jurisdictions are creating "regulatory sandboxes" to allow innovators to test new green technologies in a controlled environment without the usual regulatory constraints. This approach helps in understanding the implications of new technologies before they are introduced on a larger scale.
3. Low-Interest Loans: For projects related to renewable energy or energy efficiency.

Using policy and patent data for a large sample of 194 countries and territories, Hille et al. (2020) found that more comprehensive portfolios of renewable energy support policies increase patenting in solar- and wind-power-related technologies. This inducement effect is strongest for public Research, Development, and Demonstration (RD&D) programs, targets, and fiscal incentives. The results also reveal the positive effect on patenting activity increases significantly over time, with an increase in duration of the implemented RD&D programs and targets. The findings of Maestre-Andrés et al. (2019) revealed that many people prefer using revenues for environmental projects of various kinds. Maestre-Andrés et al. suggested increasing policy acceptability by combining the redistribution of revenue to vulnerable groups with the funding for renewable energy and other environmental projects.

These climate policies not only aim to reduce GHG emissions and dependency on fossil fuels but also stimulate economic growth in the green technology sector. They can create jobs, drive innovation, and make renewable energy more competitive compared to traditional energy sources. However, the effectiveness of these policies can vary based on their design, implementation, and the specific energy profile of a country or region.

Drawing on a dataset of policy reports, Meckling and Allan (2020) showed how economic ideas influenced climate policy advice by major international organizations, including the OECD and the World Bank Group, from 1990 to 2017. Meckling and Allan identified a major transformation from a neoclassical paradigm to a diversified policy discourse, suggesting that climate policy has entered a postparadigmatic period. The diversification of ideas broadened policy advice from market-based policy to green industrial policy, including deployment subsidies and regulation.

By putting the EGD in a boarder perspective of evolving, constitutional rationale of environmental protection in the EU legal order, Sikora (2021) suggested that the challenge ahead of the EU is how to transform the ambitious climate agenda into efficient legal and economic instruments "in a fair way, leaving no one behind." Sikora argued that EGD is a great opportunity, but in order to turn it into a success, it must be strongly anchored in the concepts pertaining to the constitutional framework of the EU legal order, in particular, the concepts of solidarity, sustainable development, and high level of environmental protection.

In the context of the U.S. subsidies for clean energy deployment, which has become a major component of federal energy and climate policy, Newell et al. (2019) suggested upfront subsidies provide more bang-for-the buck than subsidies spread into the future, other things equal. Popp (2020) argued that while state-level policies could promote clean-energy innovation, it is overall market size that matters most.

Climate Stress Testing

The increasing regulatory focus on climate risk disclosure, exemplified by frameworks like the TCFD, has elevated the importance of climate stress testing as a vital component of compliance. *Climate stress testing* involves simulating a range of climate-related scenarios, including both physical risks and transition risks. Over the last years, central banks and financial regulators, particularly in Europe, North America, and parts of Asia, are beginning to incorporate climate stress tests into their regulatory frameworks. For instance, the BoE and the ECB have initiated climate stress tests for banks and insurers. The primary goal is to evaluate how financial institutions would perform under various climate-related scenarios.

Central banks and financial supervisors have also started to design scenarios for climate stress tests to assess how vulnerable the financial system is to climate change. Organizations such as the Network for Greening the Financial System are working to promote best practices and consistency in climate risk management and stress testing across countries.

Regulators have recommended asset owners and asset managers to assess their exposure to climate-related financial risks. Regulators are also increasingly expecting financial institutions to disclose the results of their climate stress tests, thereby improving transparency and informing asset owners, policy makers, regulators, and other stakeholders. The outcomes of the climate stress tests can help them understand the systemic implications of climate risks and to design appropriate regulatory responses. As methodologies improve and data availability increases, climate stress testing is expected to become more sophisticated and integral to financial risk management and regulatory processes.

Summary

This chapter delves into the dynamic and increasingly pivotal role of regulatory frameworks in shaping climate-conscious investment portfolios. It underscores the multifaceted nature of these regulations, highlighting four key areas: disclosure requirements, carbon pricing, other climate policies, and climate stress testing.

The chapter begins by exploring the evolving disclosure requirements, emphasizing their critical role in providing transparency and accountability in climate-conscious investing. It discusses frameworks, such as the TCFD, the SFDR, and the EU taxonomy for sustainable activities. These evolving standards are reshaping how companies and financial asset-management companies report their environmental impact and how asset owners assess and manage climate-related risks in their portfolios.

Next, the chapter delves into the various climate policies and regulations implemented globally to mitigate climate change. A key focus is on carbon-pricing mechanisms, such as carbon taxes and cap-and-trade systems, which aim to reduce GHG emissions by assigning a cost to carbon emissions, thereby incentivizing lower emissions. The section also explores other climate policies, including renewable energy mandates, energy efficiency standards, and subsidies for green technology. These policies are designed to complement carbon pricing by directly promoting sustainable practices and technologies. The effectiveness, challenges, and economic impacts of these policies are discussed.

Finally, this chapter addresses the emerging practice of climate stress testing within the financial sector. It outlines how regulators and financial institutions are increasingly assessing the resilience of portfolios to climate-related risks. This section underscores the importance of these tests in understanding potential future losses under various climate scenarios and informs asset owners about the long-term sustainability and viability of their investments. Overall, this chapter provides a comprehensive overview of the evolving regulatory landscape for climate-conscious investing, illustrating how these regulations are integral in guiding investment strategies toward a more sustainable and environmentally responsible future.

CHAPTER 8

The Future of Climate-Conscious Investing

This chapter embarks on a forward-looking journey through the evolving landscape of investment, where the urgency of climate change is reshaping the very foundations of investment decision making. This chapter delves into the emerging trends in climate-conscious investing, a movement gaining unprecedented momentum as asset owners increasingly recognize the critical intersection between environmental stewardship and economic viability. This chapter examines the cutting-edge technological innovations that are not only influencing investment strategies but also driving the transition toward a more sustainable global economy.

A critical focus will be placed on the pivotal role that asset owners play in achieving the ambitious goals set forth in the Paris Agreement, highlighting the synergy between financial returns and environmental stewardship. As we navigate through these transformative themes, the chapter will culminate in a comprehensive discussion on "The Road Ahead," offering insights into the challenges and opportunities that lie in the future of climate-conscious investing. This chapter aims to provide a nuanced understanding of how investment practices are adapting in the face of global climate imperatives, and what this means for the future of finance and our planet.

Emerging Trends in Climate-Conscious Investing

The emerging trends in climate-conscious investing reflect a paradigm shift in the world of finance, where environmental stewardship is increasingly viewed as integral to economic viability. This shift reflects a growing recognition of the impact of climate change on the economy and the role of investment in addressing environmental challenges. This movement is characterized by several key trends.

Net-Zero Commitments

Many asset managers are making commitments to align their portfolios with net-zero emissions targets by a specific date, in line with the goals of the Paris Agreement. For instance, many are pledging to achieve net-zero GHG emissions in their investment portfolios by 2050, aligning with the Paris Agreement's goal to limit global warming to well below 2°C above preindustrial levels.

To meet these commitments, asset managers are reassessing and rebalancing their portfolios. This involves divesting from fossil fuels and other high-emission sectors and increasing investments in renewable energy and other sustainable industries. The findings of Mbanyele (2022) suggest that companies curtail their investment expenditure to suboptimal levels if exposed to severe climate-change shocks. Aligning portfolios with net-zero targets also involves managing the financial risk as a result of climate change more effectively.

Investees and financial institutions are making their net-zero commitments public and are increasingly transparent about their progress. This public commitment is crucial for establishing a clear stance on climate action. To maintain credibility, investees and financial institutions are also providing regular updates on their progress. These reports often include milestones achieved, challenges faced, and adjustments to strategies, offering a transparent view of their journey toward net zero.

Many institutions are aligning their reporting with global standards and frameworks, such as the TCFD and the *Science-Based Targets initiative (SBTi)*. This ensures consistency and comparability of data across the industry. To enhance credibility, many institutions are seeking verification and audits from independent third parties. This external validation ensures that their disclosures are accurate and in line with best practices. The risk assessments and scenario analyses that conducted by different organizations are often shared publicly, highlighting their proactive approach to managing climate risks.

Focus on Scope 3 Emissions

Scope 3 emissions are becoming a critical component in investment decisions, recognizing that a company's carbon footprint extends beyond its direct operations. This includes emissions from sources such as purchased goods and services, transportation and distribution, and the use of sold products. This focus requires more detailed data collection and analysis across the supply chain, leading to greater transparency in environmental reporting.

The focus on Scope 3 emissions reflects a more comprehensive understanding of a company's overall carbon footprint and how it manages its supply chains. Companies with sustainable supply chain practices are viewed more favorably. Understanding Scope 3 emissions also helps asset owners identify potential risks and liabilities that may not be apparent from only considering direct emissions. This includes risks related to regulatory changes, reputational damage, and shifts in consumer preferences.

Calculating and managing the full scope of emissions, particularly Scope 3, is challenging because it involves activities not directly controlled by the company and due to complex and opaque supply chains. Le Guenedal and Roncalli (2022) assessed the different climate-risk metrics, including carbon footprint, carbon transition pathway, and physical risks. The analysis shows that portfolio decarbonization is more difficult when including Scope 3 carbon emissions. This is primarily due to that optimizing using the sum of Scope 1, 2, and 3 emissions leads to a portfolio with more tracking-error risk than using direct plus first-tier indirect carbon emissions.

The result of Le Guenedal and Roncalli (2022) also indicates that portfolio alignment is more complex than portfolio decarbonization. As aligning portfolios with Scope 3 is becoming the standard approach to climate-conscious portfolio construction, the impact on portfolio management may be substantial, and the divergence between carbon investing and traditional investing will increase. The focus on Scope 3 emissions aligns with global standards and frameworks such as the GHG Protocol and the SBTi. A GHG emissions inventory guide, which is derived from the GHG Protocol, can be found in Appendix C.

Integration of Climate Science

Climate science is becoming a crucial component of climate-conscious investment analysis. It provides a more robust framework for evaluating how companies are prepared for and responding to climate-related issues. Integrating climate science into investment analyses is crucial for aligning investment strategies with the broader goal of sustainable development and climate resilience.

Asset managers are incorporating climate science, scientific data, and climate modeling into their investment analyses to better understand the impacts of climate change on portfolios, conduct more sophisticated risk assessments, and mitigate the impacts. This involves analyzing how different climate scenarios, such as increased frequency of extreme weather events or gradual changes in climate patterns, could impact investments, and stress testing based on climate models. For investments in real estate and infrastructure, climate modeling is used to assess risks such as sea-level rise, extreme weather events, and changing weather patterns.

Asset managers are using insights from climate science to communicate more effectively with asset owners about the climate risks and opportunities in their portfolios. There is a growing trend of collaboration between financial institutions and the scientific community. This partnership helps in translating complex climate data into actionable financial insights.

Growth of Sustainable Finance and Green Funds

There is a growing demand among asset owners for mutual funds, ETFs, and other investment vehicles that focus on companies with strong sustainable practices. The availability of sustainable index funds and ETFs is growing, providing asset owners with easy access to diversified, climate-conscious portfolios.

Some prominent green and sustainable ETFs include:

1. iShares Global Clean Energy ETF (ICLN): Tracks an index composed of global companies in the clean energy sector, including solar, wind, and other renewable sources.
2. Invesco Solar ETF (TAN): Focused specifically on the solar industry, this ETF tracks companies involved in various aspects of solar energy.
3. First Trust Global Wind Energy ETF (FAN): Focuses on the wind energy sector, including both manufacturers of wind energy equipment and wind farm operators.

4. VanEck Vectors Environmental Services ETF (EVX): Tracks companies involved in environmental services, including waste management and pollution control.

5. SPDR S&P 500 Fossil-Fuel Reserves Free ETF (SPYX): Offers exposure to the S&P 500 while excluding companies that own fossil-fuel reserves.

Some notable sustainable mutual funds include:

1. Parnassus Core Equity Fund (PRBLX): A sustainable mutual fund focusing on companies with long-term competitive advantages and ethical practices.

2. Teachers Insurance and Annuity Association of America (TIAA)-College Retirement Equities Fund (CREF) Social Choice Equity Fund (TICRX): Seeks long-term capital growth by investing in a diversified portfolio of stocks that meet certain ESG criteria.

3. Pax Global Environmental Markets Fund (PGRNX): Invests in companies around the world that are involved in environmental markets and sustainable economies.

4. Calvert Equity Fund (CSIEX): Focuses on companies that demonstrate positive ESG performance relative to their peers.

5. Domini Impact Equity Fund (DSEFX): Aims to create long-term value with a portfolio of companies that meet rigorous standards of social and environmental performance.

The issuance of green bonds and other sustainable debt is also on the rise. New investment products and solutions are being developed to support climate-conscious investing, such as sustainability-linked loans, which have interest rates tied to sustainability performance targets, and insurance products related to climate risks.

Evolving Renewable Energy Investments

Renewable energy investments are continuously evolving as new trends and innovations emerge to drive the transition to clean energy. Some notable emerging trends and innovations in renewable energy investments

include floating solar power, offshore wind power, green hydrogen, electrification of transportation, community-based renewable energy, hybrid
renewable energy systems, and corporate renewable power purchase
agreements (PPAs).

1. Floating Solar Power: Floating solar PV installations are gaining
   momentum as a promising solution for maximizing renewable
   energy generation. These solar PV systems are installed on water
   bodies such as reservoirs, lakes, and ponds. Investing in floating
   solar projects offers advantages such as land conservation, increased
   energy output due to the cooling effect of water, and potential
   synergies with hydropower facilities.

2. Offshore Wind Power: Offshore wind energy is rapidly expanding as
   technological advancements enable the development of wind farms
   in deeper waters. Investing in offshore-wind projects presents significant opportunities due to the vast wind resources available in offshore areas. Technological innovations in floating wind turbines and
   foundation designs are further enhancing the potential for offshore
   wind investments.

3. Green Hydrogen: Produced through electrolysis powered by renewable energy, green hydrogen is gaining attention as a versatile and car-
   bon-free energy carrier. Investments in green hydrogen production
   facilities and infrastructure are growing. This includes investments
   in electrolyzer manufacturers, hydrogen storage, and transportation
   systems and applications. Hydrogen, and to a certain extent, synthetic carbon-neutral hydrocarbons, are critical elements among the
   disruptive options (Capros et al. 2019).

4. Electrification of Transportation: The electrification of transportation is a major trend shaping renewable energy investments. Investments in EV manufacturing, charging infrastructure, and related
   technologies offer significant potential. Investing in EV battery
   technologies, including advancements in battery chemistry and
   manufacturing processes, also supports the growth of the electric
   transportation sector.

5. Community-Based Renewable Energy: Community-based renewable energy projects, such as community solar and wind coopera-

tives, are becoming popular. These initiatives allow community members to collectively invest in and benefit from renewable energy installations. Investing in community-based renewable energy projects can support local energy generation, community engagement, and decentralized energy systems.

6. Hybrid Renewable Energy Systems: Hybrid renewable energy systems combine different renewable energy sources to create integrated power systems. Investments in hybrid renewable energy projects and technologies offer opportunities to optimize energy generation, increase system reliability, and enhance grid integration of renewables.

7. Corporate Renewable PPAs: Corporate renewable PPAs involve long-term contracts between renewable energy developers and corporations to purchase renewable energy. This trend allows companies to meet their sustainability goals, secure a long-term renewable energy supply, and support the development of new renewable energy projects. Investments in corporate PPAs provide stable revenue streams and support the expansion of renewable energy generation.

Innovative Water and Waste Management

Water- and waste-management investments are continuously evolving as new trends and innovations emerge to address sustainability challenges. Some notable emerging trends and innovations in water- and waste-management investments include smart water management, water recycling and reuse, and circular economy initiatives.

1. Smart Water Management: The integration of IoT devices, sensors, and data analytics is driving the development of smart water management systems. These systems monitor water usage, detect leaks, optimize irrigation, and enable real-time data analysis for efficient water management. Investments in smart water technologies offer opportunities to improve water conservation, enhance infrastructure efficiency, and reduce operational costs.

2. Water Recycling and Reuse: Water recycling and reuse projects play a crucial role in addressing water scarcity and ensuring sustainable

water management. Investments in wastewater reuse infrastructure, including treated wastewater for industrial processes, irrigation, or nonpotable uses, offer opportunities to support water conservation and reduce reliance on freshwater sources.

3. Circular Economy Initiatives: Circular economy principles are being applied to water and waste management, aiming to minimize waste, maximize resource recovery, and reduce environmental impact. Investments in circular economy initiatives, such as extended producer responsibility programs, eco-industrial parks, and waste management start-ups with circular economy business models, align with sustainable resource management goals.

Innovations in Sustainable Agriculture

Sustainable agriculture and food investments are driven by evolving trends and innovations that promote environmentally friendly and socially responsible practices in the food system. Some notable emerging trends and innovations in sustainable agriculture and food investments include indoor vertical farming, regenerative agriculture, alternative protein sources, sustainable aquaculture, farm-to-consumer traceability, sustainable supply chain management, and urban farming and rooftop gardens.

1. Indoor Vertical Farming: Indoor vertical farming, where crops are grown in stacked layers using artificial lighting and controlled environments, is gaining traction. Investments in indoor vertical farming operations or companies specializing in vertical farming technologies can enable year-round, climate-independent food production, reduce water usage, and minimize land requirements.

2. Regenerative Agriculture: Regenerative agriculture focuses on soil health, biodiversity, and carbon sequestration. Investments in regenerative agriculture practices, such as cover cropping, crop rotation, and holistic grazing management, contribute to soil regeneration, enhanced ecosystem services, and climate-change mitigation.

3. Alternative Protein Sources: Investments in alternative protein sources are driven by the increasing demand for sustainable and plant-based

protein options. Startups focusing on plant-based proteins, cultured meat (cellular agriculture), and insect-based proteins offer investment opportunities aligned with the growing shift toward more sustainable and ethical protein production.

4. Sustainable Aquaculture: Sustainable aquaculture practices that minimize environmental impact and prioritize animal welfare are gaining momentum. Investments in sustainable aquaculture ventures, such as land-based RAS or offshore aquaculture operations, support responsible fish farming and promote sustainable seafood production.

5. Farm-to-Consumer Traceability: Consumer demand for transparency and traceability in the food supply chain is driving investments in technologies that enable farm-to-consumer traceability. Blockchain-based platforms, IoT sensors, and data analytics solutions can provide real-time visibility into food production, processing, and distribution, enhancing food safety and sustainability.

6. Sustainable Supply Chain Management: Investments in sustainable supply chain management initiatives focus on promoting responsible sourcing, fair trade practices, and reducing environmental impacts. Companies involved in sustainable sourcing, ethical certifications, supply chain traceability, and impact measurement offer investment prospects aligned with sustainability goals.

7. Urban Farming and Rooftop Gardens: Urban farming and rooftop gardens leverage underutilized urban spaces to grow fresh produce locally. Investments in urban farming start-ups or infrastructure projects can contribute to food security, reduce food miles, and provide opportunities for community engagement and education.

Trends in Green Buildings and Infrastructure

Emerging trends and innovations in green buildings and infrastructure investments are shaping the future of sustainable development. Some notable trends and innovations in this field include net-zero energy buildings, zero-carbon materials, biophilic design, circular economy practices, healthy building certifications, green data centers, resilient infrastructure, and prefabricated and modular construction.

1. Net-Zero Energy Buildings: Net-zero energy buildings are designed to produce as much energy as they consume over the course of a year. These buildings typically integrate energy-efficient design, on-site renewable energy generation, and energy storage systems. Investing in net-zero energy buildings or technologies that enable their implementation can contribute to the advancement of sustainable and self-sufficient building solutions.

2. Zero-Carbon Materials: The focus on reducing embodied carbon in building materials is gaining prominence. Innovations in manufacturing processes, such as carbon capture and utilization and the development of low-carbon cement alternatives, are emerging to address the carbon footprint of construction materials. Investments in companies developing zero-carbon or low-carbon building materials can support the reduction of embodied carbon in the construction industry.

3. Biophilic Design: Biophilic design incorporates natural elements and features into building design to improve occupant well-being and connection with nature. This can include the integration of green spaces, natural lighting, indoor plants, and water features. Investments in biophilic design solutions, green roofs, or vertical gardens can enhance the sustainability and livability of buildings.

4. Circular Economy Practices: Circular economy principles are being applied to the construction industry, focusing on resource efficiency, material reuse, and waste reduction. Investments in companies that specialize in construction waste recycling, modular construction, or deconstruction services can contribute to the circularity of building materials and the reduction of construction waste.

5. Healthy Building Certifications: Healthy building certifications, such as the WELL Building Standard or Fitwel, emphasize occupant health, wellness, and indoor environmental quality. Investments can be made in companies that provide healthy building certification services or in properties seeking these certifications, supporting the growing demand for health-focused buildings.

6. Green Data Centers: Data centers consume significant amounts of energy. Investing in green data centers that prioritize energy efficiency, renewable energy integration, and waste heat recovery

can reduce the environmental impact of the digital infrastructure sector.

7. Resilient Infrastructure: As resilience strategies become a prominent orthodoxy in city planning, resilient infrastructure is increasingly deployed to enhance protection from climate risks and impacts. Resilient infrastructure investments focus on adapting to climate-change impacts. Opportunities include investing in climate-resilient building materials, flood-resistant infrastructure, and renewable energy microgrids that can enhance the resilience of buildings and communities.

8. Prefabricated and Modular Construction: Prefabricated and modular construction methods offer benefits in terms of reduced waste, shortened construction timelines, and improved energy efficiency. Investments in companies specializing in prefabricated building components or modular construction solutions can support sustainable construction practices.

Emerging Climate Resilience and Adaptation Investments

Emerging trends and innovations in climate resilience and adaptation investments are driving the development of new approaches and solutions to address the challenges posed by climate change. Some notable trends and innovations in this field include nature-based solutions, social and community-based adaptation, urban heat island mitigation, climate adaptation in health systems, and climate education and awareness.

1. Nature-Based Solutions: Nature-based solutions involve harnessing the power of ecosystems to enhance climate resilience and adaptation. Examples include restoring wetlands, creating urban green spaces, implementing green infrastructure, and using natural coastal defenses. Investments in nature-based solutions can provide multiple benefits such as flood mitigation, carbon sequestration, and biodiversity conservation.

2. Social and Community-Based Adaptation: Recognizing the importance of local knowledge and community engagement, social and community-based adaptation approaches are gaining prominence.

These approaches involve empowering communities to develop adaptation strategies, implement resilience projects, and build social cohesion. Investments in community-driven adaptation initiatives, participatory planning processes, and capacity building programs can strengthen community resilience.

3. Urban Heat Island Mitigation: Urban heat islands are urban areas that experience significantly higher temperatures compared to surrounding rural areas due to human activities and the built environment. Investments in urban heat island mitigation measures, such as cool roofs, green roofs, and urban tree planting, can help reduce heat-related risks and improve urban climate resilience.

4. Climate Adaptation in Health Systems: Climate change poses risks to public health, and investments in climate adaptation within health systems are becoming more important. This includes investments in climate-resilient health care infrastructure, disease surveillance systems, and community health programs focused on addressing climate-related health risks. Collaborating with health care organizations or investing in climate-resilient health care projects can contribute to health system resilience.

5. Climate Education and Awareness: Building climate literacy and raising awareness about climate change and its impacts are critical for fostering resilience. Investments in climate education programs, public awareness campaigns, and digital platforms that provide climate information can enhance climate awareness and empower individuals and communities to take adaptive actions.

Technological Innovations Shaping
Future Investments

The cutting-edge technological innovations are playing a pivotal role in driving and shaping the future of climate-conscious investments. These technologies not only address current environmental challenges but also open up new avenues for sustainable growth and investment. Technology is also enabling more effective, efficient, and scalable solutions. The key innovations include renewable energy technologies, green transportation technologies, CCS, sustainable agriculture technologies, advanced water- and waste management, green-building technologies, and climate data analytics and AI.

Renewable Energy Technologies

Advances in renewable energy technologies, such as solar photovoltaics, wind turbines, and battery storage, are revolutionizing the energy sector. Innovations in efficiency, storage (e.g., advanced battery technologies), and grid integration are making renewable energy increasingly viable and cost-effective. Technological advancements in solar energy are also driving the development of next-generation solar technologies. Investments in innovative solar technologies, such as perovskite solar cells, tandem solar cells, and solar windows, can offer improved efficiency, flexibility, aesthetics compared to traditional solar PV, and lead to breakthroughs in the solar industry. In addition, the development of new materials and the application of nanotechnology are leading to more efficient solar panels, wind turbines, and batteries. These advancements are enhancing the performance and reducing the cost of renewable energy technologies.

Blockchain technology is also being explored in the renewable energy sector to facilitate *peer-to-peer (P2P) energy trading*, track renewable energy certificates, and enable transparent and secure transactions. Investments in energy blockchain platforms and projects can drive the decentralization of energy systems and democratize renewable energy trading.

Digital business practices positively contribute to reducing CO_2 emissions and promoting renewable energy, although the impact on final energy consumption varies across different indicators. Kwilinski et al. (2023) provided evidence that digital business has a significant negative effect on energy intensity, implying that increased digital business leads to decreased energy intensity. The findings also underscore the significance of integrating digital business practices to improve energy efficiency, lower energy intensity, and advance the adoption of renewable energy sources within the EU. Based on the findings, Kwilinski et al. argued that policy makers and businesses should prioritize the adoption of digital technologies and e-commerce strategies to facilitate sustainable energy transitions and accomplish environmental objectives.

Green Transportation Technologies

The automotive industry is undergoing a transformation with the rise of EVs and autonomous driving technology. Innovations in battery technology, charging infrastructure, and software for autonomous vehicles are driving investments in this sector. Low-carbon transportation investments are constantly evolving as new trends and innovations emerge to drive the transition to sustainable mobility. Some notable emerging trends and innovations in low-carbon transportation investments include electrification of heavy-duty vehicles, hydrogen fuel cell vehicles (FCVs), sustainable aviation solutions, mobility-as-a-service (MaaS), connected and autonomous vehicles (CAVs), micromobility solutions, vehicle-to-grid (V2G) technology, renewable energy-powered charging infrastructure, last-mile delivery innovations, and green hydrogen infrastructure.

1. Electrification of Heavy-Duty Vehicles: The electrification trend is expanding beyond passenger cars to heavy-duty vehicles such as trucks, buses, and commercial fleets. Investments in electric trucks and buses, charging infrastructure for larger vehicles, and battery technology advancements can contribute to reducing emissions in the transportation sector.

2. Hydrogen FCVs: Hydrogen FCVs are gaining attention as a zero-emission alternative to traditional internal combustion engine vehicles. Investments in hydrogen fuel cell technology, hydrogen infrastructure development, and hydrogen production methods can support the growth of FCVs and the establishment of a hydrogeneconomy for transportation.

3. Sustainable Aviation Solutions: The aviation sector is exploring various low-carbon solutions, including electric aircraft, biofuels, and sustainable aviation fuels (SAFs). Investments in sustainable aviation technology companies, biofuel producers, and SAF projects can help reduce GHG emissions from air travel and support the development of sustainable aviation alternatives.

4. MaaS: MaaS platforms integrate various transportation modes into a single service, allowing users to access different modes through a single app or platform. Investments in MaaS companies, digital

platforms, and technology providers can enhance transportation efficiency, encourage modal shifts, and reduce overall carbon footprint.

5. CAVs: CAV technologies have the potential to improve transportation efficiency and reduce emissions through optimized traffic flow, route optimization, and platooning. Investments in CAV technology, data analytics platforms, and infrastructure to support CAVs can contribute to low-carbon transportation solutions.

6. Micromobility Solutions: Micromobility options such as e-scooters and bike-sharing systems are gaining popularity as convenient and sustainable modes of transportation for short-distance travel. Investments in micromobility platforms, e-scooter and bike-sharing companies, and associated infrastructure can support sustainable urban mobility and reduce congestion.

7. V2G Technology: V2G technology enables EVs to act as mobile energy storage units that can supply electricity back to the grid during peak demand periods. Investments in V2G infrastructure, smart charging technologies, and energy management platforms can optimize energy usage, support renewable energy integration, and enhance grid stability.

8. Renewable Energy-Powered Charging Infrastructure: Investments in charging infrastructure powered by renewable energy sources, such as solar or wind, can enhance the sustainability of EV charging. This includes investing in renewable energy generation projects specifically for EV charging stations, as well as integrated renewable energy and charging infrastructure companies.

9. Last-Mile Delivery Innovations: Last-mile delivery is a critical aspect of the transportation sector that can benefit from low-carbon solutions. Investments in electric delivery vehicles, smart logistics platforms, and innovative last-mile delivery models can contribute to reducing emissions in the delivery sector and support sustainable urban logistics.

10. Green Hydrogen Infrastructure: Green hydrogen, produced from renewable sources through electrolysis, is gaining attention as an energy carrier for transportation. Investments in green hydrogen production facilities, hydrogen storage and transportation infrastructure, and hydrogen fueling stations can support the adoption of hydrogen-based low-carbon transportation solutions.

Energy Efficiency Solutions

Energy efficiency investments are continuously evolving as new trends and innovations emerge to improve energy efficiency practices. Smart grid technologies, energy-efficient appliances, and advanced building materials are contributing to significant reductions in energy consumption. Investments in these areas are growing as they offer both environmental and economic benefits. Innovations in energy efficiency, including smart building technologies, LED lighting, and advanced heating and cooling systems, are creating opportunities for investment in reducing energy consumption and emissions in the residential and commercial sectors. Some notable emerging trends and innovations in energy efficiency investments include digitalization and IoT, EPC, AI for energy optimization, blockchain for energy efficiency, deep retrofits and net-zero buildings, behavior change and gamification, energy efficiency as a service (EEaaS), integrated energy systems, and data-driven energy efficiency financing.

1. Digitalization and IoT: Digital business plays a crucial role in driving energy efficiency and sustainability by enabling innovative solutions. The integration of digital technologies and IoT is transforming energy efficiency investments. Smart sensors, meters, and building automation systems enable real-time data collection, analysis, and optimization of energy consumption. Advanced analytics, ML, and AI algorithms help identify energy-saving opportunities and provide insights for efficient operations. Investing in digital energy management platforms and IoT-enabled devices is a growing trend.

2. Energy performance contract (EPC): EPC is an innovative financing mechanism for energy efficiency projects. Under an EPC, an ESCO undertakes the upfront costs of implementing energy efficiency measures in a facility. The ESCO is then repaid from the energy savings achieved over a defined contract period. EPCs enable energy efficiency investments without requiring upfront capital, making them an attractive option for building retrofits and industrial projects.

3. AI for Energy Optimization: AI technologies are being applied to energy optimization, allowing for advanced algorithms to analyze

energy data, predict patterns, and optimize energy consumption in real-time. AI-driven systems can autonomously adjust settings, control energy usage, and optimize operational efficiency. Investing in AI-based energy optimization solutions can deliver significant energy savings and operational improvements.

4. Blockchain for Energy Efficiency: Blockchain platforms can facilitate the tracking and verification of energy savings, enable P2P trading, and streamline transaction processes. Investing in blockchain start-ups focusing on energy efficiency applications presents opportunities to transform the way energy efficiency projects are managed and monetized.

5. Deep Retrofits and Net-Zero Buildings: Deep retrofits involve comprehensive and extensive energy efficiency upgrades that significantly reduce energy consumption in buildings. Net-zero energy buildings, which generate as much energy as they consume, are also gaining momentum. Investments in deep retrofits and net-zero building technologies offer opportunities to transform existing building stock and achieve substantial energy savings.

6. Behavior Change and Gamification: Engaging building occupants and promoting behavior change can significantly contribute to energy efficiency. Gamification platforms and mobile apps incentivize users to adopt energy-saving behaviors, monitor energy usage, and compete with others. Investing in start-ups that leverage gamification and behavior change techniques can drive energy efficiency improvements and create energy-conscious communities.

7. EEaaS: Similar to energy as a service, the EEaaS model provides energy efficiency solutions to customers without upfront costs. Service providers implement and maintain energy efficiency measures in buildings or facilities, and customers pay based on the achieved energy savings. EEaaS models enable wider adoption of energy efficiency measures, particularly for smaller businesses or organizations that may have limited capital.

8. Integrated Energy Systems: The integration of multiple energy systems, such as electricity, heating, cooling, and transportation, allows for holistic energy optimization. Investments in integrated energy systems, including district energy systems and microgrids, promote

energy efficiency, renewable energy integration, and grid resilience. Integrated energy solutions contribute to overall energy efficiency gains and support the transition to decentralized and sustainable energy systems.

9. Data-Driven Energy Efficiency Financing: Leveraging data analytics and digital platforms, data-driven energy efficiency financing models are emerging. These models utilize energy consumption data, building performance metrics, and other relevant data to assess the potential savings and financial viability of energy efficiency projects. Data-driven financing mechanisms enable more accurate risk assessment and help optimize investment decisions in energy efficiency.

Carbon Capture and Storage

CCS is a technology that plays a crucial role in efforts to mitigate climate change. While still in its developmental stages, CCS is considered a key technology for meeting global climate goals, especially in industries where reducing emissions is particularly challenging, like cement and steel production. The first step in CCS is capturing CO_2 emissions at their source, such as power plants or industrial facilities. This is typically done using one of three methods: postcombustion (capturing CO_2 from fuel gases after combustion), precombustion (removing CO_2 before combustion), and oxy-fuel combustion (burning fuel in pure oxygen to produce a CO_2-rich gas stream). Once captured, the CO_2 needs to be transported to a storage site. This is usually done via pipelines, which is currently the most cost-effective and efficient method for large quantities of CO_2. The final step is storing the captured CO_2, typically deep underground in geological formations. These can include depleted oil and gas fields, deep saline aquifers, or unmineable coal seams. The goal is to store the CO_2 securely and permanently to prevent it from escaping back into the atmosphere (Capros et al. 2019).

One of the challenges of CCS is its cost, which includes expenses related to capturing, transporting, and storing CO_2. As such, ongoing R&D are focused on improving the efficiency and reducing the costs of CCS technologies. Innovations in this field are making CCS more efficient and cost-effective. Innovations in capture methods, increased storage options, and enhanced monitoring techniques are areas of active exploration.

Sustainable Agriculture Technologies

Precision agriculture, food waste reduction and upcycling, agri-fintech and digital platforms, and genetically modified crops are examples of innovations improving agricultural efficiency and reducing environmental impacts. These technologies are attracting investments due to their potential to enhance food security and sustainability.

1. Precision Agriculture: Advancements in AgTech and precision agriculture are transforming farming practices. Investments in AgTech start-ups that leverage technologies such as sensors, drones, robotics, and data analytics can improve crop yield, reduce resource use, optimize irrigation, and enhance overall farm management.
2. Food Waste Reduction and Upcycling: Investments in technologies and initiatives that reduce food waste and promote upcycling of food by-products present opportunities to tackle both environmental and economic challenges. Start-ups focusing on food waste prevention, recovery, and upcycling can contribute to a more sustainable and circular food system.
3. Agri-Fintech and Digital Platforms: Agri-fintech platforms facilitate access to finance, insurance, and marketplaces for smallholder farmers. Investments in digital platforms that connect farmers with financial services, weather information, and market opportunities can improve productivity, resilience, and livelihoods in agriculture.

Many climate-smart agricultural (CSA) technologies fail to achieve their full potential impact due to low levels of adoption by smallholder farmers and difficulties in scaling CSA. Drawing on the evidence of India, Groot et al. (2019) argued that one of the critical issues is distortive government subsidies on energy and the lack of market intelligence affecting the profitability of the business model of small- and medium-sized enterprises. The findings of the study indicate that scaling is enhanced through market intelligence and a favoring regulatory landscape.

Water and Waste Treatment and Technologies

Innovative water and waste treatment, recycling technologies, and water-efficient agriculture technologies are becoming increasingly important in managing the world's water resources. Investments in these technologies are growing in response to global water scarcity challenges.

1. Decentralized Water and Wastewater Treatment: Decentralized water and wastewater treatment systems are gaining popularity due to their flexibility, scalability, and potential cost savings. These systems enable on-site treatment and reuse of water, reducing the strain on centralized infrastructure. Investments in decentralized treatment technologies, such as modular systems, small-scale wastewater treatment plants, and point-of-use water purification devices, can support sustainable water management in urban and rural areas.

2. Nutrient Recovery from Wastewater: Nutrient recovery technologies extract valuable nutrients, such as phosphorus and nitrogen, from wastewater streams. These recovered nutrients can be used as fertilizers in agriculture, closing the nutrient cycle, and reducing reliance on synthetic fertilizers. Investing in nutrient recovery systems and companies that specialize in nutrient recycling from wastewater can contribute to sustainable nutrient management practices.

3. Water-Energy Nexus: The water-energy nexus focuses on the interdependencies between water and energy systems. Innovations in this area aim to reduce the energy intensity of water treatment and distribution processes while optimizing energy generation through water-related technologies. Investments in energy-efficient water treatment technologies, water-efficient energy generation, such as hydropower, or technologies that integrate water and energy systems offer potential investment opportunities.

4. Resource Recovery from Waste: Resource recovery technologies focus on extracting valuable resources from waste streams. Innovations in waste-to-energy, recycling, and anaerobic digestion processes enable the recovery of energy and valuable materials from various waste sources. Investing in resource recovery facilities, waste-to-energy projects, or companies that specialize in waste stream valorization can contribute to a more circular economy.

5. Remote Monitoring and Data Analytics: Remote monitoring and data analytics technologies enable real-time monitoring, predictive maintenance, and performance optimization of water and waste-water infrastructure. Investments in remote monitoring systems, cloud-based data analytics platforms, and AI algorithms can enhance operational efficiency, asset management, and decision making in water and wastewater management.

6. Advanced Waste Sorting and Recycling Technologies: Advanced waste sorting technologies, including robotics, AI, and ML, are transforming recycling processes. These technologies improve the accuracy and efficiency of waste sorting, enabling better separation of recyclable materials. Investments in advanced waste sorting facilities, recycling equipment manufacturers, or waste management companies adopting these technologies can enhance recycling rates and reduce landfill waste.

7. Water-Efficient Agriculture Technologies: Innovations in water-efficient agriculture technologies help optimize irrigation practices, reduce water waste, and enhance crop productivity. Investments in precision irrigation systems, soil moisture sensors, drought-tolerant crop varieties, and agricultural data analytics platforms offer opportunities to support sustainable water use in agriculture.

Green-Building Technologies

The building industry contributed to a large proportion of the global energy use and carbon emissions across material production, construction, operation, and end-of-life. Innovations in green construction, smart building technologies, and green-building data analytics are transforming the building industry. Green buildings are becoming a key focus area for climate-conscious investments.

Smart Building Technologies

Smart buildings use IoT sensors and automation systems to control lighting, temperature, air quality, and even security systems. These technologies not only improve energy efficiency but also promote the use of real-time monitoring systems to detect unfavorable scenarios for enhanced living environments (Saini et al. 2020). Innovations include building EMS, occupancy sensors, and advanced controls for lighting, HVAC systems. Investing in smart building technology companies or collaborating with solution providers can support the integration of intelligent systems in buildings.

Green-Building Data Analytics

Data analytics and ML are being applied to building operations to optimize energy performance, identify inefficiencies, and predict maintenance needs. It involves collecting and analyzing data from various building systems to optimize performance, reduce energy consumption, and predict maintenance needs. Investments in data analytics platforms, energy management software, or companies that provide building performance analytics can drive continuous improvement in building energy efficiency.

Building Information Modeling (BIM)

BIM software represents a significant technological advancement in the architecture, engineering, and construction industries. It goes beyond traditional 2D drafting and design methods, offering a more integrated, intelligent, and collaborative approach to building design and construction. BIM software allows for more efficient planning and construction processes. It enables architects and engineers to create digital models of a building, optimizing design for energy efficiency and sustainability.

Gan et al. (2020) reviewed the computer simulation and optimization studies for minimizing the life-cycle energy consumption and carbon emissions in buildings, with the aim of identifying the current practices and future research need in this field. The findings reveal that emerging digital technologies, such as ML, data-driven design, and parametric 3D modeling, enable greater automation in early design exploration and advance decision marking in design optimization. Based on the findings, Gan et al. argued that as human factors, for example, energy-related occupant behaviors, become important metrics in the built environment, multidisciplinary design should be adopted to generate social-technical solutions that encompass both environmental sustainability and human well-being.

Beyond these innovations, indoor air quality has been a matter of concern for the international scientific community. Saini et al. (2020) presented a systematic review of the state of the art on indoor air quality monitoring systems based on the IoT, and highlighted design aspects for monitoring systems, including sensor types, microcontrollers, architecture, and connectivity.

Climate Data Analytics and AI

AI and ML are also being used to analyze vast amounts of ESG data, assess ESG metrics, and identify sustainable investment opportunities and risks. Moreover, AI and big data analytics are being used to better model climate risks and long-term impacts, optimize energy use, and develop climate adaptation strategies. These technologies can process complex and diverse data sets, including satellite imagery and social media feeds, to provide insights into a company's environmental impact and sustainability practices. In addition to being used to enhance transparency and traceability in supply chains, blockchain technology is also being utilized in the issuance and trading of green bonds and in carbon credit markets, providing a more efficient and transparent way of tracking carbon emissions and offsets. Investments in these technologies are crucial for informed decision making in climate-conscious investing.

Role of Asset Owners in Achieving the Paris Agreement Goals

Asset owners play a crucial role in achieving the goals set out in the Paris Agreement, as they set the tone for the investment value chain by mobilizing capital for low-carbon technologies, influencing corporate behavior, supporting policy and regulatory changes, risk management and reporting, building sustainable financial markets, and education and collaboration.

Mobilizing Capital for Low-Carbon Technologies

Climate-change vulnerability is associated with a significant drop in investment efficiency. Mbanyele (2022) found that this impact is more pronounced after the Paris Agreement and for firms with severe financial constraints and less collateral security. The transition to a low-carbon economy presents a unique and vital opportunity for asset owners to make a significant impact on reducing GHG emissions while potentially reaping financial rewards.

Directing capital toward renewable energy projects is a critical component of this transition. In addition to supporting the generation of clean energy, investments in solar farms, wind turbines, and hydroelectric power plants also drive technological advancements and cost reductions in these sectors. As these technologies become more efficient and widespread, they offer a sustainable and increasingly cost-competitive alternative to traditional energy sources.

Beyond energy production, there is a growing need for investments in energy-efficient technologies and infrastructure. In the industrial sector, investments can be channeled into efficient manufacturing processes that reduce energy consumption and minimize waste, which can address the demand side of energy use, reducing overall carbon footprints while often providing cost savings over the long term. The impact of such investments is profound, contributing to a reduction in global energy demand and the associated emissions, while fostering a more sustainable approach to urban development and industrial processes.

VC and PE funds play a particularly influential role in shaping the future of a low-carbon economy. By funding start-ups and new technologies, these asset owners can catalyze the development of innovative solutions that might otherwise struggle to find support. This includes backing companies that are pioneering new materials to replace high-carbon alternatives, developing CCS technologies, or creating advanced energy storage solutions to complement intermittent renewable energy sources. VC and PE investments can also support the growth of companies working on sustainable agriculture, EVs, and other sectors crucial for a low-carbon transition.

Divestment from fossil-fuel companies is a more direct approach that asset owners can take to reduce the flow of capital to industries that are major contributors to GHG emissions. By withdrawing their investments from these sectors, asset owners send a clear message about the urgency of transitioning to a low-carbon economy. This strategy can be particularly impactful when adopted by large asset owners, such as pension funds, universities, and insurance companies. Divestment contributes to a shift in societal norms and expectations, increasingly framing investment in fossil fuels as not only environmentally unsustainable but also financially risky in the face of tightening regulations, shifting consumer preferences, and the advancing renewable energy sector.

The role of asset owners in driving the transition to a low-carbon economy cannot be overstated. By strategically directing capital toward renewable energy, energy efficiency, and innovative low-carbon technologies, asset owners not only contribute to the mitigation of climate change but also tap into emerging markets with significant growth potential. As public awareness and regulatory frameworks increasingly favor sustainability, these investments are likely to become even more critical and potentially lucrative. The challenge and opportunity for investors lie in identifying and supporting those solutions that offer the most effective and scalable means of reducing GHG emissions, thereby playing a pivotal role in shaping a sustainable and resilient global economy.

Influencing Corporate Behavior

Asset owners wield considerable influence as shareholders, and this power can be harnessed to drive meaningful change toward sustainability in the corporate world. By actively engaging with the companies in which they invest, asset owners can encourage, and sometimes compel, these entities to adopt more sustainable practices. One critical area of focus is the setting of GHG reduction targets. Asset owners can press companies to not only establish ambitious and scientifically aligned GHG targets but also to develop clear, actionable strategies to achieve these goals.

By evaluating companies based on their climate-conscious initiatives and sustainability practices, asset owners can direct capital toward businesses that demonstrate a commitment to sustainability, while potentially mitigating risk in their investment portfolios. This shift in capital allocation can also have a profound impact on investees, and over time, this can lead to a broader transformation in business practices, driving industries toward more sustainable and environmentally friendly operations.

The strategy of divestment from fossil-fuel companies is often complemented by a more nuanced approach of engagement. Some asset owners choose to retain their stakes in high-emission companies to influence them from within. This involves using their voting rights and engaging in constructive dialogue to push for changes in business practices, energy sources, and long-term strategic planning. This approach can be particularly effective in industries where transitioning to lower emissions is challenging but critical.

Supporting Policy and Regulatory Changes

Asset owners play a crucial role in shaping the policy landscape that supports the transition to a low-carbon economy. By advocating for progressive environmental policies, they can help create a more favorable context for sustainable investments. One key area where investor advocacy can make a significant impact is in the support of carbon pricing mechanisms. By backing such policies, asset owners can help drive a market shift away from carbon-intensive industries and toward cleaner alternatives, aligning financial incentives with environmental objectives.

Renewable energy subsidies are another critical policy area where investors can exert influence. By advocating for financial incentives for renewable energy development, asset owners can help accelerate the shift toward sustainable energy sources. These subsidies can lower the barrier to entry for renewable energy projects, making them more competitive with traditional fossil-fuel-based energy sources and more attractive to the market. Additionally, asset owners can push for stricter emission regulations, which can compel companies to innovate and adopt cleaner technologies, thereby opening up new investment opportunities in the field of sustainable technology and green infrastructure.

Beyond policy advocacy, asset owners can collaborate directly with governments and international organizations to finance large-scale infrastructure projects that are critical for achieving climate goals. This collaboration can take the form of PPPs, energy-efficient building retrofits, and public transportation systems. Such collaborations can also extend to international efforts, particularly in EM countries where the need for sustainable infrastructure is greatest, but funding is often limited. Asset owners can work with international organizations to fund projects that promote sustainable development, such as clean water systems, sustainable agriculture, and resilient urban development.

Using BRAIN-Energy, a novel agent-based model of investment in electricity generation to simulate and contrast government and market dynamics in the transition pathways of the United Kingdom, German, and Italian electricity sectors, Barazza and Strachan (2020) showed that a successful transition, which achieves the energy policy "trilemma" (low carbon, secure, affordable), requires the coevolution of the policy dimension (strong and frequently updatable CO_2 price, renewable subsidies, and capacity market) with the strategies of the heterogeneous market players. Barazza and Strachan argued that if this dynamic balance is maintained, then incentives are politically feasible and suppliers learn and evolve. If either the incentives are too weak to drive learning or too expensive so the policy regime collapses, then the transition fails on one of its key dimensions. Getting this balance right is harder in risky markets that also have players with more pronounced bounded rationality and path dependence in how they make investments.

Disclosure and Reporting

Demanding greater transparency and disclosure from investee companies regarding their carbon emissions and climate-change strategies is another critical step asset owners can take. By pushing for comprehensive and standardized reporting on climate-related issues, asset owners can assess the true environmental impact of their investments and avoid the pitfalls of greenwashing. This level of transparency is vital for evaluating a company's commitment to sustainability and its preparedness to handle the risks and opportunities posed by climate change.

Moreover, asset owners can use this information to engage with companies and encourage them to adopt more sustainable practices, set ambitious GHG reduction targets, and develop robust climate-change strategies. By holding companies accountable and driving them toward greater environmental responsibility, asset owners can play a pivotal role in promoting sustainable business practices across different sectors and industries.

Improving Lending Practices

Asset owners also have a significant role in influencing the lending practices of banks and financial institutions. By advocating for lending policies that favor environmentally friendly projects and companies, asset owners can drive a shift in how financial institutions allocate their resources. This influence can be exerted through direct engagement with banks, participation in shareholder meetings, or by choosing to invest in financial institutions that demonstrate a commitment to sustainable lending. Such actions can encourage banks to adopt stricter environmental criteria for their lending practices, increase financing for green projects, and reduce funding for activities that are harmful to the environment. The development of green financial products and the influence of asset owners on lending practices are crucial components in the broader shift toward a sustainable economy. By providing capital for environmentally beneficial projects and companies, these financial decisions play a pivotal role in mitigating climate change and promoting sustainability.

Education and Collaboration

Asset owners have a unique opportunity to support educational efforts that increase awareness about the importance of sustainable investing in achieving climate goals. Education plays a crucial role in shaping the perspectives and decisions of current and future asset owners, as well as the broader public. By funding and promoting educational initiatives, asset owners can help demystify sustainable investing and highlight its critical role in addressing climate change. This can involve supporting programs that educate individuals and institutions about the impacts of climate change on financial markets, the importance of ESG factors in investment decision making, and the potential of green investments to drive positive environmental outcomes. Such educational efforts can range from workshops and seminars to comprehensive online courses and educational content, targeting a diverse audience including students, professionals, and the general public.

Collaboration among asset owners is another powerful strategy for amplifying the impact of sustainable investing. By joining forces through climate-focused investment coalitions, asset owners can pool their resources, expertise, and influence to drive more significant changes. These coalitions allow them to share best practices, collaborate on research, and engage collectively with companies and policy makers.

One of the key strengths of such coalitions is their ability to leverage the collective voice of their members to advocate for policy changes, corporate sustainability practices, and increased transparency around climate risks and opportunities. This collective action can be particularly effective in influencing large corporations and industries that play a pivotal role in the transition to a low-carbon economy.

Furthermore, these coalitions can facilitate joint investment initiatives, pooling capital to fund large-scale sustainable projects that individual asset owners might not be able to support on their own. This collaborative approach can be especially beneficial in financing renewable energy projects, sustainable infrastructure, and innovative technologies that are essential for mitigating climate change. By working together, asset owners can also share the risks and rewards associated with these investments, making it more feasible to invest in emerging technologies and markets.

In addition to pooling financial resources, asset-owner coalitions can also serve as platforms for knowledge exchange and capacity building, and participants can benefit from shared insights into market trends, regulatory developments, and innovative investment strategies. This collective wisdom can enhance the ability of asset owners to make informed decisions that align with both their financial goals and their commitment to sustainability.

The Road Ahead

Climate-conscious investing also faces a range of challenges. Understanding these challenges is also crucial for asset owners, asset managers, and policy makers.

Obtaining Reliable Data

Obtaining reliable data for investment analyses, particularly in the context of ESG screening, presents several challenges. These challenges stem from the nature of the data, reporting standards, and the evolving landscape of ESG criteria. Some of the key challenges are related to the lack of standardization, data quality and reliability, geographic and sector variations, and access to data.

There is no universally accepted standard for ESG reporting, leading to inconsistencies in how companies report ESG data. This makes it difficult to compare companies within and across industries. Different organizations and rating agencies also use diverse metrics and methodologies to evaluate ESG performance, leading to a lack of uniformity in the data.

ESG reporting and practices can also vary significantly by region due to different regulatory environments and cultural norms. Sector-specific issues also exist—different industries face unique ESG challenges, making it difficult to apply a one-size-fits-all approach to data analysis.

Much of the ESG data relies on self-reporting by companies, which can lead to biased or overly positive portrayals of their ESG practices. Some companies may only report on certain ESG aspects, or not report at all, leading to gaps in the data. Besides, ESG data is not always updated regularly, which can be problematic in a rapidly changing environment.

In terms of costs and accessibility, high-quality ESG data is often expensive and may be inaccessible to smaller investors. Beyond these, integrating ESG data with traditional financial data for comprehensive analysis can be technically challenging.

Despite these challenges, the importance of ESG data in investment decision making continues to grow, driving ongoing efforts to enhance data quality and accessibility. To address these challenges, investors and asset managers can use a mix of third-party services and solutions and internal proprietary data and investment research, which were described in detail in Chapter 3 and Chapter 5.

Greenwashing

Greenwashing, a term used to describe the practice of companies exaggerating or misrepresenting the environmental benefits of their products, services, or practices, poses a significant challenge in climate-conscious investing. Greenwashing can mislead asset owners who are seeking to support genuinely sustainable businesses and can undermine the overall credibility of climate-conscious investing. Amidst concerns of greenwashing, reliable sustainability assessment methods are needed to ensure that funds are channeled toward priority sectors for the transition to a low-carbon and more inclusive economy.

The study of Setyowati (2023) reveals that there has been high procedural compliance by financial institutions through developing sustainable finance action plans and submitting annual sustainability reports to the financial regulator; however, there is considerable variation and inconsistency in interpreting what constitutes a "green" project among financial institutions, enabling some financial institutions to engage in little more than tokenism. Setyowati argued that with the limited regulatory oversight currently provided, it is difficult to see how financial institutions might be incentivized to do more or how tangible sustainability outcomes can be achieved.

To mitigate greenwashing, several strategies can be employed:

1. Enhanced Due Diligence: Asset owners and asset managers should conduct thorough due diligence to verify the environmental claims of companies. This involves looking beyond marketing materials and superficial sustainability reports to assess the actual environmental impact of a company's operations, products, and services.

2. Third-Party Verification and Certifications: Using independent third-party verifications and certifications can help ensure that a company's environmental claims are credible. Certifications from reputable organizations can serve as a benchmark for sustainability.

3. Regulatory Compliance and Standards: Compliance with standards such as the GRI or the SASB can provide a more accurate picture of a company's sustainability practices.

4. Transparency and Accountability: Encouraging transparency and accountability in environmental reporting is key. Asset owners can also play a proactive role by engaging with company management on sustainability issues and voting on shareholder resolutions that promote greater transparency and action on environmental matters.

5. Use of ESG Data and Analytics Tools: Leveraging advanced ESG data and analytics tools can help asset owners analyze and compare the sustainability performance of different companies more

effectively. These tools can provide deeper insights into the environmental impact of companies.

6. Portfolio Diversification: Diversifying investments across various sectors and companies that are leaders in sustainability can reduce the risk of exposure to greenwashing.

Regulatory Uncertainty

The regulatory landscape for climate-conscious investing is still evolving. Changes in policies can significantly alter market dynamics. Financial incentives and regulations can also impact the viability and attractiveness of sustainable investments.

Changes in government policies can have a direct impact on the valuations of companies, making certain sustainable investments more attractive while diminishing the appeal of others, particularly those associated with high carbon emissions. For instance, stricter environmental regulations can lead to increased costs for companies that are not compliant, whereas companies that have proactively embraced sustainable practices may benefit from regulatory changes.

In addition, the incentives used by governments and regulatory bodies, such as subsidies and tax incentives, can significantly enhance the attractiveness of investing in green technologies, renewable energy, and other sustainable initiatives. Moreover, different sectors may be affected in varying ways by climate regulations. For example, the energy sector might be more directly impacted by environmental regulations, while the financial sector might be more influenced by governance regulations.

New regulations in sustainability reporting and compliance can lead to increased costs for companies. While this may initially be seen as a burden, over the long term, it often leads to more sustainable business practices and can open up new investment opportunities in areas such as clean technology and sustainable infrastructure. As regulations evolve, companies and investors alike need to be adaptable and resilient. Staying informed and being able to quickly adjust to new regulatory environments is crucial for sustained success in climate-conscious investing.

Moving Forward

The path ahead for climate-conscious investing is both challenging and rich with opportunities. As the world grapples with the urgent need to address climate change, the role of the financial ecosystem in driving this transition becomes increasingly critical. The challenges are multifaceted, involving the need for accurate data and impact measurement, development of innovative financial products, creation of supportive regulatory frameworks, and a deep commitment to genuine sustainability practices. Navigating these challenges requires a concerted effort from asset owners, policy makers, asset managers, investees, regulatory bodies, and society at large.

Innovative financial products are central to this journey. Green bonds, climate-aligned bonds, and green and sustainably ETFs and funds are examples of instruments that have already begun reshaping the investment landscape. The future will likely see the emergence of even more sophisticated products that not only provide financial returns but also drive positive environmental outcomes. These products must be underpinned by robust data and impact measurement tools to ensure transparency and credibility.

Accurate and standardized metrics for assessing environmental impact are essential for asset owners to make informed decisions and avoid the pitfalls of greenwashing. This calls for advancements in technology and analytics, as well as collaboration with scientific experts to integrate the latest environmental research into investment strategies.

Regulatory frameworks play a pivotal role in shaping the environment for climate-conscious investing. Policies that incentivize sustainable practices and penalize unsustainable ones are crucial; however, regulation alone is not sufficient. There needs to be a cultural shift within the investment community toward valuing long-term environmental sustainability as a key component of financial success. This shift is already underway, as evidenced by the growing interest in climate-conscious investing, but it needs to be accelerated and deepened.

A commitment to genuine sustainability practices is the cornerstone of this path forward. This goes beyond mere compliance with regulations or superficial adherence to sustainability standards. It involves a fundamental rethinking of investment strategies to prioritize long-term environmental health and resilience. Asset owners, asset managers, and financial institutions alike must embrace a more holistic view of value creation, one that considers the environmental and social impact of their activities.

As awareness and concern about climate change continue to grow, climate-conscious investing is not just an option but a necessity. It represents a powerful tool for driving the transition to a more sustainable global economy. By aligning financial goals with environmental objectives, climate-conscious investing has the potential to transform the challenges posed by climate change into opportunities for innovation, growth, and sustainable development. The path ahead is complex, but with the right mix of innovation, regulation, and commitment, it is a path that leads to a brighter, more sustainable future.

Summary

This chapter navigates through the dynamic and evolving landscape of climate-conscious investing, uncovering the multifaceted aspects that are shaping its future. The journey begins with an exploration of the emerging trends in this field, where we witness a paradigm shift toward integrating sustainability considerations into investment decisions. This shift is characterized by a growing emphasis on net-zero commitments, a keen focus on Scope 3 emissions, an increasing reliance on sophisticated metrics to gauge real-world environmental impacts, innovation in investment vehicles, and development in renewable energy, water- and waste management, sustainable agriculture, green buildings and infrastructure, and climate resilience and adaptation investments. These trends underscore a broader recognition of the critical role that the financial ecosystem plays in addressing global environmental challenges.

Delving into the realm of technological innovations, we see how advancements in renewable energy, green transportation, energy-efficient solutions, and CCS are actively reshaping investment strategies. Innovations in sustainable agriculture, water- and waste treatment, green-building technologies, and the integration of climate data analytics and AI are providing new opportunities for investors to contribute to a sustainable future while seeking financial returns. These technologies represent a convergence of environmental sustainability and economic opportunity, highlighting the potential for innovative solutions to drive significant environmental progress.

It is evident that asset owners are instrumental in the global effort to combat climate change—their roles extend far beyond mere capital allocation. By mobilizing capital for low-carbon technologies, asset owners are directly fueling the innovations necessary for a greener future. Their influence on corporate behavior, through active engagement and RI choices, is reshaping business practices toward greater sustainability. Asset owners are also key players in advocating for supportive policy and regulatory changes, recognizing that a conducive regulatory environment is essential for meaningful progress. In terms of disclosure and reporting, asset owners are setting new standards and demanding greater transparency from their investees. Their efforts in building sustainable financial markets are creating a robust ecosystem where sustainable investing is not just a niche strategy, but a foundational principle. Through education and collaboration, asset owners are spreading awareness and forging alliances that amplify their impact. Collectively, these roles underscore the immense responsibility and power asset owners hold in steering the global economy toward the ambitious yet crucial goals set forth in the Paris Agreement. As stewards of capital, asset owners have the unique capability, and indeed the obligation, to drive the transition to a sustainable, low-carbon world.

Lastly, we recognize that the journey toward effective climate-conscious investing is laden with challenges, yet it is undeniably critical for our collective future. The quest for reliable ESG data remains a complex endeavor, demanding enhanced methodologies and standardization to ensure accuracy and comparability. Greenwashing poses a significant hurdle, necessitating vigilance and a commitment to deeper due diligence to discern genuine sustainability from mere marketing. Regulatory uncertainties add another layer of complexity, highlighting the need for adaptive strategies that can navigate evolving policy landscapes.

Despite these challenges, the path forward is clear. It calls for a concerted effort from asset owners, policy makers, asset managers, investees, regulatory bodies, and society at large to foster transparency, accountability, and genuine commitment to sustainability. As we move forward, the collective actions and decisions made in the realm of climate-conscious investing will not only shape the financial markets but also determine the health and sustainability of our planet for generations to come.

This chapter paints a picture of a future where financial success is inextricably linked with environmental stewardship, offering a blueprint for those eager to be at the forefront of this transformative movement. Looking ahead, this journey, though fraught with obstacles, is one of profound opportunity—to redefine the principles of investment in alignment with the urgent environmental imperatives of our time.

Appendix A

Glossary

Absolute emissions: The total emissions in metric CO_2e, indicating the total amount of GHGs emitted into the atmosphere over a specific period.

Additionality: Refers to ensuring that the carbon reduction would not have occurred without the offset project.

Best-in-class selection: A method that focuses on investing in companies that perform better than their peers in terms of ESG performance.

Cap-and-trade: Cap-and-trade systems set a cap on the total amount of GHG emissions allowed.

Carbon capture and storage: Involves capturing CO_2 emissions produced from the use of fossil fuels in electricity generation and industrial processes, and then transporting and storing it underground to prevent it from entering the atmosphere.

Carbon Disclosure Project (CDP): An NGO that solicits, collects, grades, and makes publicly available more than 8,400 issuer responses to its annual Climate Change survey. This survey includes detailed information on each responding issuer's GHG inventory in the forms of Scope 1, 2, and 3 and any relevant metrics, targets, and strategies related to measuring and managing its GHG emissions.

Carbon footprint: The total amount of GHG emissions, specifically CO_2.

Carbon offsetting: A strategy used to counterbalance the carbon emissions from investment portfolios. Carbon offsetting involves directing funds into investees that are designed to reduce or absorb an equivalent amount of GHG from the atmosphere to compensate for the emissions associated with one's investments.

Carbon tax: A carbon tax directly sets a price on carbon by levying a fee on the production, distribution, or use of fossil fuels based on their carbon content.

Climate adaptation: Involves making adjustments to social, economic, and ecological systems in response to observed or expected changes in the climate.

Climate change: The shift in climate patterns mainly caused by GHG emissions from natural systems and human activities.

Climate-conscious investing: Refers to allocating capital to assets that mitigate climate change, biodiversity loss, resource inefficiency, and other environmental challenges.

Climate-conscious SAA: A forward-looking investment approach that integrates climate-related risks and opportunities into the process of determining the mix of asset classes in a portfolio.

Climate investment themes: The broad categories or focus areas within the field of climate-related investments.

Climate resilience: The ability of a system to anticipate, prepare for, respond to, and recover from adverse climate-related events.

Climate stress testing: Involves simulating a range of climate-related scenarios, including both physical risks and transition risks.

Community investment note: A type of fixed-income security that allows asset owners to invest in community-focused projects.

Corporate governance: The process and structure for overseeing the business and management of a company.

Corporate social responsibility (CSR): A broad business concept that describes a company's commitment to conducting its business in an ethical way.

Divestment: Involves removing investments from certain industries or companies that do not align with an asset owner's values or principles.

Energy-efficiency standards: Designed to reduce energy consumption and increase efficiency in various sectors.

Emissions intensity: Emissions relative to a financial metric, such as revenue or market capitalization.

Environmental factors: Factors pertaining to the natural world.

Environmental, social, and governance (ESG): A framework used to assess an organization's business practices and performance on various sustainability and ethical issues.

ESG integration: An investment strategy that considers financially material ESG factors at each applicable step of its investment process.

ESG investing: An approach to managing assets where investors explicitly incorporate ESG factors in their investment decisions with the long-term return of an investment portfolio in mind.

European green deal: A package of policy initiatives, which aims to set the EU on the path to a green transition, with the ultimate goal of reaching climate neutrality by 2050.

G10: Group of 10, refers to the group of countries that agreed to participate in the General Arrangements to Borrow, an agreement to provide the International Monetary Fund with additional funds to increase its lending ability.

G20: Group of 20, an intergovernmental forum comprising 19 sovereign countries, the EU, and the African Union.

Global impact investing network: Focuses on reducing barriers to impact investment by building critical infrastructure and developing activities, education, and research that help accelerate the development of a coherent impact investing industry.

Global Real Estate Sustainability Benchmark (GRESB): An independent organization providing validated ESG performance data and peer benchmarks for asset owners and managers to improve business intelligence, industry engagement, and decision making.

Global Reporting Initiative (GRI): Provide guidance on disclosure across environmental, social, and economic factors.

Gold standard: A voluntary carbon offset program focused on progressing the SDGs.

Governance factors: Factors that involve issues tied to countries and/ or jurisdictions or are common practice in an industry, as well as the interests of broader stakeholder groups.

Green bond principles: Established by the ICMA, provide voluntary guidelines on transparency, disclosure, and reporting in the green-bond market.

Green bonds: A type of fixed-income instrument specifically earmarked to fund projects that have positive climate and environmental benefits.

Greenwashing: Used to describe the practice of companies exaggerating or misrepresenting the environmental benefits of their products, services, or practices.

Impact-investing funds: A type of investment fund that seeks to generate both financial return and positive social or environmental impact.

Liability risks: Arise when parties who have suffered loss or damage from the effects of climate change seek compensation from those that hold responsible.

Nationally Determined Contributions (NDCs): Where each country determines, plans, and regularly reports on the contribution it undertakes to mitigate global warming.

Paris agreement: An international treaty adopted in 2015 that aims to limit global warming to well below 2°C above preindustrial levels, and to pursue efforts to limit the temperature increase to 1.5°C.

Physical risks: The risks arising from the physical impacts of climate change, which include acute risks and chronic risks.

Positive screening: Involves selecting companies or investment vehicles that meet specific ESG criteria.

Principles for Responsible Investment (PRI): Comprises an UN-supported international network of investors—signatories working together toward a common goal to understand the implications of ESG factors for investment and ownership decisions and ownership practices.

Regulatory technical standard: A type of regulatory instrument used in the EU to provide detailed technical specifications for the implementation of certain aspects of the legislation.

Renewable energy mandates: Regulations that require a certain percentage of a country's energy production or consumption to come from renewable sources.

Responsible investment: A strategy and practice to incorporate ESG factors into investment decisions and active ownership.

Risk premium: The extra return that asset owners require to compensate for the risk of holding a particular asset.

Scenario analysis: In the context of climate change, scenario analysis involves creating and evaluating a range of plausible future scenarios based on different assumptions about GHG emissions, regulatory changes, technological advancements, and other factors affecting climate change and the transition to a low-carbon economy.

Science-Based Targets initiative (SBTi): Advocates for companies to set climate science-based targets to boost their competitive advantage in the transition to a lower carbon economy. The SBTi, which has certified 407 companies as having SBTi targets, is a collaboration between CDP, the United Nations Global Compact, the World Resources Institute, the World Wildlife Fund, and one of the We Mean Business Coalition Commitments.

Scope 1 emissions: Direct emissions from sources that are owned or controlled by the company.

Scope 2 emissions: Indirect emissions from the generation of purchased electricity, steam, heating, and cooling consumed by the company.

Scope 3 emissions: All other indirect emissions that occur in a company's value chain but are not owned or controlled by the company.

Social factors: Factors that affect the lives of humans.

Stress testing: Assessing the resilience of an investment portfolio under extreme but plausible adverse conditions.

Stewardship: An overarching term encompassing the approach that asset owners take as active and involved owners of the companies and other entities in which they invest through voting and engagement.

Sustainable Development Goals (SDGs): An agreed framework for all UN member state governments to work toward in aligning with global priorities.

Transition risks: Include policy and legal risks, technology risks, market risks, and reputation risks.

Task Force on Climate-related Financial Disclosures (TCFD): The Financial Stability Board created the TCFD to develop recommendations on the types of information that companies should disclose to support asset owners, lenders, and insurance underwriters in appropriately assessing and pricing a specific set of risks related to climate change.

United Nations Framework Convention on Climate Change (UNFCCC): Launched at the Rio de Janeiro Earth Summit in 1992, the UNFCCC aims to stabilize GHG emissions to limit man-made climate change.

Verified carbon standard: The world's most widely used GHG crediting program.

Appendix B

Carbon Offsets—Engagement Guide

Use of Offsets

1. Does the issuer's current climate strategy include the use of carbon offsets? If *yes*, proceed to Question 2. If *no*, proceed to questions 4 and 5.

   Note: Pay particularly attention to issuers that claim "carbon neutrality"

2. (a) If the issuer is using offsets, are they only for residual emissions, that is, has the company undertaken substantial efforts to reduce and remove carbon emissions from its value chain ahead of resorting to offsets? If *yes*, refer to Question 3. (b) If *no*, what are the company's plans to reduce its absolute, real-world emissions and its dependence on offsets?

3. If the issuer is using offsets, are they originated from a compliance market, such as a cap-and-trade or ETS? If *yes*, how is pricing evolving in these markets and how is the issuer preparing for that financially? If *no*, refer to Question 5.

4. Is the issuer based, or have operations, in a compliance market such as a cap-and-trade, ETS, or a market that features carbon taxes? If *yes*, refer to Question 2 (b). If *no*, how is the issuer monitoring regulatory efforts to create such mechanisms in its operational jurisdictions?

5. Is the issuer's climate strategy and/or scenario analysis based on, or include, a carbon price? If *yes*, what are the pricing assumptions and are they linked to compliance markets? If *no*, refer to Question 4.

Quality of Offsets

1. Are the offsets qualified or verified by a regulatory body or government-sanctioned or affiliated offset certifier?

Note: These can include bodies such as the Australian Carbon Farming Initiative of the California Air Resources Board. Nonprofit certifiers such as the Gold Standard, Verra, the American Carbon Registry, or the Climate Action Reserve.

2. Are the offsets nature-based (i.e., afforestation/reforestation, sequestration in mangrove or sea meadows or soil carbon enhancement) or industrial-based (i.e., CCS, or carbon sequestration in products)?

   Note: Nature-based offsets are preferable over industrial-based offsets as nature-based offsets are considered to remove carbon more permanently than industrial-based offsets.

3. Does the issuer use carbon removal offsets (i.e., afforestation, reforestation, soil carbon enhancement, or ecosystem restoration), or avoided emissions offsets (i.e., renewable energy credits)?

   Note: Avoided emissions offsets are highly controversial. Avoided emissions are those that do not occur because a product or service is a substitute for a similar but more carbon-intensive product or service. The resulting emissions are measured against a hypothetical future baseline. As a result, it is challenging to accurately quantify and measure the impact of avoided emissions.

4. What opportunities does the issuer have in investing in offset products or developing its own offsets directly? Is the issuer able to derive any ecological or social cobenefits from offsetting?

5. Does the issuer have any plans to develop carbon-neutral goods or services?

Appendix C

GHG Emissions Inventory Guide

The following standards and definitions are derived from the GHG Protocol, a multistakeholder initiative of corporations, NGOs, governments, and other stakeholders convened by the World Resources Institute and the World Business Council for Sustainable Development. The GHG Protocol, launched in 1998, has developed the most widely used and internationally recognized set of accounting and reporting standards for businesses and governments to measure and manage their GHG inventory.

Why Should Issuers Perform a GHG Inventory?

In light of the potential financial and social risks, many governments are taking steps to address climate change by reducing GHG emissions through national policies that include the introduction of emissions trading programs, voluntary programs, carbon or energy taxes, and regulations and standards on energy efficiency and emissions. As a result, companies must be able to understand and manage their GHG risks if they are to ensure long-term success in a competitive business environment. A well-designed and maintained corporate GHG inventory can serve several business goals, including:

- Managing GHG risks and identifying reduction opportunities;
- Public reporting and participation in voluntary GHG programs;
- Participating in mandatory reporting programs;
- Participating in GHG markets; and
- Recognition for early voluntary action.

Definitions and Standards

The GHG Protocol covers for issuers the accounting and reporting of the six GHG recognized under the Kyoto Protocol:

1. Carbon dioxide (CO_2)
2. Methane (CH_4)
3. Nitrous oxide (N_2O)
4. Hydrofluorocarbons (HFCs)
5. Perfluorocarbons (PFCs)
6. Sulfur hexafluoride (SF_6)

The GHG Protocol's Corporate Accounting and Reporting Standard is for issuers who are disclosing against the GHG Protocol accounting and reporting standards, the document is also a useful collection of definitions, rational, concepts, examples, and best practices for investors analyzing, researching, and engaging on, emissions.

Measuring GHG Emissions Inventory

To help issuers delineate direct and indirect emission sources, and improve transparency, Scope 1, 2, and 3 are defined for GHG accounting and reporting purposes. Details can be found in Chapter 2.

Notes

Chapter 1

1. MSCI ESG Research LLC (2023).

Chapter 4

1. CICERO (2015).

References

Agrawal, A. and K. Hockerts. 2019. "Impact Investing Strategy: Managing Conflicts between Impact Investor and Investee Social Enterprise." *Sustainability* 11, no. 15, p. 4117. https://doi.org/10.3390/su11154117.

Alekseev, G., S. Giglio, Q. Maingi, J. Selgrad, and J. Stroebel. December 2022. "A Quantity-based Approach to Constructing Climate Risk Hedge Portfolios." https://doi.org/10.3386/w30703.

Alsmadi, A.A, M. Al-Okaily, N. Alrawashdeh, A. Al-Gasaymeh, A. Moh'd Al-hazimeh, and A. Zakari. 2023. "A Bibliometric Analysis of Green Bonds and Sustainable Green Energy: Evidence From the Last Fifteen Years (2007–2022)." *Sustainability* 15, no. 7, p. 5778. https://doi.org/10.3390/su15075778.

Amenc, N., F. Goltz, and V. Liu. 2022. "Doing Good or Feeling Good? Detecting Greenwashing in Climate Investing." *The Journal of Impact and ESG Investing* 2 no. 4, pp. 5768. https://doi.org/10.3905/jesg.2022.1.045.

Atta-Darkua, V., D. Chambers, E. Dimson, Z. Ran, and T. Yu. 2020. "Strategies for Responsible Investing: Emerging Academic Evidence." *The Journal of Portfolio Management* 46, no. 3, pp. 2635. https://doi.org/10.3905/jpm.2020.46.3.026.

Autio, P., L. Pulkka, and S. Junnila. April 2023. "Creating a Strategy Framework for Investor Real Estate Management." *Journal of European Real Estate Research*. https://doi.org/10.1108/jerer-09-2022-0027.

Barazza, E. and N. Strachan. July 2020. "The Co-evolution of Climate Policy and Investments in Electricity Markets: Simulating Agent Dynamics in UK, German and Italian Electricity Sectors." *Energy Research & Social Science* 65,p. 101458. https://doi.org/10.1016/j.erss.2020.101458.

Battiston, S., I. Monasterolo, K. Riahi, and B.J. van Ruijven. 2021a. "Accounting for Finance Is Key for Climate Mitigation Pathways." *Science* 372, no. 6545, pp. 918920. https://doi.org/10.1126/science.abf3877.

Battiston, S., Y. Dafermos, and I. Monasterolo. March 2021b. "Climate Risks and Financial Stability." *Journal of Financial Stability* 54, p. 100867. https://doi.org/10.1016/j.jfs.2021.100867.

Behr, P., C.W. Mueller, and P. Orgen. December 2023. "Portfolio Allocation and Optimization With Carbon Offsets: Is It Worth the While?" *Journal of Climate Finance* 5, pp. 100019100083. https://doi.org/10.1016/j.jclimf.2023.100019.

Bender, J., T.A. Bridges, and K. Shah. 2019. "Reinventing Climate Investing: Building Equity Portfolios for Climate Risk Mitigation and Adaptation." *Journal of Sustainable Finance & Investment* 9 ,no. 3, pp. 191–213. https://doi.org/10.1080/20430795.2019.1579512.

Benedetti, D., E. Biffis, F. Chatzimichalakis, L.L. Fedele, and I. Simm. 2021. "Climate Change Investment Risk: Optimal Portfolio Construction Ahead of the Transition to a Lower-Carbon Economy." *Annals of Operations Research* 299, no. 12, pp. 847–871. https://doi.org/10.1007/s10479-019-03458-x.

Bento, N., G. Gianfrate, and J.E. Aldy. 2021. "National Climate Policies and Corporate Internal Carbon Pricing." *The Energy Journal* 42, no. 01. https://doi.org/10.5547/01956574.42.5.nben.

Bowman, M. and S. Minas. 2018. "Resilience Through Interlinkage: The Green Climate Fund and Climate Finance Governance." *Climate Policy* 19, no. 3, pp. 342–353. https://doi.org/10.1080/14693062.2018.1513358.

Bressan, G., I. Monasterolo, and S. Battiston. 2022. "Sustainable Investing and Climate Transition Risk: A Portfolio Rebalancing Approach." *The Journal of Portfolio Management* 48, no. 10, pp. 165–192. https://doi.org/10.3905/jpm.2022.1.394.

Broadstock, D.C., I. Chatziantoniou, and D. Gabauer. 2022. "Minimum Connectedness Portfolios and the Market for Green Bonds: Advocating Socially Responsible Investment (SRI) Activity." *Applications in Energy Finance* pp. 217253. https://doi.org/10.1007/978-3-030-92957-2_9.

Cakici, N. and A. Zaremba. June 2022. "Responsible Investing: ESG Ratings and the Cross-Section of International Stock Returns." *The Journal of Impact and ESG Investing.* https://doi.org/10.3905/jesg.2022.1.052.

Capasso, G., G. Gianfrate, and M. Spinelli. September 2020. "Climate Change and Credit Risk." *Journal of Cleaner Production* 266, p. 121634. https://doi.org/10.1016/j.jclepro.2020.121634.

Capros, P., G. Zazias, S. Evangelopoulou, M. Kannavou, T. Fotiou, P. Siskos, A. de Vita, et al. November 2019. "Energy-system Modelling of the EU Strategy Towards Climate-Neutrality." *Energy Policy* 134, p. 110960. https://doi.org/10.1016/j.enpol.2019.110960.

Cheema-Fox, A., G. Serafeim, and H.S. Wang. August 122, 2022. "Climate Change Vulnerability and Currency Returns." *Financial Analysts Journal.* https://doi.org/10.1080/0015198x.2022.2100233.

Chen, M., R.J. Chen, S. Zheng, and B. Li. 2023. "Green Investment, Technological Progress, and Green Industrial Development: Implications for Sustainable Development." *Sustainability* 15, no. 4, p. 3808. https://doi.org/10.3390/su15043808.

CICERO. 2015. *CICERO Shades of Green.* https://cicero.green/.

Coelho, R., S. Jayantilal, and J.J. Ferreira. 2023. "The Impact of Social Responsibility on Corporate Financial Performance: A Systematic Literature

Review." *Corporate Social Responsibility and Environmental Management* 30, no. 4,pp. 1535–1560. https://doi.org/10.1002/csr.2446.

D'Orazio, P. September 115, 2021. "Towards a Post-Pandemic Policy Framework to Manage Climate-Related Financial Risks and Resilience." *Climate Policy*. https://doi.org/10.1080/14693062.2021.1975623.

Dai, Z., Z. Luo, and C. Liu. June 2023. *Dynamic Volatility Spillovers and Investment Strategies between Crude Oil, New Energy, and Resource Related Sectors* 83. https://doi.org/10.1016/j.resourpol.2023.103681.

De Lange, DE. May 27, 2023. "Sustainable Transportation for the Climate: How Do Transportation Firms Engage in Cooperative Public-Private Partnerships?" *Sustainability* 15, no. 11, p. 8682. https://doi.org/10.3390/su15118682.

Dimitrov, R.S., J. Hovi, D.F. Sprinz, H. Saelen, and A. Underdal. 2019. "Institutional and Environmental Effectiveness: Will the Paris Agreement Work?" *Wiley Interdisciplinary Reviews: Climate Change* 10, no. 4. p. e583. https://doi.org/10.1002/wcc.583.

Duong, H.D., D.D.T. Hong, K.D. Huu, and U.D. Hai. January 1, 2023. "The Theory, Situation, and Solutions to Green Real Estate Development in Vietnam." *AIP Conference Proceedings*. https://doi.org/10.1063/5.0126137.

Dutta, A., E. Bouri, T. Rothovius, and G.S. Uddin. February 2023. "Climate Risk and Green Investments: New Evidence." *Energy* 265, p. 126376. https://doi.org/10.1016/j.energy.2022.126376.

Dye, J., M. McKinnon, and C. van der Byl. January 1, 2021. "Green Gaps: Firm ESG Disclosure and Financial Institutions' Reporting Requirements." *Journal of Sustainability Research* 3, no. 1. https://doi.org/10.20900/jsr20210006.

Elsayed, A.H., S. Nasreen, and A.K. Tiwari. August 2020. "Time-Varying Co-Movements between Energy Market and Global Financial Markets: Implication for Portfolio Diversification and Hedging Strategies." *Energy Economics* 90, p. 104847. https://doi.org/10.1016/j.eneco.2020.104847.

Fang, M., K.S. Tan, and T.S. Wirjanto. 2019. "Sustainable Portfolio Management Under Climate Change." *Journal of Sustainable Finance & Investment* 9, no. 1, pp. 4567. https://doi.org/10.1080/20430795.2018.1522583.

Fatica, S. and R. Panzica. 2021. "Green Bonds As a Tool against Climate Change?" *Business Strategy and the Environment* 30, no. 5. https://doi.org/10.1002/bse.2771.

Feridun, M. and H. Güngör. 2020. "Climate-Related Prudential Risks in the Banking Sector: A Review of the Emerging Regulatory and Supervisory Practices." *Sustainability* 12, no. 13, p. 5325. https://doi.org/10.3390/su12135325.

Focardi, S.M. and F.J. Fabozzi. 2020. "Climate Change and Asset Management." *The Journal of Portfolio Management* 46, no. 3, pp. 95–107. https://doi.org/10.3905/jpm.2020.46.3.095.

Folqué, M., E. Escrig-Olmedo, and T. Corzo Santamaría. 2021. "Sustainable Development and Financial System: Integrating ESG Risks Through Sustainable Investment Strategies in a Climate Change Context." *Sustainable Development* 29, no. 5. https://doi.org/10.1002/sd.2181.

Gaikwad, N., F. Genovese, and D. Tingley. April 13, 2022. "Creating Climate Coalitions: Mass Preferences for Compensating Vulnerability in the World's Two Largest Democracies." *American Political Science Review* 116, no. 4, pp. 1165–1183. https://doi.org/10.1017/s0003055422000223.

Gan, V.J.L., I.M.C. Lo, J. Ma, K.T. Tse, J.C.P. Cheng, and C.M. Chan. May 2020. "Simulation Optimisation Towards Energy Efficient Green Buildings: Current Status and Future Trends." *Journal of Cleaner Production* 254, p. 120012. https://doi.org/10.1016/j.jclepro.2020.120012.

Glanemann, N., S.N. Willner, and A. Levermann. 2020. "Paris Climate Agreement Passes the Cost-Benefit Test." *Nature Communications* 11, no. 1. https://doi.org/10.1038/s41467-019-13961-1.

Görgen, M., A. Jacob, and M. Nerlinger. 2021. "Get Green or Die Trying? Carbon Risk Integration Into Portfolio Management." *The Journal of Portfolio Management* 47, no. 3, pp. 77–93. https://doi.org/10.3905/jpm.2020.1.200.

Green, J.F. 2021. "Does Carbon Pricing Reduce Emissions? A Review of Ex-Post Analyses." *Environmental Research Letters* 16 (4). https://doi.org/10.1088/1748-9326/abdae9.

Groot, A.E., J.S. Bolt, H.S. Jat, M.L. Jat, M. Kumar, T. Agarwal, and V. Blok. February 2019. "Business Models of SMEs As a Mechanism for Scaling Climate Smart Technologies: The Case of Punjab, India." *Journal of Cleaner Production* 210, pp. 1109–1119. https://doi.org/10.1016/j.jclepro.2018.11.054.

Gugler, K., A. Haxhimusa, and M. Liebensteiner. March 2021. "Effectiveness of Climate Policies: Carbon Pricing vs. Subsidizing Renewables." *Journal of Environmental Economics and Management* 106, p. 102405. https://doi.org/10.1016/j.jeem.2020.102405.

Hamilton, I., H. Kennard, A. McGushin, L. Höglund-Isaksson, G. Kiesewetter, M. Lott, J. Milner, et al. 2021. "The Public Health Implications of the Paris Agreement: A Modelling Study." *The Lancet Planetary Health* 5, no. 2, pp. e74–e83. https://doi.org/10.1016/S2542-5196(20)30249-7.

Hepburn, C., J.E. Stiglitz, and N. Stern. April 2020. "'Carbon Pricing' Special Issue in the European Economic Review." *European Economic Review* p. 103440. https://doi.org/10.1016/j.euroecorev.2020.103440.

Hille, E., W. Althammer, and H. Diederich. April 2020. "Environmental Regulation and Innovation in Renewable Energy Technologies: Does the Policy Instrument Matter?" *Technological Forecasting and Social Change* 153, p. 119921. https://doi.org/10.1016/j.techfore.2020.119921.

Horan, S.M., E. Dimson, C. Emery, K. Blay, and G. Yelton. 2022. "The State of ESG Investing: A Portfolio Management Perspective." *The Journal of Impact and ESG Investing* 2, no. 4, pp. 7–29. https://doi.org/10.3905/jesg.2022.1.043.

Huij, J., D. Laurs, P.A. Stork, and R.C.J. Zwinkels. 2023. "Carbon Beta: A Market-Based Measure of Climate Risk." *SSRN Electronic Journal.* https://doi.org/10.2139/ssrn.3957900.

Irfani, M.I. and O.Y. Sudrajad. 2023. "Portfolio Optimization Using Markowitz Model on Sri-Kehati Index." *International Journal of Current Science Research and Review* 06, no. 08. https://doi.org/10.47191/ijcsrr/v6-i8-45.

Ji, X., Y. Zhang, N. Mirza, M. Umar, and S.K.A. Rizvi. November 2021. "The Impact of Carbon Neutrality on the Investment Performance: Evidence From the Equity Mutual Funds in BRICS." *Journal of Environmental Management* 297, p. 113228. https://doi.org/10.1016/j.jenvman.2021.113228.

Joshi, G.P. and R.K. Dash. 2023. "A Bibliometric Analysis of Climate Investing." *International Journal of Energy Economics and Policy* 13, no. 3, pp. 396–407. https://doi.org/10.32479/ijeep.14279.

Kasdan, M., L. Kuhl, and P. Kurukulasuriya. July 2020. "The Evolution of Transformational Change in Multilateral Funds Dedicated to Financing Adaptation to Climate Change." *Climate and Development* pp. 1–16. https://doi.org/10.1080/17565529.2020.1790333.

Kwilinski, A., O. Lyulyov, and T. Pimonenko. 2023. "The Impact of Digital Business on Energy Efficiency in EU Countries." *Information* 14, no. 9, p. 480. https://doi.org/10.3390/info14090480.

Le Guenedal, T. and T. Roncalli. 2022. "Portfolio Construction with Climate Risk Measures." *SSRN Electronic Journal.* https://doi.org/10.2139/ssrn.3999971.

Liu, W., W.J. McKibbin, A.C. Morris, and P.J. Wilcoxen. August 2020. "Global Economic and Environmental Outcomes of the Paris Agreement." *Energy Economics* 90, p. 104838. https://doi.org/10.1016/j.eneco.2020.104838.

Lu, Y., Z.A. Khan, M.S. Alvarez-Alvarado, Y. Zhang, Z. Huang, and M. Imran. 2020. "A Critical Review of Sustainable Energy Policies for the Promotion of Renewable Energy Sources." *Sustainability* 12, no. 12, p. 5078. https://doi.org/10.3390/su12125078.

Maestre-Andrés, S., S. Drews, and J. van den Bergh. 2019. "Perceived Fairness and Public Acceptability of Carbon Pricing: A Review of the Literature." *Climate Policy* 19, no. 9, pp. 1186–1204. https://doi.org/10.1080/14693062.2019.1639490.

Maiti, M. September 2022. "Does Development in Venture Capital Investments Influence Green Growth?" *Technological Forecasting and Social Change* 182, p. 121878. https://doi.org/10.1016/j.techfore.2022.121878.

Mbanyele, William. 2022. "Climate Change Vulnerability and Corporate Investment Efficiency." SSRN.com. May 4, 2022. https://papers.ssrn.com/sol3/papers.cfm?abstract_id=4317743.

McKibbin, W. J., A.C. Morris, A.J. Panton, and P.J. Wilcoxen. 2017. "Climate Change and Monetary Policy: Dealing with Disruption." *SSRN Electronic Journal.* https://doi.org/10.2139/ssrn.3084399.

Meckling, J. and B.B. Allan. 2020. "The Evolution of Ideas in Global Climate Policy." *Nature Climate Change* 10, no. 5, pp. 434–438. https://doi.org/10.1038/s41558-020-0739-7.

Mésonnier, J.S. and B. Nguyen. 2020. "Showing off Cleaner Hands: Mandatory Climate-Related Disclosure By Financial Institutions and the Financing of Fossil Energy." *SSRN Electronic Journal.* https://doi.org/10.2139/ssrn.3733781.

Monasterolo, I. and L. de Angelis. April 2020. "Blind to Carbon Risk? An Analysis of Stock Market Reaction to the Paris Agreement." *Ecological Economics* 170,p. 106571. https://doi.org/10.1016/j.ecolecon.2019.106571.

MSCI ESG Research LLC. June 2023. *ESG Ratings Methodology.* Methodology Document. www.msci.com/documents/1296102/34424357/MSCI+ESG+Ratings+Methodology+%28002%29.pdf.

Mundonde, J. and P.L. Makoni. 2023. "Public Private Partnerships and Water and Sanitation Infrastructure Development in Zimbabwe: What Determines Financing?" *Environmental Systems Research* 12, no. 1. https://doi.org/10.1186/s40068-023-00295-7.

Naeem, M.A., M.R. Rabbani, S. Karim, and S.M. Billah. 2021. "Religion vs Ethics: Hedge and Safe Haven Properties of Sukuk and Green Bonds for Stock Markets Pre- and During COVID-19." *International Journal of Islamic and Middle Eastern Finance and Management ahead-of-print* (ahead-of-print). https://doi.org/10.1108/imefm-06-2021-0252.

Newell, R.G., W.A. Pizer, and D. Raimi. May 2019. "U.S. Federal Government Subsidies for Clean Energy: Design Choices and Implications." *Energy Economics* 80, pp. 831–841. https://doi.org/10.1016/j.eneco.2019.02.018.

Newman Ao, P. 2020. "COVID, CITIES and CLIMATE: Historical Precedents and Potential Transitions for the New Economy." *Urban Science* 4, no. 3, p. 32. https://doi.org/10.3390/urbansci4030032.

OECD. 2022. *OECD Series on Carbon Pricing and Energy Taxation Pricing Greenhouse Gas Emissions Turning Climate Targets into Climate Action.* OECD Publishing.

Painuly, J.P. and N. Wohlgemuth. 2021. "Renewable Energy Technologies: Barriers and Policy Implications." *Welcome to DTU Research Database.* https://orbit.dtu.dk/en/publications/renewable-energy-technologies-barriers-and-policy-implications.

Pee, L.G. and S.L. Pan. April 2022. "Climate-Intelligent Cities and Resilient Urbanisation: Challenges and Opportunities for Information Research." *International Journal of Information Management* 63, p. 102446. https://doi.org/10.1016/j.ijinfomgt.2021.102446.

Polzin, F. and M. Sanders. December 2020. "How to Finance the Transition to Low-Carbon Energy in Europe?" *Energy Policy* 147, p. 111863. https://doi.org/10.1016/j.enpol.2020.111863.

Popescu, I.S., C. Hitaj, and E. Benetto. September 2021. "Measuring the Sustainability of Investment Funds: A Critical Review of Methods and Frameworks in Sustainable Finance." *Journal of Cleaner Production* 314, p. 128016. https://doi.org/10.1016/j.jclepro.2021.128016.

Popp, D. 2020. "Promoting Clean Energy Innovation at the State and Local Level." *Agricultural and Resource Economics Review* 49, no. 2, pp. 360–373. https://doi.org/10.1017/age.2020.15.

Rana, A., R. Sadiq, M.S. Alam, H. Karunathilake, and K. Hewage. January 2021. "Evaluation of Financial Incentives for Green Buildings in Canadian Landscape." *Renewable and Sustainable Energy Reviews* 135, p. 110199. https://doi.org/10.1016/j.rser.2020.110199.

Roelfsema, M., H.L. van Soest, M. Harmsen, D.P. van Vuuren, C. Bertram, M. den Elzen, N. Höhne, et al. 2020. "Taking Stock of National Climate Policies to Evaluate Implementation of the Paris Agreement." *Nature Communications* 11, no. 1, p. 2096. https://doi.org/10.1038/s41467-020-15414-6.

Roncalli, T., T.L. Guenedal, F. Lepetit, T. Roncalli, and T. Sekine. 2021. "The Market Measure of Carbon Risk and Its Impact on the Minimum Variance Portfolio." *The Journal of Portfolio Management* 47, no. 9, pp. 54–68. https://doi.org/10.3905/jpm.2021.1.285.

Saini, J., M. Dutta, and G. Marques. 2020. "Indoor Air Quality Monitoring Systems Based on Internet of Things: A Systematic Review." *International Journal of Environmental Research and Public Health* 17, no. 14, p. 4942. https://doi.org/10.3390/ijerph17144942.

Sanderson, H., D.M. Irato, N.P. Cerezo, H. Duel, P. Faria, and E.F. Torres. 2019. "How Do Climate Risks Affect Corporations and How Could They Address These Risks?" *SN Applied Sciences* 1, no. 12. https://doi.org/10.1007/s42452-019-1725-4.

Schmidt, R. May 2022. "Are Business Ethics Effective? A Market Failures Approach to Impact Investing." *Journal of Business Ethics*. https://doi.org/10.1007/s10551-022-05133-x.

Seltzer, L., L. Starks, and Q. Zhu. April 2022. "Climate Regulatory Risk and Corporate Bonds." *National Bureau of Economic Research*. https://doi.org/10.3386/w29994.

Setyowati, A.B. December 2023. "Governing Sustainable Finance: Insights From Indonesia." *Climate Policy* pp. 1–14. https://doi.org/10.1080/14693062.20 20.1858741.

Sharif, A., S. Kocak, H.H.A. Khan, G. Uzuner, and S. Tiwari. March 2023. "Demystifying the Links Between Green Technology Innovation, Economic Growth, and Environmental Tax in ASEAN-6 Countries: The Dynamic Role of Green Energy and Green Investment." *Gondwana Research* 115, pp. 98–106. https://doi.org/10.1016/j.gr.2022.11.010.

Shokry, G., J.J.T. Connolly, and I. Anguelovski. March 2020. "Understanding Climate Gentrification and Shifting Landscapes of Protection and Vulnerability in Green Resilient Philadelphia." Urban Climate 31, p. 100539. https://doi.org/10.1016/j.uclim.2019.100539.

Sikora, A. 2021. "European Green Deal—Legal and Financial Challenges of the Climate Change." ERA Forum 21, no. 4. https://doi.org/10.1007/s12027-020-00637-3.

Sun, G., A. Khaskheli, S.A. Raza, and S. Ali. 2023. "The Asymmetric Relationship Between Public–Private Partnerships Investment in Energy and Environmental Degradation for Sustainable Development: New Evidence From Quantile-On-Quantile Regression Approach." Environmental Science and Pollution Research 30, no. 26, pp. 68143–68162. https://doi.org/10.1007/s11356-023-27136-5.

Thompson, B.S. May 2023. "Impact Investing in Biodiversity Conservation With Bonds: An Analysis of Financial and Environmental Risk." *Business Strategy and the Environment.* https://doi.org/10.1002/bse.3135.

Tolliver, C., A.R. Keeley, and S. Managi. January 2020. "Drivers of Green Bond Market Growth: The Importance of Nationally Determined Contributions to the Paris Agreement and Implications for Sustainability." *Journal of Cleaner Production* 244, p. 118643. https://doi.org/10.1016/j.jclepro.2019.118643.

Tröger, T.H. and S. Steuer. 2021. "The Role of Disclosure in Green Finance." SSRN Electronic Journal. https://doi.org/10.2139/ssrn.3908617.

van de Ven, D.J., A. Nikas, K. Koasidis, A. Forouli, G. Cassetti, A. Chiodi, M. Gargiulo, et al. 2022. "COVID-19 Recovery Packages Can Benefit Climate Targets and Clean Energy Jobs, but Scale of Impacts and Optimal Investment Portfolios Differ Among Major Economies." *One Earth* 5, no. 9, pp. 1042–1054. https://doi.org/10.1016/j.oneear.2022.08.008.

Wang, T., Z. Qu, Z. Yang, T. Nichol, G. Clarke, and Y.E. Ge. November 1, 2020. "Climate Change Research on Transportation Systems: Climate Risks, Adaptation and Planning." Transportation Research Part D: Transport and Environment 88, p. 102553. https://doi.org/10.1016/j.trd.2020.102553.

Xiong, W., M. Dong, and C. Xu. July 2022. "Institutional Investors and Corporate Social Responsibility: Evidence From China." *Emerging Markets Finance and Trade* pp. 1–12. https://doi.org/10.1080/1540496x.2022.2088351.

Yang, J. and X. Liu. July 2022. "The Role of Sustainable Development Goals, Financial Knowledge and Investment Strategies on the Organizational Profitability: Moderating Impact of Government Support." *Economic Research-Ekonomska Istraživanja* pp. 1–22. https://doi.org/10.1080/133167 7x.2022.2090405.

Yasuda, A. April 27, 2023. "Impact Investing." SSRN.com. https://papers.ssrn. com/sol3/papers.cfm?abstract_id=4431236.

Ye, X. and E. Rasoulinezhad. January 2023. "Assessment of Impacts of Green Bonds on Renewable Energy Utilization Efficiency." *Renewable Energy* 202, pp. 626–633. https://doi.org/10.1016/j.renene.2022.11.124.

Yunus, N. March 2020. "Commonalities Across Commercial Real Estate Indexes." *Applied Economics* pp. 1–17. https://doi.org/10.1080/00036846.2 019.1708256.

Zhan, J.X. and A.U. Santos-Paulino. 2021. "Investing in the Sustainable Development Goals: Mobilization, Channeling, and Impact." *Journal of International Business Policy* 4, no. (1), pp. 166–183. https://doi.org/10.1057/ s42214-020-00093-3.

Zhang, M., Z. Zhao, T.M. Long, and X. Chen. 2023. "Carbon Footprint in Agriculture Sector: A Literature Review." *Carbon Footprints* 2, no. 3. https:// doi.org/10.20517/cf.2023.29.

Zolfaghari, B. and G. Hand. March 2021. "Impact Investing and Philanthropic Foundations: Strategies Deployed When Aligning Fiduciary Duty and Social Mission." *Journal of Sustainable Finance & Investment* pp. 1–28. https://doi. org/10.1080/20430795.2021.1907090.

About the Author

Dr. Zhong is the founder of Fundopedia. She is a former portfolio manager (PM) (strategy chief investment officer) at BlackRock, the world's largest asset management firm by assets under management (AUM). Before BlackRock, Dr. Zhong was a fund PM at UBS, the world's largest private bank by AUM. She started her career as a Wall Street analyst at Lehman Brothers.

Dr. Zhong has also been a subject-matter expert and consultant in asset management. The institutions she has actively provided advice since 2022 include McKinsey & Company, Boston Consulting Group, Bain & Company, Deloitte, PwC, and Ernst & Young. She is frequently invited to roundtable events and webcasts as a public speaker in the United States and Asia Pacific.

Dr. Zhong published the books *Alternatives Thinker: Endowment Investment Philosophy to Active Portfolio Management* in 2013 and *Strategies That Chinese Small and Medium-Sized Enterprises Used to Attract Venture Capital* in 2018.

Index

OTHER TITLES IN THE ENVIRONMENTAL AND SOCIAL SUSTAINABILITY FOR BUSINESS ADVANTAGE COLLECTION

Robert Sroufe, Duquesne University, Editor

- *Making the Connection* by Peter Sammons
- *Sustainable Investing* by Kylelane Purcell and Vivari Ben
- *Confronting the Storm* by David Ross
- *Sustainability for Retail* by Vilma Barr and Ken Nisch
- *People, Planet, Profit* by Kit Oung
- *Bringing Sustainability to the Ground Level* by Susan J. Gilbertz and Damon M. Hall
- *Handbook of Sustainable Development* by Radha R. Sharma
- *Community Engagement and Investment* by Alan S. Gutterman
- *Sustainability Standards and Instruments* by Alan Gutterman
- *Strategic Planning for Sustainability* by Alan S. Gutterman
- *Sustainability Reporting and Communications* by Alan S. Gutterman
- *Sustainability Leader in a Green Business Era* by Amr E. Sukkar
- *Managing Sustainability* by John Friedman
- *Human Resource Management for Organizational Sustainability* by Radha R. Sharma

Concise and Applied Business Books

The Collection listed above is one of 30 business subject collections that Business Expert Press has grown to make BEP a premiere publisher of print and digital books. Our concise and applied books are for...

- Professionals and Practitioners
- Faculty who adopt our books for courses
- Librarians who know that BEP's Digital Libraries are a unique way to offer students ebooks to download, not restricted with any digital rights management
- Executive Training Course Leaders
- Business Seminar Organizers

Business Expert Press books are for anyone who needs to dig deeper on business ideas, goals, and solutions to everyday problems. Whether one print book, one ebook, or buying a digital library of 110 ebooks, we remain the affordable and smart way to be business smart. For more information, please visit www.businessexpertpress.com, or contact sales@businessexpertpress.com.

www.ingramcontent.com/pod-product-compliance
Lightning Source LLC
Chambersburg PA
CBHW061152220326
41599CB00025B/4453